*Crisis and Conflicts
in the Middle East*

MIDEAST AFFAIRS SERIES

1. **ARAB RELATIONS IN THE MIDDLE EAST**
The Road to Realignment

2. **CRISIS AND CONFLICTS IN THE MIDDLE EAST**
The Changing Strategy: From Iran to Afghanistan

CRISIS AND CONFLICTS
IN THE MIDDLE EAST

The Changing Strategy:
From Iran to Afghanistan

edited by
COLIN LEGUM

HOLMES & MEIER
Publishers, Inc.
New York • London

First published in the United States of America 1981 by
Holmes & Meier Publishers, Inc.
30 Irving Place
New York, N.Y. 10003

Great Britain:
Holmes & Meier Publishers, Ltd.
131 Trafalgar Road
Greenwich, London SE10 9TX

The articles in this book are reprinted from the current volumes
of *Middle East Contemporary Survey* and *Africa Contemporary Record,*
published by Holmes & Meier Publishers, Inc.

Library of Congress Cataloging in Publication Data
Main entry under title:

Crisis and conflicts in the Middle East.

  (Mideast affairs series ; 2)
  Articles reprinted from the current volume of Middle East contemporary survey.
  1. Near East—Politics and government—1945–
I. Legum, Colin. II. Middle East contemporary survey.
III. Series.
DS63.1.C73   1981   955'.05   81-84135
ISBN 0-8419-0784-6 (pbk.)   AACR2

Manufactured in the United States of America

Dedicated to all those
who are striving for peace in the Middle East

Contents

PREFACE
The Middle East at the End of a Decade

It is hardly surprising that the political history of the Middle East in 1980, a year marking the transition from one decade to the other, was shaped by the divergent effects of continuing processes and new developments. The essays included in this volume, selected from the 1980 edition of the *Middle East Contemporary Survey,* address some of the central aspects of this interplay between lingering and more recent trends. The broader Middle Eastern political scene during the last few years can be conveniently analyzed under three headings: the super-power rivalry, regional politics and domestic politics.

The mid-1970's were years of achievement for US policy in the Middle East. American diplomacy made good use of the ambiguous outcome of the October 1973 war and its own contribution to the opening of the "peace process" in the Arab-Israeli conflict. It reestablished Washington's central position in the core area of the Middle East, expedited the Soviet Union's ouster from Egypt and began to make inroads into the Soviet Union's position in Syria. But impressive as it may have seemed at the time, the new American policy in the Middle East and the new position it created were not free from serious flaws and weaknesses such as the growing American dependence on Middle Eastern oil. These were seriously exacerbated during the last years of the decade by the Soviet counter-offensive which began in the outlying areas of the Middle East and by the errors and failures of the Carter Administration's policy in the years 1977–1979, particularly its Iranian and Afghan setbacks. Thus, the image of a vigorous and resourceful American policy was replaced at the end of the decade by that of an effective Soviet offensive encountering a helpless and less than credible American response. These developments, the Iranian crisis in particular, had far-reaching repercussions within the United States and they contributed both to Ronald Reagan's electoral victory and to his Administration's determination to restore Washington's position and credibility and to check the Soviet Union's advances.

But the Soviet perspective on these developments is not a mirror image of the Western and pro-Western anxieties. The Soviet invasion of Afghanistan seems to have been motivated by the desire to save a crumbling position and by fears of the contagious effects of Islamic revival alongside the realization that a strategic gain could be made. Likewise, the political and military price paid by the Soviet Union in Afghanistan should not be overshadowed by the impact that the invasion has had in the region.

Nor was ambivalence absent from the Soviet Union's attitude to its most prominent achievement in the core area of the Middle East—the signing of the Soviet-Syrian treaty of friendship and cooperation in October 1980. Earlier in the decade the Soviets were the party interested in such a treaty and they exerted pressure on the Syrian government to sign it. The roles had since been reversed and the same weakness which prodded Syria to ask for the signing of a treaty in 1980 made Moscow reluctant to commit itself to a regime that might have become more of a liability than an asset. Still, by signing the treaty, Moscow acquired greater influence over a variety of Middle Eastern issues including the Arab-Israeli conflict and the Lebanese crisis.

Both the Soviet Union and the United States were hard put to formulate clear-cut policies towards the Iran-Iraq war upon its outbreak in September 1980. Both perceived serious immediate risks as well as potential gains, and neither had a close relationship with either of the belligerent governments. Consequently, following a brief period of tensions the two powers kept, by and large away, from the conflict, thus enabling it to unfold without generating a serious international crisis.

The outbreak of the Iranian-Iraqi war served in regional terms to underline the evergrowing importance of the Persian Gulf area to the point at which its very definition as an outlying region has been challenged. The area not only became the focus of international tension and attention, but the growing wealth and influence of the Gulf states had altered the traditional relationship between them and the Arab states of the core area.

The rise of these new centres of influence in the 1970's also accelerated the fragmentation of the Arab state system. The system of inter-Arab relations had been adversely affected since its inception in the 1940's by the tension between a unionist ideology and particularist interests, and by conflicts between rival states and forces. But during the first two decades of the Arab League's existence these conflicts were conducted in the context of a certain pattern—the rivalry between the Hashemite and Egyptian-Saudi axes in the 1940's, and between Nasser and his rivals in the late 1950's and early 1960's. Later, in the 1960's, the system of inter-Arab relations began to disintegrate with the decline of Egypt's hegemony, the emergence of several new foci of influence and a series of bilateral rivalries. These developments continued at a still more rapid pace in the 1970's when they were also accompanied, to some extent even legitimized, by the waning of pan-Arab ideology as a compelling intellectual and emotional force.

Thus, by the end of the 1970's, Egypt was formally outside the inter-Arab pale while inside it ephemeral groupings had taken the place of erstwhile blocs and coalitions. The effect of these developments was clearly demonstrated in the final quarter of 1980. When the Iraqi-Iranian war broke out Iran was supported by two Arab states—Syria and Libya.—Then, when an Arab summit conference met in Amman, it was boycotted by Syria, her allies and clients. All in all five members of the Arab League absented themselves from Amman in addition to Egypt that was invited (and may have chosen not to attend) in the first place.

Egypt's quarrel with most of the other Arab states can be seen in the context of both inter-Arab relations and the Arab-Israeli conflict. Viewed from the first vantage point, Sadat's Israeli policy in the late 1970's could be legitimately interpreted as an assertion by Egypt's president of his right as the leader of the senior and largest Arab state to carry out the policy he regarded as best for both Egypt and the whole Arab collective. In the annals of the Arab-Israeli conflict, the same quarrel appears as the culmination of the tension between two contradictory trends which had transpired earlier in the decade.

One was the trend towards accommodation and moderation which appeared in the aftermath of the October 1973 war and was, indeed, influenced by its course and outcome. It manifested itself primarily in the series of agreements signed in 1974–5 and in the gradual modification of the national consensus in both Israel and Egypt.

But other factors—the sense of growing power in the Arab world, the Islamic resurgence, the reaction both in Israel and the Arab world to the settlement process and the growing salience of the Palestinian issue contributed to the exacerbation of other aspects of the Arab-Israeli conflict.

Consequently, while the process of settlement did lead to the signing of a peace treaty, that treaty was preceded and followed by acrimonious negotiations and the new Egyptian-Israeli relationship can at best be described as precarious and ambiguous. During the first two years since the signing of the Camp David Accords, the impact of the first Arab-Israeli peace treaty on the regional politics of the Middle East was far more limited than the expectations which preceded it and

2

possibly the potential inherent in the situation. The Israeli-Egyptian peace was certainly an important factor in preventing the outbreak of another Arab-Israeli war and its symbolic and emotional significance can hardly be exaggerated. But it did not produce a normal relationship between the two states and societies or an attenuation of the Arab-Israeli conflict as a whole.

The outbreak of war between Iran and Iraq in September 1980 represented a transition to a new phase in two of the processes which have affected the Middle East since the latter part of the 1970's. One was the "Islamic resurgence" or the rise of Islam's importance and salience as a force affecting all levels of politics in the region. This development could be discerned by the mid-1970's and was given much prominence and acceleration by the Iranian revolution in 1978–79. The success of a predominantly Islamic movement in overthrowing a powerful secularizing regime and in defeating its great Western ally released in 1979 a wave of Islamic and anti-Western eruptions which threatened for a brief moment to engulf the whole region.

Related to this has been the issue of domestic stability in the states of the Middle East. With one major exception, the 1970's were a decade of domestic stability in a region whose political history in the previous two decades was characterized by successive changes of regimes, coups d'etat and other forms of political violence. This trend could be explained by the exhaustion of the revolutionary potential which underlay the instability of the previous decades and by the sophisticated ruling techniques employed by both radical and conservative regimes. But by the late 1970's the impact of new factors could be felt which threatened to undermine the stability of several political systems in the region— the effect of enormous wealth acquired so rapidly, the challenges posed by Islamic movements, political decay and corruption and the influence of the regional and international conflicts mentioned above. The combined effect of these forces happened to have been first felt in a particularly dramatic fashion in Iran but it left its mark, in different forms, in practically all the states of the region.

The formation of Khomeyni's regime, or an Islamic government, in Iran added a new significance to these developments. For one thing the new regime claimed to offer an alternative to the model of Westernization and modernization which had predominated in the region since the 19th century. Many Muslims outside Iran followed the course of the new regime with great interest—its success could generate similar movements in other states. The new regime in Iran sought also to export the revolution, but the impact of its effects was largely confined to Shi'i areas.

Iraq, however was a neighbouring state with an underprivileged Shi'i majority and the single most important factor explaining its leadership's decision to launch war on Iran was the feeling that the agitation of Iraq's Shi'i population was endangering not just the regime but the very foundation of the Iraqi state as it had existed since 1920.

By invading the territory of Iran and by inflicting an initial defeat on its emasculated army the Iraqi government achieved results that were quite different from its own goals. The military failure of Khomeyni's regime, the loss of national territory and the aggravated internecine squabbling have further demonstrated to most interested Muslims, who had already registered their doubts and disappointments, the limitations and drawbacks of Khomeyni's formula. The very fact of war between Arab Muslims and Iranian Muslims, with an attendant underlining of nationalist themes and symbols, was a serious blow to the notion of Islamic solidarity.

The war between Iran and Iraq thus served as yet another factor which

3

PREFACE

checked, but certainly did not end, the Islamic resurgence of the 1970's. But the war was far from having a stabilizing impact on the domestic politics of the two belligerents or on the region as a whole. In this regard, the forces of instability appeared to be undiminished.

Itamar Rabinovich

OVERVIEW
The Military and Political Battleground

Few regions have seen in the last decade so many events of strategic importance as has the Persian Gulf. The first oil crisis in the wake of the October War of 1973 dramatically brought home to the West and indeed to the Third World how dependent they were on oil, and oil from the Gulf in particular. The problem was not just one of supply, important enough in all conscience, but price too, which soared, with lasting effects on the world economic system. When nations had slowly learned to live with the new situation, the revolution in Iran in February 1979 suddenly took significant quantities of oil off the market, producing a second oil crisis and a doubling of prices within a year, fuelling recession.

But the fall of the Shah also meant the collapse of the Western strategic position in the Gulf, which had been built around a friendly link with growing Iranian armed forces. The hostility of the new regime to the United States then weakened the Western position further and the taking of the US Embassy hostages drew strong US naval forces into the Arabian Sea prepared to take action against Iran if need be.

Then in December 1979 came the Soviet invasion of Afghanistan, to give these naval forces, now augmented, new purpose: to remedy Western weakness in face of the new Soviet military presence in the sensitive Gulf area and, with bitter irony, to be ready to protect Iran instead of opposing it. Finally, when the Soviet action in Afghanistan had produced almost unanimous protest throughout the world, the invasion of Iran by Iraq in September 1980 brought the familiar intra-Arab quarrels to the surface once more and divided the regional states, some for Iraq, some for non-Arab Iran.

The political scene became extremely confused and still is. The Soviet Union, for example, finds itself with friendship treaties with Syria and Iraq, which are bitterly opposed to each other. Iran, tumbling further into chaos daily, is at odds with the outside world yet seeks military supplies from such unlikely sources as Israel in order to prosecute the war with Iraq. The war itself has been at a stalemate, with most countries doing their best to remain neutral and the Islamic powers trying to bring about some form of cease-fire to two states entrenched in their own dislike of each other. Only Israel seems capable of producing some sort of unity among the Arabs by its actions against the PLO and in Lebanon.

There are of course some connecting threads in all this. One is oil; another militant Islam; a third, the Arab-Israel conflict. But regional rivalries tangle the web: between Syria and Iraq, and between Iraq and Iran, as does the Iraqi ambition, presently somewhat blunted, to dominate the Gulf militarily now that the Shah is no more. India and Pakistan; the two Yemens; Somalia and Ethiopia; all have their quarrels that must also be taken into account by any state trying to find a political and military balance in the region. But casting its shadow across everything is the East-West tension produced by an assertive Soviet foreign policy backed by a capability and willingness to use force and to supply weapons to others wishing to use it. Soviet activity spreads from the Horn of Africa to Afghanistan and its influence, to some degree or another, through the Middle East, Africa, India and beyond. At the heart of this region is the Gulf, on which the West depends vitally, but the Soviet Union hardly at all, and where the West is on land at a marked strategic disadvantage. The Soviet military presence in Afghani-

5

stan has in effect created a new front to which the West must now give urgent attention, and which competes for resources with the other theatres of confrontation in Europe and the Pacific.

The one temporary respite for the West has been the unanticipated surplus on the world market that has caused prices to fall rather than rise as had been feared. The glut partly results from conversion measures taken to offset increased energy costs, partly from reduced demand because of industrial recession, and partly because new supplies have come on stream in the North Sea and Mexico. But it was maintained because Saudi Arabia increased its own production to compensate for that lost through the Iraqi-Iranian War, not only to give some help to Western economies but also to put pressure on other Organization of Petroleum Exporting Countries (OPEC) members to bring about a more stable price regime and thus more consistent demand. OPEC found itself losing leverage over consuming countries, a welcome change but one which in no way altered the essential heavy dependence of the West on Gulf oil.

While Western navies were demonstrating their determination to keep the Gulf open for tankers, it became more than ever clear that to keep oil flowing from the fields themselves was quite another matter. The Iraqi-Iranian War showed at once, not only the instability and volatility of the area, but the weakness of the outside world in face of the disruptions to supply caused by such upheavals. And even if such cut-backs were averted, prices might still have their own volatility. To reduce dependence on oil by conservation or the development of new energy sources was an obvious policy for the West to pursue, though a costly one, to keep prices lower than they might otherwise be. But what if the Soviet Union chose to enter the market in the next decade, perhaps because of declining domestic production—and there is doubt about the extent of readily-recoverable reserves in the Soviet oilfields? The market could then become very tight once more, perhaps producing political frictions between producers and consumers. More dramatic, what if the Soviet Union, through political penetration or military expansion, aimed at gaining control or influence over supply, diverting it towards its own needs or those of the Soviet bloc? Oil was therefore the central strategic preoccupation of all in the Gulf or concerned with it, except perhaps Iran, where fanaticism seemed to rule over rationality.

THE SIGNIFICANCE OF EVENTS

If oil was inevitably the central concern, the strategic scene in the region was transformed by the Iranian revolution and the invasion of Afghanistan, and not a little affected by the Iraqi-Iranian War.

IRAN

As has been said above, the fall of the Shah destroyed the Western position in the Gulf. Until 1971, stability in the area had been underpinned by a British military presence, but when this was withdrawn the Shah took on himself the role of the arbiter of events in the Gulf, with Western acquiescence and help. The strengthening of the Iranian forces and friendly Iranian territory offered an obvious basis for the protection of Western interests. With the revolution all this collapsed. Bitter hostility took the place of friendly relation between the US and Iran and the Western position suffered accordingly, deteriorating even further when sanctions were invoked after the taking of the hostages. The West's loss was of course a gain for the Soviet Union, though not one immediately translatable into political influence since godless Moscow was hardly more acceptable to Tehran than was satanic Washington. But the Soviet leaders can hope to exploit the political

6

change in due course and no doubt looked forward to taking advantage of the political chaos that seemed eminently likely, using Marxist or left-wing elements as a vehicle, or even Islam.

AFGHANISTAN

Then came the invasion of Afghanistan, an event that was to prove a strategic and political watershed. Soviet forces suddenly moved in very large numbers into a country within easy air striking distance of the Gulf, an action which almost at once changed the whole direction of US foreign and defence policy. It ended any chance of the ratification of SALT II and put US-Soviet détente in the freezer. President Carter promptly declared that any Soviet military move into the Gulf would be met militarily and set about forming the Rapid Deployment Force (RDF) to be able to do this, and increasing the defence budget. A wave of conservatism was set off in the US that, fuelled by the unhappy record of US policy in the Gulf, eventually led to the Reagan landslide victory in the Presidential election. And, of course, President Reagan increased the defence budget still further and made containment of the Soviet Union a foreign policy priority. While the Gulf States themselves did not see events in quite the same East-West light, they also roundly condemned the invasion and began to look more closely at their own security, even if they were mostly chary of moving politically much closer to the US in order to help with this.

This essay is not the place for an examination of the precise Soviet motives for going into Afghanistan, but one was clearly the determination to prevent the overthrow of a Communist regime. Since this determination is likely to persist, and since the regime is unlikely to survive without the prop of Soviet military forces, it seems probable that a substantial garrison will remain in the country indefinitely, a factor that will have to be taken into account strategically.

The costs to the Soviet Union of the invasion have been not inconsiderable. It has been almost universally condemned, not least in the Islamic world, and Moscow has suffered a degree of political isolation. Soviet forces are now involved in a drawn-out and expensive campaign against a people long accustomed to fighting and using weapons and capable of exploiting the rugged terrain through guerilla tactics that are second nature to them, and more weapons are now reaching them. (It should be said in passing that it would be wrong if they were not to be getting more weapons: the invasion was illegal and brutal, and the Afghan people have shown themselves willing and able to resist it, a perfect case for external help if ever there was one). Even massive Soviet forces are unlikely to be able to put an end to resistance completely, and may have to settle for limited control of the country only. The building of military facilities has been going on on a scale and pattern which suggests that a long-term presence is envisaged.

Not only has the invasion resulted in Soviet forces being installed on airfields within fighter range of the Gulf; they are also on the eastern border of Iran, from which they could intervene there if they chose, and on the northern border of Pakistan. It is this latter fact that has captured some attention, as possible evidence of the historic wish in Moscow of a move one day towards the warm waters of the Ocean. A glance at the map will show that this might not be easy, since there is extremely difficult country en route. There is no doubt, though, that the Soviet presence has put pressures on Pakistan, which has been by no means a stable country politically. Fears are expressed that the Soviet Union will now do what it can to foment unrest among the Baluchis there, perhaps regarding this action as no more than the equivalent of the Western support reaching the Afghans via Pakistani territory. Be that as it may, the invasion of Afghanistan has led

7

to the US showing a close interest in the security of Pakistan and being willing to supply it with advanced weapons even if this has to be at the cost of some tensions with India, though these are to be avoided if possible. The strategic importance of Pakistan is evident—both to the US and the Soviet Union. Its geographical position and its Muslim links with the Gulf States will inevitably make it figure largely in Western strategy, and no doubt in Soviet calculations.

THE IRAQI-IRANIAN WAR

The war between Iraq and Iran has not had quite the same impact on the strategic position as the events in Iran and Afghanistan have, but it has not been without its significance. It seems clear from the pattern of the early fighting that Iraq attacked on the assumption that Iran could be defeated fairly quickly. When the Iranian armed forces seemed largely to disintegrate after the revolution the way must have seemed open for Iraq to fill the vacuum left by the Shah and assert itself as the strongest military power in the Gulf. The invasion appeared to confirm this ambition on the part of Saddām Hussayn but the indifferent performance of his forces and the surprisingly dogged defence put up by Iran has lent no strength to it. Instead of a new strong man emerging in the Gulf, which would have had considerable political inpact, there is instead a stalemate in the war and a loss of prestige for Saddām Hussayn (which may not have troubled his Gulf neighbours too much).

The war has also had the effect of loosening further the ties between Iraq and the Soviet Union, since Moscow cannot easily support Iraq in the war, despite their treaty, without offending Syria and Iran, both of which have political importance for Moscow. Conversely, it has caused Iraq to move closer to Saudi Arabia and the more conservative Arab States, away from its former radical affiliations.

The effect of the war on Iran could, however, be important. The need to defend the country seemed to have induced a degree of realism in the Ayatollahs, judged by the release of fighter pilots from jail. The Iraqi attack also helped unite the country and forced the Government (if such it is) to do something to strengthen the armed forces, even by seeking military supplies from governments that might otherwise be shunned. Whether the needs of the war and thus of the military will continue to enjoy some priority over other political considerations remains to be seen. If they did not and Iran suffered a major defeat, the country could well cease to remain under the control of a central government and provide a fertile field for Soviet political infiltration. If, on the other hand, the armed forces are kept in reasonably cohesive condition, they could provide the underpinning for more stable government one day. Whichever direction events take—and there could be others—the strategic situation in the region will be affected.

The super-power confrontation

This strategic situation is dominated at the moment by the confrontation between the Soviet Union and the US, the latter in effect the self-appointed military arm of the West but one for which there is no substitute. It is the maritime forces of the two that actually face each other, even if ground forces are held in readiness because it is on land that any decisive outcome would have to be sought.

Soviet naval vessels have been on station in the Indian Ocean since the mid-1960s, not in any large numbers for the most part. The combat strength of French forces in the area were often larger. During the same period the US Navy has had only very small permanent forces in the Gulf, but has from time to time sent powerful task forces to the Ocean. Since the Iranian revolution and the invasion of Afghanistan, however, the US Navy has been in the Arabian Sea in strength. Two

8

carrier task forces have been detached from the Mediterranean and Pacific Fleets and an amphibious unit (MAU) of c. 1,800 marines has been kept afloat there, again from the Pacific. Some seven ships carrying stores and equipment for a marine brigade have been pre-positioned at Diego Garcia, as have logistic vessels, and the airfield runway there is being lengthened for use by B-52 bombers.

In response to this US naval build-up, Soviet naval forces in the Ocean and the Red Sea have been augmented, but with ships less powerful than their US Navy counterparts, in particular lacking the defensive and offensive fighter air power that the US carriers provide. The Soviet squadron is heavily dependent on land-based air support, from Aden perhaps, or from Soviet airfields a considerable distance away. The Soviet reinforcing ships have also to be detached from other fleets, notably from that in the Far East, where the use of Cam Ranh Bay in Vietnam has now afforded a useful half-way staging post along the very long route from Vladivostok or Petropavlovsk. The Suez Canal lies, of course, between the Ocean and the Soviet Mediterranean and Black Sea Fleets and might be closed to reinforcements in a crisis, which would then have to sail the length of the Mediterranean and round the Cape.

Without doubt, the US enjoys naval superiority in the Arabian Sea area and seems likely to continue to do so, even taking into account the Soviet ability to deploy anti-shipping aircraft like the *Backfire* from Soviet airfields. Both fleets are a very long way from their home ports, but the US Navy has well-established, large forward-operating bases in the South Pacific, much nearer to the Indian Ocean than is Vladivostok. Though Cam Ranh Bay is being developed and Soviet ships may use Aden and ports in the Red Sea, these are operating facilities—and airfields, which are important—rather than major bases. The US has also negotiated naval and air facilities in a number of regional countries (so as not to be too dependent on one): Berbera in Somalia, in Kenya and Oman, and has Diego Garcia and an airbase in Egypt as well. Then not to be overlooked is the French naval base at Djibouti, with a useful French naval force there, and the bases in Singapore and Australia that are available for Western use. For both the US and the Soviet Union, maintaining naval forces on station in the huge Indian Ocean is a very expensive business, but the US does have a number of strategic advantages as a long-established naval power with maritime nations as allies.

One obvious task for the US Navy, with French and British assistance, is the traditional one of keeping the oil routes open, deterring any Soviet action against them by a presence in strength. Patrolling the Straits of Hormuz is part of this, though here there is also the subsidiary aim of dissuading any regional power such as Iran from offensive action there. However, the US Navy is also in the Arabian Sea to be able to project force on land, through air strikes and the support of marine or other landings. In any such land battle, the strategic advantage at once moves to the Soviet Union, geographically much nearer the Gulf and, now, with airfields in Afghanistan that are near enough to give fighter cover to operations on the eastern side of the Gulf. In the Soviet Union itself there are eight airborne divisions, very well equipped with light armour and the transport aircraft to enable them to mount attacks in the Gulf in a much shorter time than could forces sent from the US, 7,000 miles away.

The US is building up its RDF of army and marine formulations with air support in continental America and marines in the Pacific that can form part of it. Tactical air squadrons could be moved quickly, from Europe if need be, but the problem of moving land forces quickly and in sufficient numbers to the Gulf is an immensely difficult one. To be timely, all initial movement must be by air, which means that the ground forces can take with them only light, airportable weapons and equipment, so that heavy weapons would have to follow by sea or be pre-positioned in the area beforehand. Even then, these weapons are likely to be a considerable distance from a forward-operating area, so much time will still be taken in moving troops forward from the point at which their weapons are collected. This movement may have to be by sea or overland, for lack of suitable airlift for heavy weapons such as tanks.

The air movement from the US would have to be *via* the Atlantic, Mediterranean and ME. This entails air refuelling and transit arrangements in such countries as Egypt, Somalia, Kenya and Oman, with only the last-named affording a real jumping-off point for operations in the Gulf itself. Lacking at the moment are any forward-operating airfields or facilities further north, yet it must be clear that US forces could really only operate there if the local states wanted them to. If a Soviet military threat became more visible, facilities might be made available. In Saudi Arabia, US Air Force units are in fact operating now, with fighter and Airborne Warning and Control (Radar) System (AWACS) aircraft, and there is much compatibility with Saudi equipment. For the moment, however, the Gulf regimes are in general not ready to forge overt political and military links with the US, largely because of Washington's links with Israel.

The US is very good at solving strategic mobility problems, not least by throwing dollars at them. It will, nonetheless, be a long time before there is the necessary air and sea-lift to be able to move forces in timely fashion in the numbers that could begin to match those that the Soviet Union could deploy. At the moment it might take something over three weeks to move the men and equipment of a US airborne division and a marine brigade from the US to the Gulf, using all the heavy airlift that the US Air Force possesses. The RDF is planned eventually to have a strength of some 200,000 men. It will be many years before it is possible to move forces of this strength with their equipment within operationally acceptable timings, even if new long-range transport aircraft are built. There would also have to be a real network of forward operating facilities available, not possible, of course, without local consent and help.

While it is very easy to dwell on the difficulties that the US faces, those of the Soviet Union, while not of quite the same kind, are not so simple either. Without doubt, Soviet forces could move into northern Iran and little could be done to impede this; geography is too much on the Soviet side. Further south the problems are different. To operate in southern Iran, on the strategically very important western side of the Gulf, would have its political attractions but the distances over which Soviet troops would have to travel are great, even from Afghanistan, and the mountainous and desert terrain extremely difficult. It would not be too hard to get airborne divisions to the coast quite quickly, though the transport aircraft would be very vulnerable, but making the necessary link-up later with the heavier formations and providing logistic support would be time-consuming and costly. Both the forward bridgeheads and the troop columns that would have to travel very slowly overland, would be open to air attack mounted from US carriers and by long-range fighters. Quite light US ground forces could disrupt the bridgeheads themselves, if they could be got there early enough. The climate can be most inhospitable, and perhaps the local forces would be too. In the meantime the Soviet naval vessels in the Arabian Sea would be hard put to survive the attacks that would be made on them from the outset. Though the US land forces would be relatively weaker, the whole operation could still be singularly unattractive to the Soviet leaders.

On the western side of the Gulf, the vital one for the West, the distances from the Soviet Union to critical areas are considerable and the terrain and climate again unforgiving. An important factor here would be the attitude of Iraq, which could be a barrier to Soviet forces or a conduit, depending on the state of relations between the two states. As with southern Iran, to get Soviet airborne formations on the ground is one thing, to link them up with heavier formations and to give them air cover is quite another. US air action from airfields in the area which under the circumstances would almost certainly be made available, would make the conduct of such a campaign very costly to the Soviet Union. And that is quite apart from what is really the most important feature, the risks of a wider conventional war, almost implicit in any major Soviet action against the oilfields of the Gulf.

It is in this light that the purpose of the RDF must be seen. The US may not get to the Gulf 'fustest with the mostest', but elements of the RDF can get there fast enough to 'lay an American across the road', the form of deterrence evolved and practised in Europe but applicable here, even if it may not be quite clear just where the road will actually be. The American determination to resist any Soviet military expansion in the area presents potential risks to Moscow which include that of a major war, a very salutary consideration. While an extension of conflict from the Gulf to other areas may not include the threat of the use of nuclear weapons, which both sides would have an interest in avoiding, it is very hard to see how conventional fighting could be neatly contained within the region.

The Western position as a whole is thus protected, though the part that the allies would play may be only a limited one. France and Britain, long accustomed to being in the ME, can give some military help and contribute experience, valuable not least for not being American. Other allies could assume other burdens to take the weight off the US, such as financial help to involved countries such as Egypt or Pakistan, or Turkey, and be generally helpful politically in the Arab world.

All of this may look remarkably like the West defending its own interests rather than those of the regional states. There is obviously some truth in this, since these certainly are Western interests, but they are local interests as well. Soviet military expansion into the Gulf would menace Western oil supplies, but it would also sound the death-knell for many local regimes and freedoms. It may be American foreign policy and military preparations that attract most attention at the moment, but events in nearby Afghanistan bear witness to Soviet policies and actions.

Regional states, with the exception of large ones such as India and Pakistan, are unlikely to be able to defend themselves against any serious external threat. There has been a new awareness in the Gulf of the needs of security, as well there might be, given the political uncertainties there are and the way that military force is regularly used in the ME in the attempt to achieve political aims. Weapons are being bought by many States, and Saudi Arabia has been notable for inviting US Air Force units into the country to provide fighter and early warning coverage (with AWACS aircraft) as a result of the outbreak of the Iraqi-Iranian War. While there is much to be gained by local defensive arrangements such as those in the United Arab Emirates, there is no substitute for external military support if a real threat is present: Oman has recognized this very clearly and made successful use of it. If the shadow of Soviet military action hangs over the Gulf, the counterweight of the US is needed there too, and no regional strategic balance is likely to alter this. It seems likely that local States will be prepared to underwrite an American military presence, to grant it access, if the threat becomes evident to them.

Most of what has been said above is properly concerned with military considerations, since they are the key element in a strategy. But there are other important elements in strategy too, including diplomatic, political and economic.

11

Soviet military activity in the Gulf is almost certainly less likely than attempts at political expansion. The Soviet Union went into Afghanistan politically first, steadily expanding influence there over many years. When it intervened militarily this was not least to preserve the investment already made. Expanded political influence in the ME and Africa has given Moscow eventual military footholds in strategically valuable places, despite occasional setbacks such as in Egypt and Somalia. In the Gulf, Iran presents a scene of political turbulence, near civil war, that the Soviet Union will undoubtedly try to turn to its own advantage. Moscow might like to see a regime with Soviet leanings seize power and then invite Soviet forces in to protect it, on the pattern of Afghanistan. If that happened it would not be easy for the West to react to the *fait accompli* and a certain dubious legitimacy—but the Western strategic position would be drastically weakened.

Political action is therefore vital: military power is no substitute for diplomacy; they must go hand in hand. Some of this political action must be devoted to the all-important feature of promoting the stability of the Gulf States, perhaps through economic and technical assistance and trade. It is abundantly clear that the Western position could suffer as much through a breakdown of the internal fabric of these countries as from an attack on them from outside, as the case of Iran has demonstrated. Internal instability presents a much more complex problem than the relatively simple case of external defence. Political action must therefore not be insensitive to local needs; too strong an insistence on purely East-West considerations could actually contribute to instability by forcing local regimes to bear more political weight than they can stand. It is here that the very diversity of the countries of the West can be a strength. Japan and Europe may add little to the military component of the strategy, but their contribution to the political and economic elements, from standpoints often discernibly different from that of the US, can be a help rather than the hindrance that it can sometimes appear to be in Washington. It must be said roundly that American diplomacy in the ME will need to be more sensitive than it has been in the recent past, if the Western strategy in the region is to have any chance of success.

Brig. Kenneth Hunt

12

PART I
Crisis and Conflicts

The Middle East in Perspective

The promised imminent upheavals of 1979 were amply fulfilled in 1980—but not necessarily at what had appeared to be the pivotal points of impending disruption. Rather than the collapse of existing regimes, or the onward surge of the "Islamic tide," it was armed conflict and the menace of further wars which marked off 1980 from its predecessors: the Iraqi-Iranian war; the Syrian show of force on the Jordanian border; Libya's plunge into Chad with its concomitant threat to Sudan and other countries in the area. For a generation, actual or threatened war in the Middle East had always meant an Arab-Israeli conflagration: in 1980 it was either Muslim fighting Muslim or Arab threatening Arab—and with Arab States dividing their allegiances.

THE IRAQI-IRANIAN WAR

The 1980 Iraqi-Iranian war crossed territory which had been an area of regional confrontation for many centuries. Geo-political pressure lines, the blurred ethnic frontier of Arabs and Persians, the equally blurred religious demarcation line between Sunnīs and Shī'īs, had made the area a major "seismic fault" in southwest Asia long before it became the Iraqi-Iranian border after World War I. In 1979, the new Iranian regime had revived all these historic, religious and ethnic tensions and infused them with a new and unrelenting vigour. What had started as a vague malaise in Iraqi-Iranian relations in the early Spring of 1979 had become outright hostility by the end of the year. During 1980, tension escalated from propaganda warfare to subversion and sporadic border fighting before erupting into full-scale war.

The build-up to the war resulted from two miscalculations: Iran's was in believing that it could continue its political, ideological, and subversive assaults against Baghdad without inviting retribution; Iraq's was in believing that the in-fighting among Khomeyni's supporters, its purges of the officer corps and the failure to maintain the armour and logistics in the armed forces had left the country an easy prey to Iraq's better equipped army.

The Iranian political offensive, carried forward by ceaseless destabilizing propaganda and subversive activities, was aimed at the overthrow of the Iraqi Ba'th regime and, it must be assumed, by its replacement with a leadership (possibly Shī'ī?) holding ideas similar to those of Ruḥollah Khomeyni. The Iraqi military offensive was aimed at ridding President Saddām Ḥusayn of what had become his obsession with Khomeyni—by humiliating, perhaps even bringing down his regime or, at the very least, making it desist from its anti-Iraqi campaign. The more lasting gains would be the realization of Baghdad's maximalist territorial and navigational claims along its land and riverine borders—perhaps to be made all the more unassailable by establishing some form of Iraqi overlordship over the ethnic Arabs of the province of Khuzistan.

When it became clear during October 1980 that the war had turned from a *blitzkrieg* into a slogging match, some of the consequences for both the parties involved in the conflict, and for the region as a whole, began to emerge. Moving outwards from the two capitals, the following points stand out:

• In Iran, the first reaction was to close ranks in the face of a foreign enemy. Yet, before long, the power struggle was resumed. However, rather than being

15

fragmented into multiple centres of power, the political scene now became more clearly polarized: at one end was President Abul-Ḥasan Bani Sadr, building up his own power base among the armed forces; at the other, a group of clerics, heading the Islamic Republican Party, led by Khomeyni's heir-presumptive, Ḥusayn 'Ali Montazeri, and Muḥammad Beheshti. By the end of 1980, the conduct of the war had to some extent become a function of their struggle, with the parties using the changing fortunes of war to score against each other.

• In Iraq, the regime had to cope with the public reaction to a struggle which had been expected to last a few days or weeks, having turned into a protracted war. The inherent weaknesses of the regime were thrown into sharper relief. The disaffection of the Shī'īs and Kurds, and the persisting hope of the Communist Party to regain lost ground, all made themselves felt: their hatred for the Ba'th provided a possible—indeed the only—common interest. Moreover, Saddām Ḥusayn's political future now became dependent on the army's performance—an army which he distrusted as a group. His natural inclination at times of crisis has been to rely on the party militia and the secret services; but this was impractical in the new situation.

• Iran's external relations did not change radically during the first phase of the war. Its already evident international isolation was simply underscored. Its regional isolation in the Gulf area was rendered complete. Further afield, support from Syria and Libya was welcome; but this turned out to have even greater repercussions on the inter-Arab setting than on the war itself. (See below.) Algeria's support was more qualified and, for that very reason, proved an asset in ending the US hostage affair. Elsewhere in the Muslim and Third World, Iran found no friends.

• For Iraq, the unexpected prolongation of the war was a major foreign-policy setback. It halted what had earlier seemed to be the start of a real breakthrough on the road to regional hegemony in the Gulf; to a centre-stage, if not an outright leadership position, in the Arab world; and to a major role in the Non-aligned movement. Baghdad's Pan-Arab Declaration of February 1980 had been intended to mark a new phase in each of these three directions, with the war as the next major step along that road. A speedy, decisive victory would establish Iraq as the military overlord of the Gulf and earn it all-Arab recognition as the defender of Arab causes against non-Arabs (Iranians today, Israelis—it was hinted from Baghdad—tomorrow). Instead, Iraq's claim to superior military capability proved hollow. What was worse: Iraq was no longer seen as the Arab country capable of taking the lead in Arab affairs. Its military forces were tied down in the east, facing away from the Arab world, and its political attention was riveted on a non-Arab rival. This, it was generally believed, was likely to remain the position for a long time to come. Even an eventual ceasefire would not release Baghdad's energies because political and ideological hostility and irridentist claims would persist. So, therefore, would the prospect of renewed fighting. Furthermore, Iraq's economic strength— which had only recently become a potent instrument of political influence— was being sapped by the war. An instructive example of this political and economic downgrading is provided by comparing Iraq's stance at the Amman conference of Foreign and Economic Ministers in July 1980 with that at the summit conference at the same venue in November, after the outbreak of the war. At the July meeting, Iraq had presented, with great fanfare, a plan for an Arab "decade of development" with the oil-rich States putting up $1.5 bn per year to strengthen the economies of the poorer Arab countries. At the

November summit, Iraq was almost exclusively concerned with drumming up support against Iran, and hardly even protested when its economic plan was reduced to a mere third of its original scope.
• The Iraqi-Iranian war continued the process—begun by the invasion of Afghanistan—of relegating the Arab-Israeli conflict from being the central issue in the ME, which it had been for so long. Rhetoric at Arab and Islamic meetings, notwithstanding, it was the disputes in their immediate neighbourhood that were of greater concern for most Arab countries in 1980 than Arab-Israeli issues. This was most of all true of the Gulf and Peninsular states with regard to Iran; but hardly less so for Sudan with its preoccupation with Chad and the Horn of Africa, and for Morocco with its struggle in the West Sahara. Libya, always eager in the past to promote Arab action against Israel, shifted the focus of its attention to its Saharan *lebensraum* until, by the end of the year, the thrust of its policies was almost exclusively concentrated there. (In the process, the Libyan-Syrian merger plan, announced in September 1980, was set aside.) Moreover, the fate of Afghanistan, and its perceived Soviet threat to the ME, remained a powerful issue preoccupying (and dividing) Arab countries. Despite resolutions on *jihād,* for most Arab countries the Arab-Israeli conflict had in fact, moved down to second or even third place in the order of their national foreign policy priorities. Only for Syria and the Palestine Liberation Organization (PLO) did Israel remain the overriding concern. Being alone in that attitude, their standing in overall ME affairs declined quite sharply.
• Gradually, this began to register in the West as well. The concept that if only the Palestinian issue were solved, the ME would become a more tranquil place was obviously no longer tenable. Yet, the powerlessness of Europe to produce any impact whatsoever on either the Gulf war or the Afghan situation, led to European statements revolving around the ME issues of 1974–77 rather than those of 1980.
• The "demotion" of the Israeli issue was underscored by the evident inability of the Arab countries to reconstitute the "Eastern Command" opposite Israel. At least in the short term, any such attempt was precluded by Syria's isolation, its quarrels with both Jordan and Iraq, and Iraq's overriding concentration on the Iranian war.
• The war bore out Egypt's description of the rest of the Arab world as unstable and "disruption-prone," and strengthened it in its self-perception as an "island of stability." Whether acknowledged or not, that area of regional stability included Israel as well—and its claim to being a "strategic asset" for the West was lent greater substance by the war and its consequences.
• In terms of global policy, both Super Powers recognized that Iran was strategically the more important party to the conflict. Their profession of neutrality contained hints—phrased in the lowest possible key—suggesting that their neutrality was ever so slightly tilted in favour of Iran. But in 1980, this had virtually no practical effect: the US was still hamstrung by the hostage affair, and the USSR by the problem of Afghanistan. Moreover, *both* were almost equally unwelcome in Tehran. But other than in the two warring countries, the process of Great Power military entrenchment in the ME proceeded apace, dramatically reversing the trend of the previous decade. In this process (triggered by the invasion of Afghanistan, but accelerated by the Gulf war), the US seemed to have a slight edge over the USSR because of its growing military presence in, and strategic co-ordination with, Egypt; its (more restricted) military ties with Saudi Arabia; the "facilities" it obtained in Somalia, Oman

17

and Kenya; and because of the unspoken, yet unmistakable, attitudes of other Gulf states, and of Sudan and Morocco. On the other hand, apart from Afghanistan, the USSR's gains were in Syria, Libya, the People's Democratic Republic of Yemen (PDRY), and in maintaining its role in Ethiopia.

• The sharp drop in Iranian oil exports, and the fluctuations in those of Iraq, did not lead to a new oil crisis in 1980. The world oil market adjusted smoothly to the war situation because of increased output by other producers, stock-piling by major consumers in preceding years, and a slight drop in consumption, or at least, in the rate of increased consumption by the economically-depressed industrialized countries. By contrast, the war's impact on the oil industry of Iran and Iraq was strong. In Iran, the downward economic trend noted since 1979 became much more marked, adding to popular discontent. In Iraq, the short-term impact was cushioned by accumulated reserves. In both countries, the damage to oil installations was serious. How lasting it would turn out to be, and how strongly the need to rehabilitate the oil industry would inhibit their post-war economic recovery, remained to be seen.

THE ARAB SUMMIT DÉBÂCLE

As is evident from the above, the Iraqi-Iranian war had a profound influence on the system of inter-Arab relations—compounding, aggravating or bringing out trends that had already been at work for the twelve months preceding its outbreak. During 1980, a group of Arab States, unwilling to endanger their good relations with the USSR and risk interrupting the supply of Soviet arms because of a remote quarrel in Afghanistan, drew away from the rest and closer to each other. In a correlation that was not at all coincidental, they were also the States to which the Arab-Israeli conflict remained a high, or the highest, priority. The Syrian slogan: "Jerusalem is closer than Kabul" conveyed the inter-connection. Syria was indeed the leader of this group, membership in which was coterminous with that of the Front of Steadfastness and Resistance (also comprising Libya, Algeria, the PLO and the PDRY). Established late in 1977 after Sādāt's visit to Jerusalem, it had virtually ceased to function in 1978 when Syria had hoped to come to terms with Iraq. When that attempt proved a failure, Syria turned back to its former allies. The revival of the Front during the last quarter of 1979 and during 1980, and its growing antagonism to the rest of the Arab world, was one of the most striking features of inter-Arab developments in that period. As Iranian-Iraqi tensions mounted during the year, Front members sided with Iran rather than with Iraq. On this point, too, Syria took the lead—acting from enmity towards Iraq rather than from sympathy for Iran. Libya had more regard for Khomeyni, partly from a shared perception of the role of the US, partly from an affinity for some (but not all) of Khomeyni's Islamic precepts. As noted above, Algeria was less committed. The PLO and Iran were, by now, rather disappointed with each other; but the PLO may still have entertained hopes for some political benefits for itself and was, in any case, compelled to defer to Syria. Among the Front members, the PDRY was the most reluctant partner, having to weigh the advantage of co-operating with a regime as anti-American as its own against the danger of supporting a religious revolution abroad, while preaching "scientific socialism" at home.

As the dividing lines over Afghanistan and Iran sharpened, the Arab quarrel with Egypt receded into the background: the anti-Sādāt forces were now more significantly divided among themselves than at any time since the beginning of President Anwar al-Sādāt's peace policy. While anti-Sādāt rhetoric and the total rejection of "the Camp David conspiracy" remained *de rigueur,* and continued to

18

make the participation of Egypt in Arab or Islamic meetings unthinkable in 1980, practical policy decisions no longer dealt with the issue of Egypt's ostracism.

All these trends came to a head with the approach of the Arab summit scheduled to meet in November 1980 in Amman, in accordance with a decision taken a year earlier at the summit conference in Tunis. Syria wished to avoid a confrontation at the highest Arab level in which it would be castigated by the majority as "un-Arab" for siding with Iran, and as "un-Islamic" for failing to condemn the Soviet presence in Afghanistan. It was unwilling to sit at the same table with Jordan and Iraq, both of whom it accused of actively supporting the violent domestic opposition to its regime. Most of all, perhaps, it wanted to torpedo a meeting which, in its view, was likely to assent to a special Jordanian role in negotiating with the incoming US Administration over a new political approach to a ME settlement—a development almost as deleterious to its interests as Sādāt's "defection." When a Syrian request for a postponement went unheeded, Damascus rallied the Steadfastness Front members (for once sufficiently disciplined to follow) for a collective boycott of the summit, and bullied Lebanon into staying away as well. For the PLO, which owed its existence to the first summit in 1964 and its legitimacy to that of 1974—the decision to remain absent must have been an agonizing one.

The conference was thus attended by only 15 countries (22 members, minus six absentees and minus Egypt, suspended since 1978). This was no longer a case of an odd country or two staying away in angry protest over an issue of special interest, as had happened on a number of earlier occasions. The absence of over a quarter of the members cast a shadow over the very future of the Arab summit as a political institution—after a career of 16 years and after the ten previous conferences had come to be regarded as the main symbol of Arab unity of purpose. If Syria was not strong enough to force a postponement on the majority, it could still—even from its position of isolation in the Arab world—make the empty seats conspicuous and render much of the deliberation pointless.

But boycott was not enough. To underscore the point it was making by "organized absenteeism," Syria concentrated troops, mainly armour, along its border with Jordan and began a threatening propaganda campaign in which Amman's aid to the opposition in Syria and its putative intention of joining a (modified) Camp David process figured most prominently. ("We will not tolerate the emergence of a new Sādāt on our border," was the way one Syrian spokesman put it.) For several weeks, in November and December, war seemed imminent. Following several rounds of Saudi mediation, both sides stopped sabre-rattling and dispersed their forces. The Saudis may not have *caused* that reversal since it was, after all, doubtful whether Syria had intended any more than intimidation in the first place; and Jordan had in any case deployed its troops only in reply to the Syrian moves. But mediation made it easier for both to climb down.

Had the Syrians attained their aims? There was no simple answer. In military terms, their venture was clearly less than a success. Military commitments in Lebanon and the need to keep a massive military presence in and around its own main cities prevented Syria from bringing the full weight of its intrinsic military power to bear along the Jordanian border. Jordan seemed able to match the forces Syria could field under such circumstances, and gave every indication of being fully determined to fight back. But, in political terms, Syria's action left its mark both on the course of the summit meeting (Amman wags were quoted as saying that Syria had been "represented at the conference by two armoured divisions 100 kms away") and on Jordan's subsequent conduct. The final summit resolutions contained no passages really objectionable to Syria. King Ḥusayn (who had pointedly omitted any reference to the PLO in his opening speech at the conference) went on to make a series of statements disclaiming any intention of becoming involved in the ME peace process, let alone of displacing the PLO as the representatives of the Palestinians. In short: while instant intimidation by the threat of force clearly had not worked, the Syrian message pointing out the cost to Jordan of antagonizing Syria—whether over the domestic situation or whether over the Arab policies towards Israel—had obviously registered with Amman. A draw of sorts, then, but one achieved at the price of a menacing public display of inter-Arab hostility. Coming on top of the developments sketched above, the spectacle of two States, which had co-operated in 1978 and 1979 in forming the broadest possible anti-Sādāt alignment, almost coming to blows in 1980 was striking evidence—keenly felt in the Arab world—of the extent to which Arab interests had diverged, Arab policies become contradictory, and Arab forces splintered. The lesson of the "three-quarter" summit was driven home even more forcefully by the fact that, to an extent unprecedented in the past, non-Arab states had become part of the pattern of inter-Arab relations. Libya, Syria and *Iran* now formed as much of a ME axis as did Iraq, Jordan and Saudi Arabia facing them. Egypt's peace treaty and its incipient ties with Israel had, in effect, created another "mixed" regional alignment—however much this contradicted Egypt's own perception of its regional role. And just as the alignment of Syria and Libya with a country outside the accepted Arab framework was one major reason for their non-participation in the summit, so Egypt's new relationship with Israel was reason enough for the summit to keep Sādāt away.

EGYPT AND ISRAEL

Along with other Arab-Israeli issues, the development of Egyptian-Israeli relations was not only less central to the overall picture of the ME in 1980 than it had been in 1978 and 1979; but it also registered little movement in itself. The pattern of partial and somewhat one-sided "normalization" which had emerged in 1979 continued into 1980 through a series of ups and downs which did not affect the basic situation; nor did the autonomy talks break out of the pattern of the strongly divergent interpretations which the parties had already put forward in 1979. The divergences stemmed, most of all, from attempts by both Egypt and Israel to conduct the autonomy talks with an eye to pre-judging—each in the direction desirable to itself—the nature of the *post-autonomy* order of things, rather than laying down rules on how to handle the five-year period of autonomy itself. Israel conducted the autonomy talks largely with an eye to domestic politics; for Egypt and the US, they were primarily an issue affecting their future relations with the rest of the Arab world. If in the course of 1980 the arguments over autonomy lost some of their acerbity, it was because first Egypt, then Israel, and eventually the US, too, accepted as inevitable that the talks could not be concluded by the end of that year. They would have to mark time until the new US Administration had established its guidelines, some time in early 1981, on an issue that was obviously not its top priority, and until the outcome of the Israeli Knesset elections would become known later that year. While outside Arab voices seized on the lack of progress of the autonomy talks to declare them bankrupt, Sādāt regarded their slow-down as no more than an intermission to be endured with patience. Israel had at first allowed the talks to mark time, but towards the end of the year official quarters and Press comments began to emphasize that it would not be in Israel's best interest for the autonomy issue to stay unresolved at the time of the final withdrawal from Sinai in the Spring of 1982.

MIDDLE EAST REGIMES: AN UNSTABLE EQUILIBRIUM

In strong contrast with the unsettled climate in the ME caused by the conflicts described above, the year was relatively quiet on the domestic front of the main countries in the area. Regimes that had looked particularly vulnerable in 1979 survived without serious upsets in 1980, but they did little towards even beginning to tackle the fundamental problems in their troubled societies. Other regimes, which had felt themselves as being reasonably free of serious domestic opposition in 1979, found this was no longer true in 1980. But the "tide of Islam" made no spectacular progress anywhere in the ME, no doubt partly due to the experiences of the Iranian Islamic Republic which had failed to offer new social policies and had proved itself incapable of running the economy; caught up in interminable in-fighting between its various power groups; showing as little regard for human rights as the Shah's regime, despite its own earlier slogans. It projected a grim image of Islamic justice and, eventually, ended up fighting a war with fellow-Muslims. Another contributory reason for the slowing up of the "tide of Islam" was that most ME regimes, having closely watched the Iranian scene, took more stringent security measures against local groups with a similar outlook to Khomeyni's. Yet the resurgence of political Islam was by no means halted. The Muslim Brotherhood—or some of its more militant offshoots—made further gains in attracting support in many countries, among them North Africa, Sudan, Kuwait, Jordan, the West Bank and Gaza. It also promoted its influence over Muslims residing in the West through the Federation of Muslim Students in Europe, which it dominated. In Turkey, Necmettin Erbakan, leader of the National Salvation Party, had seemed on the point of launching his own version of Khomeynism and had met with some initial response before his venture was cut short by the military takeover in September 1980.

The Turkish army coup was the only radical change of regime in the region in 1980. Political violence approaching the point of anarchy, economic disruption and party manoeuvring which had almost paralysed parliament combined with Erbakan's challenge to one of the pillars of Kemalism (viz. secularism), prompted the reluctant Generals to act. By their own testimony, the military coup would have a more lasting imprint on Turkish politics than that of either 1960 or 1971. Army rule would be more prolonged, and power would be returned into civilian hands only after the Turkish Constitution was sufficiently reshaped to satisfy the Generals that the disastrous conditions of the 1970s would not recur. It was by no means clear what policies the military would pursue other than to make war against political violence, take a firmer grip on the economy and produce a new Constitution.

Of the Arab leaders, President Ḥāfiz al-Asad of Syria stands out for having weathered the storm of Sunnī opposition and withstood the assault of Muslim activists. He did so by severe and forcible repression and not shirking to liquidate his opponents physically. By the end of the year he had clearly shifted the balance of violence and counter-violence in his favour. But his regime's success had also increased the resentment which had been among the root causes of turbulence since the mid-1970s; and it was achieved at the cost of reversing one of the basic components of its domestic policy over the preceding decade: correcting its image as an exclusively party-oriented and narrowly sectarian ('Alawī) clique by winning grass-roots' support and by ostensible power-sharing. By radicalizing and polarizing politics without mitigating the 'Alawī-Sunnī tension—without addressing itself to the contradiction of governing a mostly religious population in the name of a party professing a secular ideology, and without accommodating the "new middle class" through genuine participation in power—it took a lien on the future rather than improved its viability beyond the most immediate short-term.

Saudi Arabia also successfully overcame an immediate challenge—the Mecca attack in November 1979—without dealing with any of the more fundamental challenges posed by its society or political system.

In Iraq, Saddām Ḥusayn's accession to the Presidency in the Summer of 1979, had brought about a notable change in the style of government, but hardly in basic policies. In contrast with his predecessor Aḥmad Ḥasan al-Bakr, Saddām Ḥusayn developed a strong personality cult, which projected the image of a populist leader of historic genius. He was, however, even quicker now than in his ten years as the country's number-two leader to suppress the slightest signs of disloyalty. Half-hearted attempts to win over the Shī'ī community (e.g. by stepping up a campaign to recruit Shī'īs into the Ba'th party) soon gave way to repressive measures intended to stop the spread of Khomeynist ideas. As noted above, the war made Shī'ī, Kurdish and Leftist opposition more dangerous. Whether it also brought into question the officer corps' loyalty to Saddām Ḥusayn, and its subservience to the party apparatus (a unique feature of the Iraqi Ba'th) remained an important but speculative question.

Opposition, actual and potential, was also on the increase in Libya. Qadhdhāfī's erratic social policies successively alienated and antagonized most strata of the population. Expatriate opponents—more vocal and better organized than before—were subject to an assassination campaign; at home, opposition activities were obscured by tight official control of the media; but there could be no doubt that the regime was forced to act repressively on a number of occasions.

Most other Arab regimes—Egypt, Sudan, the Gulf Emirates—just held the line in 1980. For the latter—considering their fragility and their tempestuous environment—this was a considerable achievement. Egypt found it had to cope with Coptic-Muslim tensions—a spill-over from the "Islamic tide." Its perennial problem of reconciling a basically paternalistic political society with some form of a participatory democracy surfaced in 1980 mainly in the controversy over the Law for the Protection of Ethics (generally known as the "Law of Shame"), and over the *Majlis al-Shūrā* (Consultative Council; a kind of Upper House). In Sudan, "national reconciliation" remained incomplete for yet another year, and regionalism became more of a problem. Of the major Arab countries, Jordan seemed least troubled by domestic apprehensions. The Israeli Government having been buoyed up in the Spring of 1979 by the signing of the peace treaty with Egypt, became more listless as the year wore on. At first the Begin Coalition was mainly concerned to prolong its tenure for the maximum term legally possible (i.e. until November 1981); but it eventually resigned itself to its inability to do so and, early in 1981, decided on an earlier dissolution of the Knesset and mid-year elections. Compared with roughly a decade earlier when new leaders in Egypt, Sudan, Syria, Iraq, Libya and Turkey were attempting to develop new political systems, ME domestic politics did not present a memorable record in 1980.

Survival was made easier for the region's regimes by economic success. The oil producers could hardly fail with oil prices rising almost as steeply as in 1973–74. To give just one example: Saudi oil rose by 120% between December 1978 and August 1980. Even more remarkable was the relative economic success of some other Arab countries. Egypt made important gains in improving its balance of payments, accumulating a surplus for the first time in many years, and tripling its foreign currency reserves during the last quarter of 1979 and the first two quarters of 1980. Oil played a part in this; but so did the Suez Canal, greater tourism and, most particularly, foreign (mostly Western) aid and investments. However, these gains did not, as yet, "filter down" in 1980 to improve the standard of living of the great majority of Egyptians, or to alleviate the Government's economic concerns. Even Sudan—economically speaking the most embattled country in this group—ended the year on a note of hope after oil finds were announced. The worst economic difficulties were experienced by the region's non-Arab countries. Iran, first suffering from self-inflicted economic wounds, was left to face the damage done by the war. Turkey, struggling with inflation (c. 100% for 1980) was faced with severe balance-of-payment problems, with industries running far below capacity. Finally, Israel was faced with severe constraints on its economic growth, and a seemingly uncontrollable inflation reaching 133% for 1980.

CONCLUSION

It was a bad year for old concepts. Arab unity and Islamic cohesion, which only a year before seemed to have acquired a new lease of life, suffered seriously. Khomeyni had translated theological tenets into the formal clauses of a novel kind of Constitution which—so it had appeared to many Muslims—would make it possible to combine the world view of early Islam with the techniques of the twentieth century. Similarly, Pan-Islam had appeared in 1979 to be on the point of being turned into a foreign policy programme. Yet, before the end of its second year in power, his regime had become a deterrent rather than a model for Middle Eastern believers in a latter-day "Islamic State;" and Khomeyni, who had so often spoken of Islam as "one nation," was at war with another Muslim country—even if he had to declare it "a country of infidels."

Arab unity had taken a similar turn for the worse. Goaded into action in late 1978 and early 1979 by the need to articulate, and act out, a reply to Sādāt, the Arab countries had formed what at first looked like a solid, almost comprehensive, common front against the Camp David accords and against the Egyptian-Israeli peace treaty. Their charge against Sādāt was that he had *ignored* Arab solidarity; their justification for ostracizing a major Arab State was that they were acting to *uphold* their solidarity. Yet, a year later, the same countries could not bring together as many as three-quarters of their own number for the Amman summit, and their deliberations took place against the background noise of Syrian armour being concentrated to threaten the conference's host country.

Even at this low point, though, the ideals of Arab and Islamic unity of purpose remained strong and the concept of Arab and Islamic solidarity (i.e. of a more practical and pragmatic version of that ideal) remained potent in its broad appeal. The damage they had suffered activated built-in defence mechanisms which made an immediate salvage operation possible. The Arab group did so mainly by adopting, at its rump summit, resolutions couched in a language which the absentees would not, by and large, have hesitated to subscribe to. The Islamic grouping held a summit of its own—almost fully attended—in Mecca and Tā'if in January 1981, and turned it into a forceful reassertion of the concept that Islamic nations (though not, perhaps, "the Islamic nation") were a power in global politics.

Daniel Dishon

The Changing Strategic Tapestry in the Middle East

By any measure 1980 was a threshold year in the evolving strategic relationships in the Middle East. Although the traditional focus of conflict—the Arab-Israeli dispute—was relatively quiet, the Soviet invasion of Afghanistan, the hostage crisis between the US and Iran and, finally, the outbreak of war between Iran and Iraq in the Autumn of 1980 convinced all but the most naive observers that the worrying predictions that have been made for the past four or five years, namely, that the emerging crisis in the Middle East could be the most dangerous for the world today, has become reality. It is no longer possible to isolate the nuances of the various conflict regions from each other. Furthermore, the upsurge of militant Islam in the politics of the region has become as important a factor in determining alliances between the various national groups, as have traditional East-West allegiances and the "radical" vs "moderate" labels which have been applied so freely in the past.

Although the war in Afghanistan continued to be the most important strategic issue because it involved the direct use of Soviet military forces, the other two crises commanded equal, if not more, headline news during the year, because of the US involvement in the hostage crisis and also because the Iraqi-Iranian war vividly demonstrated the vulnerability of oil facilities and the willingness of major oil-producing countries to destroy each other's assets in pursuit of traditional geopolitical goals. Furthermore, since the Iraqi-Iranian war and the hostage crisis were more readily accessible to Western journalists than the war in Afghanistan, television screens were filled nightly with views of burning oilfields and fighting soldiers. The long-term implications of these conflicts for the stability of the region were difficult to foretell. Certainly, the events had a sobering impact upon the rhetoric of some of the more radical Arab leaders, and Saudi Arabia appeared to be taking more concrete steps towards shoring up its defences, although not necessarily with direct American participation. Meanwhile, towards the end of 1980, other events in Northern Africa once again highlighted the important linkage between the Southern Mediterranean and the ME itself. Libya's involvement in the war in Chad gave rise to fears about its potential hegemony in Northern Africa and its threats to Egypt. While Colonel Qadhdhāfī established himself as the most reckless and radical of all the Arab leaders, the Algerian Government, in contrast, by playing such an important role in the negotiations for the release of the American hostages in January 1981, emerged as a more "responsible" power—one that some Western observers felt should be courted in the years ahead as a way of diminishing both Libyan and Soviet influence along the North African littoral.

One ironic effect of these events was to downplay, at least temporarily, the significance of the Palestinian problem as a catalyst for ME conflict. With some justification, supporters of Israel pointed to the irrelevance of Palestine as a factor in the region's ongoing wars. To this extent, the penchant of the United Nations and the pro-Palestinian supporters there to blame future stability on Israeli intransigence suffered a setback. However, to balance this point of view, other observers felt that the events of 1980 merely postponed the Palestinian issue and in no way downgraded it.

Finally, perhaps the most important external non-military event of the year was the election of Ronald Reagan as President. He came to power on a platform committed to redressing the slide in American prestige which had occurred under the Carter Administration. Reagan, unlike many of his Republican counterparts, has had a long track record of support for Israel and it was clear that the early composition of his Administration would reflect a more pro-Israel stance than was the case under Carter. How this would translate into American decisions on such controversial issues as arms sales to the Arab countries remained an open question.

SAUDI ARABIA—INTERNAL AND EXTERNAL THREATS

Saudi Arabia significantly increased its defence and internal security budgets in 1980 at a time when indications of its vulnerability to both internal and external threats had visibly increased. Defence spending was raised by 18% to over $20 bn. However, by the end of the year this massive, focused expenditure had succeeded in expanding army manoeuvre units by only one—from one armoured and one mechanized brigade, to two armoured and one mechanized brigades. Saudi security doctrine continues to concentrate on low-to-medium threats and contingencies: infiltration of irregular units, maritime surveillance and patrol, and limited air defence, built around high-performance interception of single reconnaissance aircraft or small "spoiling" groups on high-value raider missions.

It is in this context that the Saudi-Iraqi *rapprochement* brought about by the Iraqi-Iranian war can be best appreciated. Riyadh is well aware that it is incapable of resisting a major Iraqi invasion. On the other, more image-laden facet of Iraqi-Saudi hostility, the Saudis can afford to concede some of the emotional badge of "leadership" of the Arab world to Saddām Husayn in return for collaboration in stabilizing a Fertile Crescent rent by radical ambitions.

More ominously, while certain short-term external security assurances were exchanged, Saudi Arabia's internal security deteriorated. The seizure of the Grand Mosque in Mecca by Libyan-supplied opponents of the House of Al-Sa'ūd underscored the relative instability of the National Guard, some members of which supported the sedition of 'Utayba's anti-Sa'ūd Wahhābi sect. For 1981, the Saudi defence budget included $168m for an upgraded "internal security programme." The Kingdom, it must be remembered, is not a "nation-state" according to Western definition. It is a well-managed coalition of tribal interests, balanced and, at times, harshly dominated by the Sa'ūd family. The bloody battle of Mecca in late November 1979 can only serve as a warning to the ruling house that the tribal fragmentation, which has kept the Arabian peninsula so disunited, is not yet history.

Notwithstanding its security dependence on the US and a decade-long exclusive arms connection, the Saudi regime continued its *pas de deux* with France. For the ground forces, 370 AMX-30 tanks, 200 AMX-10 APCs, *Panhard* M-3s, *Shahine,* and *Crotale* are on order, giving French equipment the majority in the ground order of battle. A deal with French shipyards for $1.75 bn for a 20-ship coastguard package was doubled in September 1980 to include four 2,000-ton missile frigates and, interestingly, two 17,000-ton replenishment ships of the proven *Durance* type. These will give the *Otomat*-equipped frigates and *Harpoon*-equipped corvettes, being built in the US, the ability to maintain long-ranging patrols in the Persian Gulf, and will help to compensate for the relative growth of potentially hostile Iranian and Iraqi naval forces.

The Saudi regime is now apparently committed to underwriting heavily the development costs of the *Mirage* 4,000 fighter, a twin-engined export version of the *Armée de l'Air Mirage* 2,000. Out of an estimated $1.45 bn programme, the Saudis will finance $968m. Tilting to France for combat aircraft was but one sign

25

of Saudi displeasure with US arms transfer policies, especially the controversial F-15 bomb-rack clause.

In the first week of January 1981, there were reports that the Saudi Government had signed a multi-billion Mark deal with West Germany for "several hundred" *Leopard* II main battle tanks. At the time of writing, this deal had not been confirmed by Bonn in view of anticipated criticism from Israel and the Christian Democrats.

EGYPT: THE NEED FOR ALLIES

The United Arab Republic remains, in name, the heir to Nāsir's modern brand of Pan-Arabism and, in spirit, the inheritor of more ancient glories. Yet Egypt today is increasingly beset by economic woes and by uncertain national security. The Sādāt regime is still unable to sustain the traditional aspirations of Egypt to leadership of the Arab world. Libya's drive to dominate Saharan Africa and build a radical, Almoravid empire around Qadhdhāfī's standard of a "Saharan Islamic Republic", must be met forcibly by Sādāt. Toward this end, the *rapprochement* with Israel has eased Egypt's obsessive focus on future military action in the Sinai, and freed those Army and Air Force units still combat-worthy for possible action against Libya and its surrogates throughout North Africa. But peace with Israel has not been without difficult diplomatic consequences. Egypt has been publicly ostracized by most of the Arab world, and its main hope for indigenous arms production and some measure of military self-sufficiency, the Arab Organization for Industrialization, has been scuttled by the Saudi financial pullout.

Faced by a pressing need to extricate itself from an exhausting hostile posture against Israel and to redeploy ready units to face Libya, Sādāt has attempted to rebuild both his military capabilities and construct a regional coalition of modern states in North-east Africa. Alliances are the key. *De facto* alliance with the US will bring a needed influx of sophisticated American weapons and advisers to help pull Egypt out of the military doldrums. Careful construction of bilateral support relationships and informal military co-ordination with local states, especially the Sudan and Somalia, might well form the basis for a traditionalist counter-offensive against Libya, the Soviet Union and their allies in Saharan Africa.

The Egyptian military is at present not capable even of sustaining containment operations against Libyan forces beyond its own frontiers, yet as recently as 1977, it was able to defeat such a challenge in short order. Even then, shortages in the predominantly Soviet-equipped force constricted the scope of operations. By 1981 the situation had become critical. Of c. 668 combat aircraft listed officially, only c. 363 were considered capable of active duty, and recent reports indicate that even this roster of Soviet machinery is to be reduced. None of the advanced MiG-23s can fly; several have been given to China in return for some 40 MiG-21s—the Shenyang F-6—for which, at least, some spares are available. Libya's gross order of battle continues to grow by contrast. Egypt's aging tank arsenal has fallen below post-1973 replacement levels. According to Maj.-Gen. Muhammed Abū Ghazāla, Egypt's Chief of Staff, Libya now possesses c. 2,750 tanks, including Soviet T-72s and Italo-German *Lions (Leopard* I). Even though Libya cannot possibly man the majority of its tanks, Qadhdhāfī's arsenal still outnumbers Egypt's by more than 70%. With MiG-25 and Mig-27 aircraft included in a Libyan air force of 384 combat aircraft, Egypt is clearly in trouble in any comparison of North African arsenals.

Sādāt would now find it difficult to engage successfully and quickly terminate a border conflict with Qadhdhāfī on Egyptian terms. Yet tensions remain high along the frontier. In the last five months of 1980 alone, there were more than 460 reported infiltration attempts by Libyan armed groups. In addition, Qadhdhāfī has pushed the construction of what Egyptian sources call a Libyan "Bar Lev Line" along its frontier with Egypt.

Sādāt has sought to reinvigorate his rusting arsenal with direct American military aid. In August, he placed a formal request for c. $10 bn in arms and assistance. The Carter Administration whittled this down to $3.5 bn to be spread over five years. In 1981 a $961m US aid package will include 35 used F-4Es, 67 M60A3s (244 by 1982), 550 M-113A2s, 52 M901 Improved *TOW* Vehicles (ITV), with 40 F-16s and 11 *HAWK* batteries earmarked for 1982 delivery.

With so many of Egypt's aircraft and tanks "just rusting away," as one Pentagon aide reported, this modest injection will barely equip two mechanized division-equivalents. Of Egypt's ground combat units, the 127th, 129th, 139th, 145th, and 136th Commando Brigades, the 28th, 182nd, and 170th Airborne Brigades, the 213th Cavalry Brigade, and the armoured and mechanized brigades of the Republican Guard are probably at the highest readiness levels. These groups also represent the potential order of battle of an Egyptian mobile intervention force. Egyptian counter-moves against Libya throughout Saharan Africa should be focused on task groups built around commando, airborne and Guards units. American re-equipment, by extension, should go directly towards endowing Egypt's army with the short-term capability to confront Libyan, Soviet, or Soviet-surrogate (Cuban/Ethiopian) forces in brief insertion/engagement fire-brigade contingencies. US aid and equipment are simply not generous enough to fully re-equip Egypt's major manoeuvre units; Sādāt, and others, have agreed that a $10 bn short-term investment would meet only minimum needs. With only c. $3.5 bn to work with over the next five years, Sādāt would do well to emphasize a limited, though long-range, combat force. This kind of power projection capability is exactly what is needed to counter the zealous ambitions of Libya.

LIBYA: THE SOUTHWARD EXPANSION

Libya, as isolated in the Saharan sphere as Syria is in the Levantine, has played a much more adventurous game than Asad, made far greater short-term gains, and enjoyed the pleasure of a relatively stable domestic polity. With very little to work with in terms of human resources—a population of less than 3m—Libya's oil revenues, and supportive military and infrastructural relationships with both the Soviet Union and Italy, have provided Qadhdhāfī with many counters to play his game, and pursue his dream of a Saharan Empire. As the spiritual successor to the radical 11th and 12th century Islamic radical empires of the Almoravides and Almohads, he can choose from an almost endless array of weaponry to fuel his fantasies. An enormous tank park of 2,500 main battle tanks, soon to be supplemented by 200 *Leopold* 1 *(Lion)* tanks built in Italy, sits in Soviet-maintained storage. A splendid air arsenal of c. 350 French and Soviet combat aircraft must rely on Soviet and North Korean pilots, for there are no more than 150 Libyans jet-qualified. A navy sporting the finest missile corvettes and sub-marines (from Italy and France) must rely on European technicians to keep the seas.

However undeveloped, however dependent on Soviet and Italian personnel support, Qadhdhāfī's armed forces have been undeterred in an escalating pattern of Saharan ventures: Chad, Mauritania, the Gambia, Mali, Senegal, Tunisia, Liberia and even Nigeria have all been victims in varying degrees of Libyan intrigue. Even sympathetic radical states have begun to express concern over

27

Libyan intentions. Algeria, especially, has misgivings over the construction of a Libyan airbase in Mauritania, which will allow aid and support for the Polisario movement to be delivered without first going through Algerian territory. (See essay on developments in the Maghrib and their ME dimensions.) The assault in July 1980 by Libyan-trained guerrillas on the Tunisian mining town of Gafsa, followed by a belligerent massing of Libyan regular forces on the Tunisian frontier, brought Libya into military confrontation with yet another North African neighbour.

Qadhdhāfī's adventures to the South, however, have created the more significant instability. Central Saharan states—Chad, Mali, Niger, Mauritania—all share a common poverty, sparse population, and excitable Islamic minority problem. Libyan subversion has focused on manipulating the Islamic nomad groups along the fringes of the Sahara. The so-called Islamic Legion much trumpeted by Qadhdhāfī in 1980, is a useful front to infiltrate Libyan regular army units into neighbouring states. Although Qadhdhāfī may "declare the frontiers of Libya open to the sons of the Tuaregs in Mali and Niger," and "call on them to revolt, raise their heads, and take up arms," there is the likelihood that they will be used as a media crust for the insertion of regular Libyan armoured and mechanized units throughout the region.

Support for such an interpretation of Qadhdhāfī's strategy comes from his tactics in Chad. Having already "annexed" a 60-mile wide strip of Chad along the Libyan frontier in 1975, Qadhdhāfī in 1980 moved Libyan units into the very suburbs of the capital city, N'Djamena. Tu-22 bombers were used in October to bomb sections of N'Djamena loyal to Hissene Habre, opponent of Libya's current ally, Goukkouni Wuedei. By December, Libyan armoured forces had installed themselves in Douguia, transformed into a staging base 35 miles north of N'Djamena. On 12 December, some 5,000 Libyan troops of an armoured brigade equivalent, took the capital. Repeated air strikes were required for the final push. Undeterred by the outcry of influential members of the Organization of African Unity (such as Nigeria, Sudan, Senegal and Egypt), Qadhdhāfī finalized plans to formally integrate Chad with Libya. It remains moot whether this plan will prove any more successful than Qadhdhāfī's other attempts at unification—alternatively with Egypt, Sudan, Tunisia and currently Syria. (Also see chapter on Libya.)

THE JORDANIAN-SYRIAN CONFRONTATION

Jordan pursued a shrewd and largely successful national strategy throughout 1980, culminating in a dramatic, and victorious, military face-off with Syria—whose drive to dominate both Lebanon and Palestine—in fact, the entire Mediterranean-Crusader littoral—although disguised in formal diplomatic behaviour, has been the focus of King Husayn's strategy of survival for his country.

With a weak economy—but $2.79 bn GDP in 1980—and a limited population—3.1m—Jordan's defence effort could not hope to match a sustained Syrian assault. Its four divisions are still poorly equipped with M-47 and *Centurion* tanks now obsolescent. The majority of the divisional artillery is still towed. The air force is constrained by medium-performance aircraft: F-5E/F. A major re-equipment effort by the US and Britain will rectify this situation within three years. In 1980, 274 *Shir/Chieftain* and 100 M-60A3 tanks were ordered, while 107 self-propelled M-109A2 and M-110A2 155mm and 203mm will re-equip two divisional equivalents. In the air, 36 *Mirage* F-1 will provide a high performance dimension to Jordanian air interception capability.

28

All of these arsenal injections will be needed. Unfortunately, they are needed urgently, and the US especially is responding slowly in its delivery. The startling Syrian mobilization on the Jordanian frontier during the last week of November underscored Jordan's vulnerability to a sudden Syrian descent. Within just a few hours, two Syrian divisions had come close to within several hundred yards of the Jordanian frontier. Husayn quickly countered. The 12th Mechanized Division, stationed in the North-western triangle, bordering on Israel and Syria, had to move only a few miles to face the Syrian concentration. The Fifth Armoured Division, astride the rail link North-east of Amman, moved ten miles to cover the 12th's right. By 27 November, some 24,000 Jordanians were facing more than 30,000 Syrians. After threats and counter-threats the Syrians pulled back after 11 December. Asad's military tantrum was triggered by Jordan's enthusiastic support of Iraq in the war with Iran, combined with Husayn's continued material sympathy for the anti-Asad Muslim Brotherhood.

King Husayn's courtship of Iraq must be seen in this context. Recognizing Syria as a primary antagonist, Husayn had built a strong set of relationships with bordering conservative Arab states, and when Saddām Husayn's shifted to the "Traditionalist Camp," the King was at last able to complete a diplomatic security ring around Syria, far more effective than simply restocking his military arsenal.

Syria continued to make impressive superficial gains in the inventory of its military arsenal, while sustaining losses in almost every other sphere of political-military endeavour. After signing a special Treaty of Friendship with the Soviet Union on 7 October 1980 the Asad regime received a contract for arms and advisers that will enable Syria to far exceed the military resources of a country with a $9.2 bn Gross Domestic Product. A sixth armoured/mechanized division is in the process of formation. A reported total of 500 T-72s are in the process of delivery, supplementing an already large tank park of 2800 T-54/55/62s. At least two squadrons of MiG-27 will be delivered, pushing the total stock of combat aircraft to 450. More Mig-25s will also be included in the package. Ominously for Israel, Asad has requested, and will receive, substantial numbers of surface-to-surface missiles. These will include at least 12 SS-12 *Scaleboard* SSMs, with ranges of 490 miles, and *SCUD*-Cs, with ranges of 450 miles.

A gleaming arsenal, however, cannot conceal the extent of Syrian foreign policy failures combined with the continuing attrition of a mounting internal crisis.

Given Syria's tense domestic milieu, the readiness of its armed forces to respond to formal external threats must be questioned. Moscow has become the Alawite's only buttress and, again, the USSR has allied itself with a shaky, oppressive, unrepresentative regime—hardly a constructive springboard to further regional influence. At this point, with a gradually resolving anti-Soviet and conservative Arab axis in slow formation, this gambit remains Moscow's only ME option.

ISRAEL: NEW SECURITY DOCTRINE FOCUS

The tremendous surge in intra-Islamic conflict during 1980 created a new, if temporary, set of parameters defining Israeli security doctrine. Its defence planning will shift, at least in the mid-term, away from traditional battlefield confrontations against potential Arab coalitions. A new focus is emerging for Israeli security doctrine. In the near-term, threats to the state are likely to take the form of low-level, sub-national conflict in Southern Lebanon and the West Bank, or possible maritime interdiction of vital Israeli sea lines of communication by radical

29

or surrogate actors. Over the long-term, as intra-Islamic relations again gravitate toward commonly-stated objectives, Israel may face a hostile Arab coalition. In this context, long-range defence policy stresses military self-sufficiency and, to the fullest extent possible, indigenous re-supply through periods of external combat operations.

Continuing low-level clashes in Israeli-occupied areas, as well as commando/ guerrilla infiltration along land and sea frontiers, remain an irresolvable by-product of past wars. Given the precarious structure of any likely "political solution" to Palestinian national claims, the pace and strength of terrorist/para-military assaults on Israel can be expected to intensify. The Soviets' delivery of 60 surplus T-34 tanks to Palestine Liberation Organization (PLO) forces in South Lebanon, reported in February 1980, and Syria's reported offer of base support for future raids from the Golan Heights, extended in March, are indications of an increasing emphasis on PLO-surrogate operations against Israel.

For the major hostile states facing Israel, there is little alternative. Egypt and Jordan have absolutely no stake in antagonizing Israel. Syria came closer to hostilities with Iraq and Jordan in 1980 than it did with Israel. Even if Asad had wished to stage a short confrontation with Israel, he could not hope for any support from neighbouring Iraq and Jordan. More than six full brigades are still embroiled in Lebanon, seriously depleting Syrian war-making capacity on other fronts. If Israel wished to "Copenhagen" the Syrian Army, it could probably annihilate the Syrian order of battle in less than 96 hours.

Israel is, for the next three to five years, relatively free from large-scale military threat. Even so, the Israeli arsenal and order of battle continues to grow. At least 15 divisional equivalents can be formed on full mobilization, double that of 1967. Spares and ammunition stocks are high—1.6m artillery rounds, for example—and armoured force and air force equipment levels complete and at high readiness. Both low and high-intensity ground/air threats can be met quickly and effectively.

The situation at sea is different. Before 1973, the Israeli Navy was at best a peripheral service. Manpower and resource allocation reflected its very junior status. The stunning performance of Gabriel-equipped missile boats against Syrian and Egyptian squadrons altered this perspective. In addition to a bouyant, post-war popular image, the acquisition of sophisticated Western naval technology by radical states such as Libya, and the startling growth of the Soviet fleet, added momentum to a large Israeli naval building programme. *Reshef*-class missile boats, much larger than the pre-war *Saar*-class, and new Vickers Type 206 submarines, has given the Navy an extended patrol "reach." Naval protection of Israel's Red Sea and Mediterranean Sea Line of Communication (SLOC) is now possible out to Aden and the Sicilian Narrows.

Libya's growing naval strength, based increasingly on Western, not Soviet technology, is poised along more than 300 miles of Israel's vital Mediterranean SLOC. French *Daphne* class subs, *Combattante* II type missile boats, and Italian *Otomat*-armed *Wadi M'ragh* class corvettes will give Qadhdhāfī a powerful strike force at sea. To counter this, the Israeli navy has increased its production run of the highly successful, long-legged *Reshef* class missile corvettes, and fitted them out with quad *Harpoon* canisters, as well as *Gabriels*. Now, Israeli missile squadrons can reach out to 60 miles and more, if over-the-horizon targeting is available. In the central Mediterranean, beyond the range of land-based Israeli patrol aircraft, shipboard helicopters are required. To meet this need, a new type of corvette has been introduced, the *Aliyah* class. Essentially a modified *Reshef* hull, the *Aliyah* mounts only a single 40mm plus *Gabriel* canisters forward, while the quarterdeck has been configured for helicopter operations and maintenance. In conjunction with *Reshef* and *Saar* type missile boats, Israel should be able to deal with the emerging "*Otomat* threat" on equal terms.

Over the long-term, Israel's security policy must focus on military self-sufficiency. Both from a balance-of-payments perspective and a need for a secure source of arms and spare parts, Israel continues to focus on creating an indigenous military-industrial complex. It was announced in March 1980 that Israeli Aircraft Industries would undertake the development of a sophisticated new fighter aircraft, to be named the "*lavi*", or *Lion*. The Pratt and Whitney 404 engine, the same as is mounted in the F-18, will be the powerplant. This programme will allow Israel to substitute an indigenous aircraft for further F-16 acquisition. The level of arms exports is an indication of both the health of Israeli military industries, as well as making a significant economic contribution. In 1977, the figure hovered at $250m. Three years later, it exceeded $1 bn. This effort involves the sale of *Galil* assault rifles to the Netherlands, and several Latin American states; *Gabriel* missiles to Taiwan; *Westwind* aircraft to West Germany; *Skyhawk* bombers to Indonesia, and *Reshef* class missile corvettes to South Africa. At every level of fabrication, Israel is capable of some degree of self-supply. The sole *complete* exception is jet aircraft engines, which must still be imported from the US.

THE IRAQI-IRANIAN WAR

The critical event in the Islamic world in 1980 was the outbreak of war between Iraq and Iran in September. In its intensity and in its implications, this conflict represented a watershed. From an Islamic perspective, it marked the end of post-colonial unity of rhetoric, if not policy, against perceived Western-Zionist enemies. The material scale of the new war harks back to traditional Muslim rivalries through the centuries following the breakup of the Abassid Caliphate. National, even "Imperial," state ambitions have replaced the dreams of both fundamentalist and revolutionary unifiers. (For background and analysis, see essay on Iraqi-Iranian war.)

Given Baghdad's perceived desuetude of the ex-Imperial Persian armed forces, a strictly limited campaign, in schedule, theatre boundaries and combat units employed, seemed to make a great deal of sense. It was thought that objectives could be gained swiftly, consolidated and held against a meagre anticipated Iranian response. Geography also seemed to favour the contained approach. South of Basra, the Eastern/Iranian bank of the Shatt al-'Arab is flanked farther to the East by an extensive semi-flooded, marshy region 20–30 miles deep. This often impassable terrain effectively limits communication with the two key Iranian cities along the Shatt al-'Arab—Abadan and Khorramshahr—to North-South roads. There is but one East-West link between Abadan and Bandar Khomeyni, 50 miles to the East. If Iraqi forces could cut the two main North-South links between Abadan, Khorramshahr and Ahvaz, they might expect to isolate and encircle their objectives. Iranian units, cut off and without succour, could then be reduced at leisure. The war would be won in weeks, with massed artillery doing the job.

As with many war plans, reality contradicted forecasted expectation. Iraq played a very conservative opening game. Of a 12-division ground order of battle, only three divisions were committed initially, probably the First and Fifth Mechanized, and either the Tenth or Sixth Armoured. So it was with confidence that Iraqi forces bridged the Tigris South of Basra and moved in strength against Khorramshahr, the first objective. Then the campaign stalled. Apparently—it

31

must be stressed that there has thus far been *no* reliable report from the fighting fronts—the Iraqi reliance on Soviet-style offensive movement, with a very slow kick-off, prevented the noose from being drawn. Khorramshahr was assaulted by artillery. Iranian defenders were given precious time to consolidate, resupply and reinforce. The very campaign plan of Iraq, based as it was on an optimistic intelligence assessment of Iranian combat capabilities, was rigidly linked to a low-level response.

On the contrary, the Iranian revolutionary "rabble" not only held their riverine cities, they responded with unexpected counter-attacks, especially in the air. As the battles for Khorramshahr and then Abadan devolved into neo-Stalingrads, dominated by surfeiting artillery barrages, snipers, and reluctant—on the part of casualty-conscious Iraqis—house-to-house combat. Reporting in the Western Press emphasized the only fluid and eye-witnessed combat theatre: the air war.

It was in the audacity and doggedness of their air strikes against Iraq that a discounted Iran surprised the world. Iran's air order of battle was listed at 445 combat aircraft, including 188 F-4D / E, 166 F-5E / F, and 77 F-14A. In response to widespread, though generally ineffective Iraqi air attacks on the first day of the war, Iranian F-4s struck hard at Iraqi airbases and petroleum facilities. The unexpected ferocity of the Iranian sorties, combined with the effective penetration of low-flying F-4s in the face of an air defence network boasting more than 3,000 major SAMs, forced the Iraqi Command to pull back large numbers of mobile SA-6 batteries that had accompanied ground units into Iran. Attacks on Baghdad and the oil complex at Basra were made consistently over the first four weeks of war, in spite of the steady losses sustained and the low readiness of combat aircraft: only 60 % of F-5s, and 40% of F-4s were reported as operationally ready for combat. Often, combat sorties were flown with only one aircraft in a strike, equipped with working radar and electronics, acting as the "eyes" for its sister *Phantoms*.

Both sides, in fact, employed their available air strike assets as raiders, rather than as integrated components of either tactical front operations, or in pursuit of clear and single-minded strategic objectives. Much wastage resulted, both in terms of aircraft losses and collateral damage, but little real economic or communications disruption was achieved by either side. More important ramifications were evident. By not carefully husbanding their available airpower for concentrated use along the Forward Edge of the Battle Area, Iran essentially threw away its only real asset in the opening weeks of war. Close air support, particularly in the form of *TOW* equipped Huey *Cobra* anti-tank helicopters, was withheld until the third week of war when hostilities expanded northward, toward the Persian heartland.

In the teeth of intensive artillery concentrations, Iranian forces continued to cling to the rubble of Khorramshahr after three long weeks. Husayn, far from achieving his initial aims, faced the prospect of long sieges at both reverine cities without effectively shutting out Iranian reinforcements, while at the same time exposing the besiegers to counterattacks. Well into the war, the decision was made to enlarge the theatre of operations and, by extension, Iraqi war aims. If Khomeyni would not yield when faced with the eventual loss of Abadan and Khorramshahr, then perhaps the loss of the entire province of Khuzistan (determinably labelled Arabistan by the Iraqis) would bring the Imam to his knees.

Accordingly, by the middle of October, the Iraqi high command struck North towards the vital provincial nexi of Ahvaz and Dezful. With these strongholds—astride key communications links—surrounded, the ports of the Shatt al-'Arab would fall like overripe fruit. Had these northern cities been immediately assaulted instead of the nearer riverine cities, Iranian resistance might have been neutralized from the start. By the third week of war, both Ahvaz and Dezful had been transformed into potential launching points for Iranian counterstrokes. Reducing these nutshells has, in more than 100 days of war, proved beyond Iraq. At this time, Iran began to employ *Cobras, TOWs,* and *Mavericks* for the first time. With 205 AH-1J *Cobras* and 2,500 *Mavericks,* Iran possessed just the range and depth of sophisticated weapons necessary to blunt Iraqi armoured columns that undisciplined ground forces were unable to contain. These efforts were propelled by the regime's decision to release 1,000 jailed air force pilots, the victims of recent purges. With a renewed stock of skilled operators, the Iranian air force was able to sustain a 100 combat sortie average through the twelfth week of war. These efforts may not have been enough to stop the Iraqi advance, but combined with the hesitant operational behaviour of the Iraqi manoeuvre forces, the Persian airwar may well have allowed Iranian ground forces to dig in around Ahvaz and Dezful. There are, of course, no real measures of effectiveness for Iranian *TOWs* and *Mavericks* against Iraqi armour.

Iran's major problem, aside from equipment maintenance, has been logistic resupply of forward units. Transport has been disrupted by a growing shortage of gasoline and motor oil, the result of severed pipelines from Ahvaz. The tenacity of Iran's revolutionary defenders, who can perform well in static, entrenched, and sheltered urban positions like Khorramshahr, Abadan, Ahvaz, Dezful, and Susangerd, had forced the Iraqis to stop their advance at each point and attempt to "smoke out" the defenders through massed artillery concentrations. Essentially, war prosecution on both sides has been stalemated. After six weeks of siege, for example, besieging Iraqis had still not cleaned out the last of the defenders of Khorramshahr, thereby holding needed Iraqi units vital to the reduction of Ahvaz, nine miles to the South.

As the rainy season approached during the first week in November, signs and by-products of the stalemate along the Khuzistan Front became increasingly evident. So, too, did the evidence of protracted war. Reports came filtering through heavy belligerent censorship that Iraq was constructing a paved highway from the southern sector, through Ahvaz, all the way north to Dezful. This indicates not only a logistical freedom of operation from Iranian interference, but a determination to remain in "liberated Arabistan" for a long time to come.

During November, reports also began to trickle in describing abortive Iranian attempts to break out of encircled cities: Ahvaz and Susangerd, and of haemorrhaging losses incurred. At this time reports began to circulate of a declining daily sortie rate for the Iranian air force. The war was taking its toll.

The war was also expanding. On 4 November, Saddām Husayn warned that "Iraqi demands might increase if Iran persisted in its rejection of Iraq's rights." Fighting spread northward beyond the boundaries of Khuzistan into the mountainous centre of Iran. Heavy fighting was reported around Mehran and Kermanshah in the heart of the Zagros massif. At this point, Iraq was going full-throttle in its commitment of military resources. By November, nine full divisional units were deployed in the battle area: eight engaged in combat, one in army reserve. Unlike Iran, though, Iraq possessed the monetary reserves to continue its war effort. With some $40 bn in ready reserves, Iraq could sustain its war and see to the needs of 14m people without resort to further oil exports for perhaps another two years. Even so, Iraq's oil pipeline through Turkey was restored to operation by 20 November. Iran, by contrast, faces dwindling financial and petroleum resources that may soon bring both military and social operations to a standstill.

If the onset of the rainy season in the South brought a noticeable slackening of the combat pace, the coming of the snows to the Western highlands only seemed to intensify operations there. At Gīlān-e Gharb and at Ilam, along the mountain lines around Kermanshah, fighting raged in mountain landscape dominated by peaks topping 11,000 feet. The main centre of both Iraqi and Persian activity, however, was around the cities of Ahvaz and Dezful. There, through immense effort, Iranian high command had by early December managed to mass nearly two divisions, and the working balance of Iran's depleted arsenal. There were reports that significant numbers of 175mm self-propelled guns had been moved forward to counter the concentrated battery-fire of Iraqi guns ringing Ahvaz and Dezful. Iranian artillery must have been at least partially successful in blocking Iraqi artillery interdiction of the few remaining lines of communication to the beleaguered cities since Iranian efforts to concentrate at Dezful during December were successful.

Just after the New Year, 1981, Iran launched its long-awaited counter-offensive. Apparently, small gains were made at the expense of several major units, which were reported by the Iraqis as having been "wiped out." Within a week, the Winter offensive had been halted and contained. Even more damaging to Iran than the failure of its trumpeted offensive—a media signal the Iraqis could hardly have failed to ignore—was the opening of an Iraqi offensive in the far North, in tenuously-held Kurdistan. Working with Kurdish irregulars, the Iraqis may well succeed in detaching another province from traditional Persian suzerainty.

While the war awaits the Spring, both sides dig in to plan and to reflect. Iran's prospects for victory can be termed simply as "bleak." Without working capital, without major sources of military re-supply, without access to its own petroleum fields to renew dwindling energy stockpiles, Iran will eventually be brought to its knees, provided Iraq can withstand the effects of protracted attrition. Iraq, by contrast, may well win this war; but it has irretrievably lost the war it set out to fight. Far from projecting the image of a strong and decisive leader-state, able to set national objectives and achieve them in the same breath, Iraq's war performance is perceived worldwide as bumbling and inept. Overwhelming force was first withheld, then hesitantly extended. The uncontainable escalation of the conflict forced first an editing and then a complete rewriting of stated war aims. Now, in order to justify the enormous national effort involved in the "Persian War", national objectives, and the negotiating terms they take, must be enlarged. Measures of victory must equal perceived measures of sacrifice.

This pattern of escalation can only harm Iraq in the long term. If Husayn could have achieved a lightning seizure of his original, strictly limited objectives along the Shatt al-'Arab, Iran might eventually have acquiesced to a *fait accompli*. Having been forced to expand the war into the heart of old Persia, triggering a national resistance in the process, Husayn must literally knock the proud Persian to his knees. A satisfactory settlement would of necessity involve the detachment of one or more provinces, probably Khuzistan and possibly Kurdistan, from an historically frozen image of Iranian sovereignty. Like the excision of Alsace and Lorraine in 1871, this settlement could lead only to revanchist wars to come. Iraq would pay a bitter price for the image of present victory, a victory made necessary by an increasingly rigorous definition.

THE BROADER STRATEGIC IMPLICATIONS

It can be seen from the above country-by-country analysis that strategic activity, both in the form of on-going conflict as well as defence procurement, has continued at high intensity over the past year. Thus 1980 ended on a very sombre note, which was only marginally alleviated by the return of the American hostages in January 1981. At the time of writing (January 1981), the most ominous clouds on the horizon continue to be the threats to the Western world and the ME posed by the Soviet Union: in this context, the traumas that occurred in Poland cannot be ignored. Increasingly, most Western observers see the Soviet Union as a sprawling, inefficient bureaucracy beset with internal problems both of an economic and spiritual nature, a country with an aging leadership and no clear-cut prescription for overcoming its internal difficulties. If one adds to this list the external problems the Soviet Union faces—not merely in the East-West context but in its relations with China and Eastern Europe and Afghanistan—then a very gloomy picture can be drawn concerning the Soviet Union's prospects in the years ahead. But for precisely this reason, a note of caution must be injected: the fact remains that Soviet military power is presently second to none in many arenas. The Soviet Union may well be tempted to use its military muscle in the absence of any other remedy and, as writers such as George Feifer and Harrison Salisbury have noted, the renaissance of pure, unadulterated nationalist chauvinism in the Soviet Union, including a more virulent anti-Semitic tinge, has grown significantly in the past three or four years.*

The possibilities that military adventurism may be a way of solving the domestic problems of the Soviet empire gained credence during the year. Some observers went so far as to conclude that if the Soviet Union had an opportunity for intervention in Iran it might take this ultimate gamble on the grounds that the one way to ensure Western impotence would be to occupy Iran and thereby threaten the oil supplies of the US, Europe and Japan. While such a scenario may sound extreme, this type of thinking was uppermost in the minds of many of the new appointees to the Reagan Administration, and it is unlikely that in the near-term the shadow of the Soviet Union over the ME will be diminished.

Michael Vlahos and Geoffrey Kemp

*See, in particular, George Feifer, "Soviet Disorders," *Harpers,* New York, February 1981, and Harrison E. Salisbury, "The Russia Reagan Faces," *The New York Times Magazine,* 1 February 1981.

The Iraqi-Iranian War

HISTORICAL BACKGROUND*

The outbreak of war between Iraq and Iran in late September 1980 was the culmination of a long-standing border dispute between the two countries, which revolved mainly around the issue of control of the Shatt al-'Arab River (in Persian: Arvand Rud). The lower part of the Shatt al-'Arab, formed by the confluence of the Tigris and Euphrates, is a vital economic and strategic artery for both Iraq and Iran since it is Iraq's main lifeline to the sea and provides Iran with its only access to the oil ports of Abadan and Khorramshahr. Although the river has long served as their boundary, discord has often arisen over the precise location of the border line. An agreement between the Ottoman and Persian Empires in 1847 provisionally set the border at the edge of the east bank of the waterway, leaving open its exact demarcation as well as navigation arrangements stemming from it. These questions were settled by a protocol signed in 1913 which gave "the river and all islands therein" to the Ottomans (and eventually, to Iraq as the successor state), except for two strips of about four miles each opposite the ports of Khorramshahr and Abadan, where the boundary was shifted to the *Thalweg*, i.e. the mid-channel line. However, the agreement came under constant attack from Iran which demanded the application of the *Thalweg* principle to the entire length of the river. During a temporary *rapprochement* between Iran and Iraq, another treaty was signed in 1937 which left the 1913 demarcations unchanged, but provided for a joint navigation commission for the Shatt al-'Arab. In the long run, these arrangements did not prove satisfactory to Iran either, and tension persisted. In April 1969 Iran—then at a peak of military strength, while the newly established Ba'th Party regime was still struggling to consolidate its power in Iraq—unilaterally abrogated the 1937 treaty. Instead, it declared the mid-channel line to be the boundary between the two countries.[1]

On 6 March 1975, an International Border and Good Neighbourly Relations Treaty was concluded in Algiers by Saddām Ḥusayn, then Deputy Chairman of the Iraqi Revolutionary Command Council (RCC), and the Shah. Iraq, facing mounting difficulties in suppressing the Kurdish rebellion, was at that time prepared formally to cede sovereignty over a part of the Shatt al-'Arab waterway to Iran, in exchange for the ending of Iran's substantial support for the Kurds. Iraq thus accepted the *Thalweg* line as its boundary. Without Iranian support, the Kurdish rebellion quickly collapsed, thus ending what had, over the preceding years, become a costly drain on Iraq's national resources. But success in Kurdistan had been bought at a price involving the Shatt al-'Arab which was hurtful to Iraqi national pride. Moreover, the 1975 treaty provided for the re-demarcation of the land border further to the north. No details of the changes involved were disclosed at the time.[2] Alleged Iranian violations of the 1975 treaty (especially over the land border) served as Iraq's justification for its abrogation on 17 September 1980—an act which marked the beginning of the Iraqi-Iranian war.

---

*The present essay gives an account of the course of the war from the start of fully-fledged warlike operations on 22 September 1980 until roughly 20 October. The period of mounting tension preceding the outbreak of war is described in the chapters on Iraq and Iran in this volume. A short account, as well as a chronological table, of the pre-war border incidents are included in the chapter on Iraq.

36

IRAQ'S MOTIVES AND WAR OBJECTIVES

From the earliest days of Khomeyni's regime, Iran had sought to export its brand of Muslim radicalism across the border into Iraq. The main threat posed for Iraq, by Khomeyni's aggressive policies lay in the potential attractiveness of his message to the large Iraqi Shī'ī population. Khomeyni incited Iraqis to rise against their rulers—whether by appealing to Shī'īs to rid themselves of a Sunni-dominated establishment, or by calling on Sunnis and Shī'īs alike to end the Ba'th Party's secular and "un-Islamic" rule. During 1979–80, Iranian hostility and the need to contain its potential dangers forced their way to the top of Iraq's scale of national priorities.

By mid-1980, the Iraqi leadership had obviously concluded that the menace posed by Iran could best be countered by transposing the dispute from the sphere of ideological and psychological warfare to military action—and that such an undertaking was feasible. Iraq was confident of its own growing military capability, while its evaluation of Iranian strength was that Khomeyni's revolution had weakened his armed forces to the point of jeopardizing their ability to defend the country's borders. Many senior officers had fled, resigned or been dismissed, and some had been jailed or executed (see *Middle East Contemporary Survey* [*MECS*] 1979–80, pp. 503–505). Not only had the structure of the army been impaired, but the rise of Revolutionary Guards as a rival armed force had created conflicts, while political infighting had left its mark on the regime's ability to lay down clear-cut domestic, foreign or defence policies (see chapter on Iran). Furthermore, the break with the US had caused a serious shortage of military spare parts and had interrupted the flow of new supplies. Baghdad also perceived Iran as having no allies and little or no international support.

All these factors suggested that, at little risk to itself, Iraq could humiliate and, in consequence, destabilize Iran by the use of armed force. President Saddām Husayn saw a promising chance of shifting the struggle away from the domestic political sphere, where he had been on the defensive since 1979, and onto the military plane. Saddām Husayn had one other important reason for his action: the need to remove the stain on Iraq's national pride caused by the 1975 concessions for which he had been personally responsible. In his speeches on 17 and 28 September 1980 (see below), Saddām Husayn spoke of the cession of part of the Shatt al-'Arab as "bitter and grave" for Iraq. Frequent statements by other Iraqi officials echoed Husayn's words, and added that it had been acceptable as an "interim solution" only.[3] If Iraq had been unable to recover the ceded territory earlier, Saddām Husayn argued it now had both the strength and the opportunity to do so—and at the same time to press its territorial claims in the central sector. However, irredentism was not the whole story. Husayn's aspirations extended to making Iraq the predominant power of the Gulf area as a whole, now that strife-ridden Iran could no longer police the region. A convincing demonstration of Iraqi military superiority would not only eliminate the Khomeynist threat, but also serve as the most effective starting point for such wider aims. This interpretation was borne out by Husayn's reference to the war as a battle "waged for the sake of the Gulf's Arabism,"[4] and by his repeated insistence upon Iran's returning to Arab (though not Iraqi) sovereignty three small islands in the Straits of Hormuz—islands whose seizure by Iran in 1971 had symbolized Iran's regional dominance. A successful operation against Iran would also have greatly enhanced Iraq's emergence as a new major force in the Arab world at large—a process Iraq had already launched by exploiting the Egyptian-Israeli peace treaty. (See essay

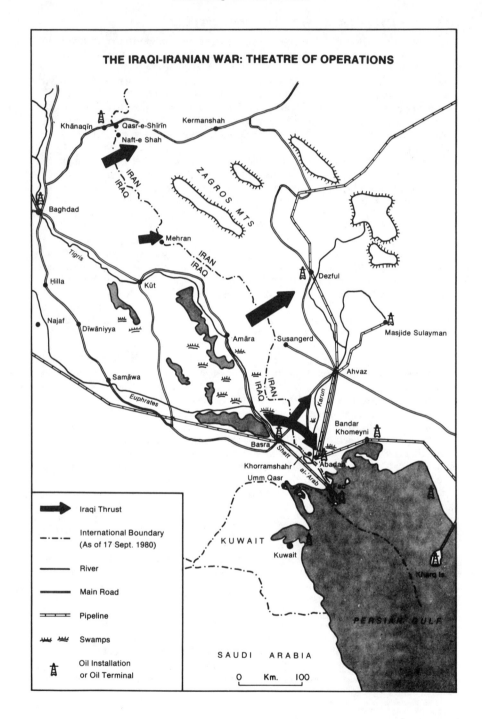

THE IRAQI-IRANIAN WAR: THEATRE OF OPERATIONS

38

on inter-Arab relations.) In short, Ḥusayn held that, at this juncture, far-reaching gains were available to Iraq at little cost.

SETTING THE STAGE

Since early September 1980, sporadic clashes along the central and southern sectors of the Iraqi-Iranian border had escalated both in intensity and through the more frequent employment of heavier weapons, including aircraft. (See chapter on Iraq.) The escalation was clearly initiated by Iraq, which took the military initiative throughout the first three weeks of September, though on a local scale. The transition from local incidents to full-scale war was heralded by Saddām Ḥusayn on 17 September in an address to the National Assembly, which he had convened in extraordinary session for this purpose.[5]

The central theme of his speech was the formal abrogation of the 1975 agreement. At the time, Ḥusayn asserted, the agreement had been accepted by Iraq under the most difficult circumstances: a costly struggle against the Kurds combined with a grave shortage of war material. Signing it had "saved Iraq from real dangers which were threatening its unity, security and future." It was from this consideration that Iraq had been prepared to put up with the "bitter reality" of ceding sovereignty over Iraqi territory to Iran. The latter, however, had subsequently ignored its obligations—agreed upon as part of the 1975 treaty—to return to Iraq a stretch of territory in the central sector (roughly 300 square kms). More recently, Ḥusayn went on to say, Iran had further violated the agreement by renewing its links with the Iraqi Kurds. Iran was therefore "legally, totally and actually responsible for the abrogation of this agreement," which, Ḥusayn announced, was now being "abrogated from our side also. . . . The legal relationship concerning the Shatt al-'Arab should now return to what it was before 6 March 1975. This Shatt shall again be, as it has been throughout history, Iraqi and Arab in name and reality." The Iraqi leadership, Ḥusayn warned, had decided "to wage all valiant battles, no matter what the sacrifice" to defend its stand.

The speech set the tone for subsequent announcements which consistently stressed that Iraq was not protecting its own narrow national interests alone, but was defending the pan-Arab cause by resisting what was in effect "Persian racism," even though it sought to disguise itself behind a "false religious mask."

President Abul-Ḥasan Bani Sadr acknowledged in an interview on the same day that Iran had not applied the 1975 agreement with regard to the land border (i.e. the central sector). He insisted, however, that "between two Muslim states there is no frontier, so the problem does not lie there." Rather, the dispute emanated from Iraq's "hostile attitude towards the Islamic Revolution;" its territorial claims were "merely a pretext."[6] On the following day, the Iranian Foreign Ministry issued a similar statement denouncing Iraq's "vague and imaginary claims", and warning that "the Muslim Iranian nation shall defend its territorial integrity and independence to its dying breath."[7]

THE ARMED CONFRONTATION

The course of military events which followed these verbal exchanges hardly matched the expectations of Iraqi leaders (or, for that matter, of many outside observers). After a five-day "warming up" period (17–21 September), there followed a short, initially successful and rapid, advance of Iraqi troops towards their targets. In the second week of fighting, however, the Iraqi troops were halted by stiff Iranian resistance and a stalemate developed along the main front in the south.

Tension mounted between 17 and 21 September, but military activity remained limited. Land and air clashes in the northern sector continued much as before, but now spread to the southern region as well. Implementing its declared sovereignty over the entire Shatt al-ʻArab, Iraq required all ships sailing there to fly the Iraqi flag. This immediately led to Iraqi-Iranian naval clashes. The armed confrontations around the Shatt al-ʻArab escalated rapidly, and soon came to include artillery duels and air activity.

The next phase—the full-scale Iraqi offensive—was initiated on the afternoon of 22 September when two waves of Iraqi aircraft attacked ten Iranian airfields including Tehran international airport, as well as targets chosen in an effort to paralyse Iranian air capability. Iran struck back at economic targets in Iraq's southern region. The war now spread to several separate fronts along the border, while deep-penetration air raids were carried out against cities and other, mainly economic, targets far inland. Iraqi units invaded Iran along four sectors, chosen for their strategic importance as well as their immediate relevance to the 1975 agreement. These were: the northern sector, between Qasr-e-Shīrīn (on the main Baghdad-Tehran highway) and Naft-e Shāh, where the Iraqi columns headed east towards the Iranian provincial capital of Kermanshah; an area near the town of Mehran, in the same sector but somewhat further to the south; the central sector, where the thrust was towards the town of Dezful, with its crucially important pumping station for the pipelines linking Iran's southern oilfields with Tehran, its air base and its hydro-electric dam, and towards the provincial capital of Ahvaz; and in the Shatt al-ʻArab around the oil port of Khorramshahr and the huge Abadan refinery. (For details, consult accompanying map.)

Expecting easy progress, the Iraqi command at first committed only a small portion of the army to the battle—apparently three or four divisions out of thirteen. The Iranian ground troops—two badly depleted divisions—were, for the most part, thrown onto the defensive, but displayed remarkable steadfastness. Within a week from the beginning of the major offensive, Iraqi forces seemed successful in the northern sector, where they took Qasr-e- Shīrīn and Mehran and occupied several hundred square miles of mostly desert territory before halting their advance.[8] In the central sector, the Iraqi units moving towards Dezful and Ahvaz made only slow progress. By the second week, they were stopped at the approaches to the two towns.

The fiercest battle took place along the Shatt al-ʻArab. The area held major Iranian and Iraqi strategic sites and economic assets. On the Iranian side were oil installations including the Abadan refinery (the world's largest), and the oil and commercial ports of Khorramshahr and Bandar Khomeyni. On the Iraqi side, too, were some of the country's most important oil installations, petro-chemical plants and the ports of Basra and Fao. Beginning on 22 September, this relatively small area—largely marshy and thus extremely difficult for movement and combat by infantry or armour—became the scene of intense artillery exchanges, mutual shelling by gunboats and bombing from the air, resulting in heavy damage to its installations. Simultaneously, Iraqi troops crossed the Shatt al-ʻArab waterway and proceeded eastwards. Approaching Khorramshahr, they were stopped at the town's north-western outskirts on 25 September. There, west of Karun river, they were immobilized for the next 16 days.

The second and third weeks of war (29 September-12 October) may best be characterized as a stalemate on all sectors. Iraqi ground forces, contained by stubborn Iranian resistance, were hardly able to advance. Battles took place outside Dezful, Ahvaz and Khorramshahr, whose defence forces kept repelling the attackers. On 2 October, Iraqi units captured Khorramshahr port, but were

40

prevented from entering the city itself across the Karun River. Air raids continued almost daily during this period, with the Iranian air force considerably more active than its Iraqi counterpart: Iranian planes attacked military, civilian and economic targets in and near Baghdad, Mosul, Basra, Kirkuk, Khānaqīn, and elsewhere. On 30 September, they raided the French-built nuclear centre outside Baghdad, still in the course of construction, apparently hitting auxiliary buildings and causing some damage to the site. Observers were surprised at the poor performance of the Iraqi forces, particularly the air force; on the other hand, they were astonished by the capability displayed by the Iranians, despite the new regime's purging of the top echelons of the armed forces.

In the absence of significant achievements, the Iraqi High Command announced on 2 October that since their forces had "reached their basic objectives, their military activities will henceforth be limited to retaining the targets gained."[9] Western reports concluded that the Iraqis were "inexorably bogged down in the Iranian desert."[10] However, on 11 October, Iraqi reinforcements broke the stalemate around Khorramshahr and succeeded in crossing the Karun ten miles northeast of the city over an improvised pontoon bridge. Infantry and armour advanced eastwards, cut the important Ahvaz-Abadan road and, by-passing Khorramshahr, moved in the direction of Abadan. Blocking all approaches from the north and east, Iraqi forces laid siege to the city—only to be involved, once again, in a snail's pace battle against Iranian resistance as relentless as they had faced in Khorramshahr.

No major change occurred during the fourth and fifth weeks of the war along other sectors of the front. The Iraqi forces moving against Dezful and Ahvaz continued to be kept at bay by the defenders outside both towns. In the northern sector, Iraqi units occupied a long but narrow strip of Iranian territory, including the towns of Qasr-e-Shīrīn and Mehran; but they were incapable of deepening their thrust by proceeding eastwards into the steep mountainous desert.

By 18 October, President Husayn judged it necessary to urge the Iraqi people to make greater efforts. Taking pains to explain why the war had not yet reached its victorious conclusion, he gave as the reasons Iran's superior military equipment and what he termed "geographical injustice." "Their aircraft" he told his listeners, "can, from a technical point of view, reach any spot in Iraq with a full load, because their range is greater than that of many of our aircraft, and because Iraq has a smaller area than Iran . . . If their aircraft want to bomb Baghdad they have only to cross 120 kms, whereas yours [i.e. Iraq's] have to cross 800 kms if they want to bomb targets in Tehran. Their artillery pieces have a greater range, fire heavier shells, and are more numerous than yours. Their tanks are among the most sophisticated Western tanks. Their navy is greater in number and can operate at a greater range than your naval forces." Husayn also conceded that there were "among this huge assembly of brave men [some people] who protested or dissented during the battle" (presumably an allusion to Iraqi Shī'īs reluctant to fight their Iranian co-religionists). All these factors, he urged, required patience as well as great exertions until the promised triumph was secured.[11]

THE POLITICAL AND DIPLOMATIC SCENE

The tenacious Iranian resistance and the fluctuating fortunes of the Iraqi offensive were reflected in the two countries' respective political positions and declarations during the war. While Iran firmly refused to consider a ceasefire or to respond to mediations, Iraq made great diplomatic efforts whenever its military momentum slackened below its leaders' expectations. Anything short of swift, decisive and

41

convincing success along the sectors it had chosen to attack, not only threatened eventually to undo the gains Iraq's leaders had expected to make, but also added risks both from abroad and, graver still, on the home front. When it became clear, during the second week of fighting, that a quick and smash victory had eluded Iraq, its leaders began searching for means to discover an acceptable way out of their military enterprise, which had turned out to be both risky and costly.

However, Iraq's first political statements were made when Saddām Husayn and his closest aides still believed they were on the verge of victory; they were therefore couched in terms reflecting a position of strength. Three days after the launching of the offensive, the Defence Minister, 'Adnān Khayrallah, stated that Iraq "will continue to pressure Iran at its vital points deep into Iranian territory until Iran responds completely to our legitimate interests . . . What can we do with people who do not appreciate the honour of responsibility and do not respect the international community? . . . I would like to assure you, my friends, that we are in a position to reach any target in the Iranian interior."[12] On the same day the Deputy Prime Minister, Tāriq 'Azīz, said that Iraq had been "forced to fight. . . . to bring those rulers in Iran to their senses so that they may establish good-neighbourly relations between Iran and the countries in the area, in order to make the rulers of Iran give up their arrogance."[13] He added that, in addition to Iraq's assertion of its sovereignty over its own land and territorial waters, it also expected Iran to return to Arab sovereignty (namely, to the United Arab Emirates: UAE) the three islands in the Straits of Hormuz which the Shah had seized in 1971.

Iranian statements at that stage struck a similar note. On 26 September, President Bani Sadr rejected mediation attempts by the Palestine Liberation Organization (PLO) leader, Yāsir 'Arafāt, as well as by Pakistan's President Ziya al-Haqq, and Tunisia's Foreign Minister, Habīb Shattī (Chairman and Secretary-General of the Islamic Conference Organization [ICO] respectively). He declared: "There is no need for mediation. It would be sufficient if they went [to Baghdad] and forced some sanity into this mad government to make it stop this sort of behaviour."[14] Iran's Prime Minister, Muhammad Ali Raja'i reiterated this stand on the next day, declaring that Iran would "accept neither mediation, nor reconciliation, discussion or anything . . . Our dispute with [Saddām Husayn] is a dispute between Islam and blasphemy, and as long as Saddām remains in his blasphemy it is essential for us to continue this *jihād*."[15]

On 28 September, when a slow-down of the Iraqi advance was plainly evident, Saddām Husayn announced another initiative in an address to the nation. Iraq, he said, was prepared "to stop the fighting if the other side responds to this sincere appeal on the basis of acknowledging our legitimate rights. We are also ready to negotiate with the Iranian side directly, or through a third party." Husayn put forward the following conditions for ending the war:

"We demand that the Iranian Government openly, legally and in deed recognize the historical and legitimate right of Iraq over its land and water. We demand that Iran adhere to good neighbour relations; . . . abandon its evil attempts to interfere in the domestic affairs of the region's countries; and return every inch it has usurped from the homeland."

Husayn also repeated the "call on the Iranian Government to give up its occupation of the three islands . . . in the Arab Gulf."[16]

Whatever Husayn's view of Iraq's military position at that point, or of its short-term prospects, it is difficult to imagine that he believed such terms stood a chance of eliciting a positive Iranian response. It is more likely that he was then still concerned with projecting an image of Iraq as being led by reasonable men who made no more than minimal legitimate demands, and who were seeking a speedy termination of hostilities. The broad diplomatic backing he had expected to gain by adopting this line would, he seemed to feel, be of help in bringing outside pressure to bear on Iran to consent to further (possibly somewhat toned-down) Iraqi proposals.

On the same day that Husayn had announced his new initiative, the Security Council (SC) issued an appeal to the parties to stop fighting and to settle the dispute through negotiations. Iraq immediately notified Dr. Waldheim of its acceptance, provided Iran did so too.[17] Iran's response, however, was negative. In a radio address to the nation on 30 September, Ayatollah Ruḥollah Khomeyni emphasized that there was "absolutely no question of peace or compromise, and we shall never have any discussion with them . . . We cannot compromise with a perpetrator of corruption. We shall fight against them right to the end."[18]

On the following day, Iraq announced its intention to cease hostilities for four days, from 5–8 October, on condition that Iran did likewise. Iran turned down this proposal.[19]

On 5 October, Iraq once more declared its readiness to end the war. Proclaiming "to the entire world" that the Iraqi army had "fulfilled its obligations," its ruling Revolutionary Command Council announced that Iraq was prepared "to cease fighting immediately . . . We are also ready to negotiate with the Iranian side to reach a just and honourable solution which guarantees our rights and principles."[20] The demand was ignored by Iran. Its President stated that Iraq would lose the war "whatever they do and however much it costs us." His assessment was that the war would last "fifteen days if Iraq receives no external aid, otherwise until the last of 36,000,000 Iranians are dead."[21]

On 9 October, Iraq was reported to have approached Turkey and India with a request for mediation.[22] Iran's stand, however, remained unchanged. Another mediation attempt on 19 October by Habib Shatti (in his capacity as Secretary-General of the ICO) was similarly rejected by President Bani Sadr. With the Iraqi failure to turn its breakthrough near Abadan into a quick victory, Khomeyni reiterated that Iran "will not rest until the downfall of the decadent Iraqi Ba'thist regime."[23] This must have sounded especially ominous to the Iraqi leadership.

It is instructive to follow the tone and *motifs* employed by the two parties in their announcements and communiqués throughout this period. They brought into sharper focus Iraqi and Iranian claims (frequently made in the preceding months) to speak for pan-Arabism, and to lead a pan-Islamic movement. Yet, despite the opposing thrust of the main arguments adduced by the two sides, there were also areas of overlap, with both claiming to defend Islam. The partial contradiction and partial parallelism of the line they set forth illustrated the problems both sides had in formulating a convincing rationale for going to war.

Iran's spokesmen presented their cause as an Islamic *jihād* against unbelief. For them the struggle against Iraq was only a stage in the Islamic revolution. "At the moment," Khomeyni asserted, "Islam is completely confronted by blasphemy . . . Sadām Husayn . . . is a person who is an infidel." Other Iraqi Ba'th leaders were similarly labelled "atheists" and "pagans."[24]

Islamic notions, with their obvious propaganda value, were likewise adopted by Sadām Husayn and his supporters. They recalled Muslim conquests of classical and medieval times in which Islam was confronting its non-Muslim enemies, including the Persians. They evoked the spirit of "the battles of Badr, al-Qādisiyya, al-Yarmūk and Hittīn";[25] and designated the war itself as "the

43

Qādisiyya-Saddām operation."[26] The foe was once again "the Persian magians," (i.e. the pre-Islamic Persian priests), the "grandsons of Khosrow [Persia's last important ruler before the advent of Islam], and Rustam [the commander of the Persian troops at Qādisiyya]." No less important were the Arab nationalist overtones in the Iraqi statements. They claimed to be fighting a pan-Arab war and to be defending "the Arab nation's sovereignty, honour and right." The battle against an external, non-Arab enemy was an inevitable stage in the grand Arab struggle to achieve more far-reaching goals: "Those who fought in Zayn al-Qaws, Safi Sa'd [both in the Qasr-e-Shirīn sector] al-Muhammara [the Arabic name of Khorramshahr] and Ahvaz were asphalting the road to Jerusalem, Rāmallah, Hebron and Jaffa."[27] However, in trying to make the war a springboard for securing a leadership role in the Arab world, Iraq achieved only a limited success, as its leaders were soon to realize.

INTER-ARAB REPERCUSSIONS

While the war did not create new alignments or rivalries in the Arab world, it certainly enhanced existing trends and brought them into sharper focus. (For pre-war developments in this regard, see essay on inter-Arab relations). Jordan and Saudi Arabia, Iraq's recently acquired allies, took Baghdad's side with markedly different limits of commitment. On the other side, Syria stuck to its anti-Iraqi stance and, along with Libya, joined hands with Iran. Other Arab countries displayed little inclination—at least initially—to become involved in the dispute; they either gave non-committal verbal support to Iraq, or remained neutral. Finally, the PLO—inevitably a loser in any Middle-Eastern war not involving the Palestinian issue—was searching for some middle ground, though with an obvious lack of self-confidence.

From the very start of the war, Jordan became Iraq's most enthusiastic and vociferous supporter. Such an attitude was dictated by King Husayn's urge to consolidate his country's emerging alliance with Iraq, which assured Jordan a place close to the centre of the inter-Arab stage, and which was becoming all the more valuable to him as Jordanian-Syrian relations deteriorated. Husayn had probably shared Iraq's expectations of major gains. His own country, geo-graphically remote from Iran and with no Shī'ī population susceptible to Iranian appeals, was relatively safe and he could afford to support Khomeyni's enemy. He had his own reasons for wishing to see the end of the present Iranian regime since its spokesmen had come out against monarchy as an "un-Islamic" institu-tion, while the Iranian media had called him "the Shah of Jordan."

Presiding over an emergency Cabinet meeting on 23 September, King Husayn called for "a unified Arab stand in support of fraternal Iraq to defend every particle of its dear Arab . . . national soil and its legitimate rights." He sent a message to President Saddām Husayn expressing "Jordan's sentiments to fra-ternal Iraq in assertions of the essence of Arab unity and [a] pan-Arab stand". He visited Baghdad on 4–5 October to reiterate his firm commitment to the Iraqi cause in "the battle . . . of the Arab nation to regain its rights and sovereignty."[28] Led by the King, Jordanian officials and the media conducted an intensive campaign in support of Iraq, emphasizing that Jordan upheld "the Arab right wherever it may be."[29]

Jordanian support went beyond declarations of alliance. At an early stage of the war, a number of Iraqi planes moved to Jordanian airfields as a safe shelter from possible Iranian air strikes against Iraqi airfields.[30] The Jordanian army was placed on alert immediately following the outbreak of war. Early in October there were reports of a 40,000-strong Jordanian force concentrated close to the Iraqi-Jordanian border.

King Husayn confirmed on 9 October that Jordan was "prepared to give military aid to Iraq if the latter asked for it," and that "the Jordanian [army] is ready and alert."[31] However, Jordanian sources denied subsequent reports claiming that a Jordanian contingent had actually crossed into Iraq. As the Iraqi port of Basra became inaccessible soon after the beginning of hostilities, Jordan allowed Iraq free access to 'Aqaba port. This opened a convenient transit route for Iraq to bring in ammunition and spare parts, as well as civilian supplies. The 'Aqaba-Amman-Baghdad route was used intensively, and many of the cargoes moving along it originated in the Soviet bloc.[32] (For earlier Iraqi aid to Jordan to develop 'Aqaba port and the overland route from there to Baghdad, see essay on inter-Arab relations.)

Iraq's other and, initially, closer ally, Saudi Arabia, was bound to be much more cautious in determining its position. With its vulnerable oil installation on the shores of the Gulf, and with a Shī'ī population susceptible to Iranian incitement in its eastern regions, the Saudis were reluctant to give Iran cause to create trouble in Saudi Arabia. (For unrest among Saudi Shī'īs earlier in 1980, see chapter on Saudi Arabia.) Moreover, an Iraq strengthened by a decisive victory could, in the long run, pose a threat to the stability of the Gulf—to the detriment of Saudi interests. Moreover, as a country taking its Islamic responsibilities as seriously as its Arab responsibilities, Saudi Arabia could not be too overtly partial in a war pitting Muslims against Muslims. Thus, when it eventually decided to back Iraq (having concluded that the threat from Khomeyni outweighed all other considerations) it did so with a great deal of circumspection. No official statement of the Saudi position was issued during the first few days of fighting. Its Press took a cautiously pro-Iraqi attitude, speaking of a "war between an Arab and a stranger" and emphasizing, in rather vague terms, the value of Arab solidarity. Only on 25 September did King Khālid telephone President Saddām Husayn. According to the Iraqi account of the conversation, Khālid had "affirmed the support of the Kingdom of Saudi Arabia for Iraq in its pan-Arab battle", and had spoken of Iran as "the enemy of the Arab nation."[33] Iraqi (but not Saudi) sources also quoted other Saudi officials as having expressed their country's support for Iraq. On 12 October the Jordanian Prime Minister, Mudar Badrān, returning from a visit to Jidda, said that the two countries had agreed to join hands with Iraq.[34] The Saudis themselves were extremely careful, though, not to spell out such a position. In an interview in New York on 5 October, the Saudi Foreign Minister Sa'ūd al-Faysal, summarized his Government's stand. The war, he said, was "a conflict between two brother Muslim countries that has to be brought speedily to termination. It is not a conflict [in which] we want to support one side against the other in order to gain advantage over the other . . . It's a fratricidal war"; therefore, it needed to be considered "in a rather different fashion" from a "conflict between Iraq and an enemy country." He insisted that his Government had never considered Iran an enemy of the Arab people: "They were never an enemy in the past. Iran is not an enemy of the Arab people now."[35]

Syria had been hostile towards Iraq for well over a decade and the failure in 1979 of a short-lived attempt at reconciliation had led to increased tension. (See essay on inter-Arab relations.) Since Khomeyni's rise to power, Syria had also been on better terms with his regime than any other Arab country. Its decision, very early on in the war, to side with Iran was thus consistent with its earlier policies. Nonetheless, it further exacerbated Syrian-Iraqi tensions. This was true, even though Syria—from considerations of its own isolation in the Arab world,

45

and because of Iraq's presentation of the war as an "all-Arab battle"—expressed its pro-Iranian stand with marked prudence and restraint. The main theme in its declared positions was to disprove Iraq's claim of fighting for the all-Arab cause and to assert that Baghdad was fighting the wrong war, thereby exhausting Arab potential needed elsewhere. "It is a pity," said a Syrian radio commentator "to see Arab countries engrossed in struggle which has nothing to do with the national struggle against imperialism and Zionism."[36] The Syrian Chief of Staff, Ḥikmat al-Shihābī, accused Iraq of "serving imperialism by fighting marginal battles which weaken the Arab nation's fastness."[37]

Syria's pro-Iranian stand was not limited to verbal support. Iraqi accusations that Syria was sending troops and military equipment to Iran were confirmed by outside sources. Syrian soldiers were reported to have been taken prisoner on the Iranian front.[38] The Iraqi media bitterly attacked Syria, while the latter's stance remained basically defensive. On 12 October, Baghdad broke diplomatic relations with Damascus in protest against the latter's military support of Iran.

Libya, another Arab foe of Iraq and, like Syria, with few friends in the Arab world, also sided with Iran. Mu'ammar al-Qadhdhāfī was apparently motivated by his rivalry with Saddām Ḥusayn over Arab leadership, as well as by his strong sympathy for Khomeyni's Islamic revolution. After some initial hesitation, Libya began an airlift of arms from Tripoli to Tehran early in October, and Libyan soldiers fighting with Iran were reported captured by Iraq.[39] In a cable to several Arab Heads of State on 9 October Qadhdhāfī publicly declared his unequivocal support for Iran and urged the other countries to follow suit, declaring: "Islamic duty dictates that we ally ourselves with the Muslims in Iran in this crusade instead of fighting them on behalf of America."[40] Two days later, Iraq severed its diplomatic relations with Libya.

The line marking off pro-Iraqi from pro-Iranian Arab states was unmistakably clear with regard to the countries mentioned so far. This was less true in the case of other Arab countries, some of whom had only a limited interest in the conflict and therefore no reason to needlessly abandon a neutral stance; others were in the delicate position of being weak neighbours of what looked to be, from their perspective, quarrelling giants; they thus attempted to appear as impartial as they possibly could. The latter category included the Gulf States. Like Saudi Arabia, they had sensitive and extremely vulnerable economic, political and security interests in the area, which they were in no position to defend militarily. All had important Shī'ī populations, and their ruling families were keenly aware of Iran's deeply-felt rejection of any kind of royal regime. While they all had reason to be apprehensive of a victorious Ba'thist Iraq, they, like Saudi Arabia, viewed the Iranian threat as more immediate and dangerous than the potential Iraqi threat, and hence tilted towards Iraq—a position they all endeavoured to coat with careful ambiguity. Kuwait, especially, allowed its media to present a pro-Iraqi stand, while its officials refrained from openly confirming such an attitude.[41] Kuwait repeatedly denied reports from Western sources of military aid to Iraq. Other Gulf States—the UAE, Qatar and Bahrain—kept a strict silence. Nonetheless, their tacit siding with Iraq was indirectly confirmed by a strong Iranian warning that Tehran would expand the theatre of operations and hit hard any country in the area whose support for Iraq was translated into active co-operation.

Egypt, too, adopted a neutral course, but for very different reasons. President Anwar al-Sādāt's attitude towards the leaders of both belligerents was one of distaste and contempt; he was unlikely to be upset by the spectacle of their warring against one another. Moreover, Egypt saw an advantage to itself in its ceasing to be, at least temporarily, the principal object of animosity in the region.

THE IRAQI-IRANIAN WAR

Thus, it could afford to do little more than follow the war developments with "extreme interest and sorrow in view of the bloodshed, the waste of resources and the destruction that is taking place."[42] Discussing the war with newsmen, President Sādāt commented with undisguised disdain that "it is a great tragedy to place armaments in the hands of such teenagers. . . We condemn both sides and both leaders of Iraq and Iran." Egyptian officials, too, declared their country's strict neutrality, and repeatedly called for a peaceful settlement of the conflict. Sādāt and his senior officials also emphasized Egypt's emergence as a credible island of stability in the ME: "I must look after the balance and the security of this area," announced Sādāt. "This is my responsibility." Acting on the same premise, he offered "facilities to the US to reach any Arab or Muslim states that are in danger."[43] Egyptian observers were also visibly pleased to point to another lesson of the war, viz. that "the Arab-Israeli conflict was not 'the conflict' but rather 'a conflict', namely one of many conflicts."[44] (In a subsequent switch, Sādāt abandoned his earlier even-handed stance and spoke of Iraq as the "aggressor." In so doing, he aligned his policy with that of the US. He may also have sensed that Iraq and Saudi Arabia were no longer as close as they had been before the war and that Egypt now had a chance of prying Saudi Arabia loose from the "Saddām Ḥusayn-Fahd axis", which Sādāt had often decried earlier in 1980. (See essay on inter-Arab relations.)

If Egypt derived some advantage from the war, the PLO was a clear loser. Not only was it embarrassed by its allies quarrelling (with the divergent attitudes of Saudi Arabia and Syria weighing more heavily than the open Iranian-Iraqi hostility); but its own struggle was being eclipsed. From the PLO's perception, the conflict was likely also to have long-term repercussions, carrying the risk of scaling down the Palestinian problem in a region where world-wide interests of a more vital nature were being endangered at other foci of instability. Immediately after the outbreak of the war, PLO representatives embarked on feverish mediation efforts. 'Arafāt spent a week in the area (24–29 September), dividing his time between Baghdad and Tehran, in a hectic search for a formula which would end the fighting. Having no substantial or feasible solution to offer, he was snubbed by both countries. The PLO then decided to keep a low profile and maintain strict neutrality. From time to time, its leaders proposed new formulae for terminating the conflict, but they found both sides unwilling to listen.

Morocco and the Yemeni Arab Republic expressed full support for Iraq at an early stage in the war. The People's Democratic Republic of Yemen (PDRY), Sudan, Algeria, Lebanon and Tunisia showed little overt interest in the dispute; their reactions were limited to expressions of sorrow at the shedding of Arab and Muslim blood and to calling for an end to hostilities. Turkey, the only country bordering both belligerents, was engaged in its own domestic problems and maintained a scrupulous neutrality. (See chapter on Turkey.)

THE GREAT POWERS

Both the US and the USSR declared their neutrality in the war. The strategic sensitivity of the area as well as previous steps taken by both sides (the Soviet invasion of Afghanistan, and President Carter's declaration of America's readiness to use military force in the Gulf, if necessary) now dictated extreme caution. Thus, while the two Great Powers by no means related to the war with detachment, their involvement was kept at a remarkably low level—incomparably lower, for instance, than their activities at the time of the 1973 Arab-Israeli war.

The US position was relatively easy to formulate. It had no diplomatic relations with either Iraq or Iran and, with the exception of its hostages in Iran, had no

47

political stake in either. On the contrary, it was at loggerheads with both regimes. (The most damning charge these could level was each to accuse the other of collaborating with "American imperialism".) The major US interest was to secure the flow of oil from the Gulf and, for that purpose, to protect its allies in the region, notably Saudi Arabia. As the war broke out, President Carter declared his country's adherence to a policy of non-intervention and called upon the Soviet Union to similarly keep out of the conflict. Early in October, the US sent four Airborne Warning and Control System (AWACS) radar aircraft to Saudi Arabia, to patrol the Gulf and monitor movements at the front. It also put its naval units in Bahrain on alert as well as those in the Indian Ocean (where their number had recently been increased to 37). They moved a number of warships closer to the Straits of Hormuz. Reports that the US was on the point of negotiating a "hostages for spare-parts" deal with Iran were vehemently denied by both parties; but on 23 October, the US came out openly against Iraq and for Iran. At a session of the SC the US Ambassador, Donald McHenry, condemned the Iraqi invasion and added that, in the US view, "the cohesion and stability of Iran is in the interests of stability and prosperity of the entire region."[45] (See essay on the US and the ME.)

The USSR position was much more complex. It had a Treaty of Friendship and Co-operation with Iraq (signed in 1972), and was its main arms supplier. Yet, in recent years, Iraq had drifted away from the Soviet orbit and, early in 1980, had taken a markedly anti-Soviet stand over Afghanistan. At the same time, the USSR was energetically seeking closer relations with Iran, trying to overcome the estrangement caused there, too, by the Afghanistan invasion. Furthermore, the Soviet Union had close relations with Syria. After prolonged preparations a 20-year Treaty of Friendship and Co-operation was signed between them on 9 October. It also had close military ties with Libya, Iran's other supporter. Moscow thus found itself in a complex situation, with both the warring sides and their allies making their claims on Soviet support a test of Moscow's credibility.

Like Washington, Moscow professed neutrality in the war. However, it practised neutrality of a different kind by simultaneously aiding both combatants. Soviet non-military and military supplies, including ammunition and spare parts, were ferried to Iraq from the PDRY, Ethiopia and some Soviet bloc countries via 'Aqaba. At the same time, Soviet arms and supplies were flown to Iran from Syria, Libya and North Korea. The USSR, meanwhile, tried to keep out of the limelight, closely watching for a turn of events promising possibly substantial Soviet gains, while guarding against the risks of incurring political damage. (For a wider consideration of Soviet policies, see essay on the USSR and the ME.)

THE WAR AND ITS REPERCUSSIONS: A PRELIMINARY EVALUATION

Iraqi expectations of an easy victory in a brief war were disproved by the course of developments in the battlefield—even during the short span reviewed here. Instead of the expected swift operation, Iraq found itself fighting a prolonged slow-moving war. Its estimates that internal strife would produce a collapse of Iran's military command and political structure, assuring the Iraqi army of decisive military superiority, proved just as erroneous. A month after Iraq launched its full-scale offensive, the two armies were locked in a struggle whose continuation would depend on the resilience and durability of both regimes, and would require new military planning and the kind of morale-building capable of sustaining a long-haul war effort.

48

Already, during the first 4-5 weeks, the material damage sustained by both parties was heavy. Major, vulnerable strategic and economic targets were bombed from the air or shelled by artillery. A few days after the beginning of full-scale hostilities, both countries were forced to stop exporting oil, thereby losing tremendous revenues. (Iraq had been exporting c. 3.2m barrels per day, and Iran c. 700,000m barrels per day before the war.) The shortfall in the world oil markets was largely compensated for by increased Saudi Arabian and Gulf States' production. The Iraqi refineries at Kirkūk, Mosul and Basra, and pipeline and pumping installation in Kirkūk and Mosul, and the Iranian refineries at Abadan and Tehran, as well as its tanker terminal at Khārg Island, were bombed and put out of commission. Some of the damage was so extensive as to require repairs lasting many months. Other infra-structure targets in both countries were severely hit. Most of the damage was caused early in the war by deep-penetration air raids. Saddām Husayn's regime proved stable enough to withstand a measure of discontent over the country's unsatisfactory military performance in the initial weeks. By the end of the period under review, there were no signs of his tightly-run government being destabilized. Yet there were at least two important centres of potentially dangerous opposition: the Shīʿī population (many of whom served as soldiers under Sunnī officers); and the Kurds. Unrest among the latter would have been particularly ominous for the regime as it would have signified the loss of the one advantage the 1975 agreement had given it. Some indications that such disquiet was developing began to appear during the first weeks of the war. (See chapter on Iraq.)

In Iran, on the other hand, the war initially had something of a stabilizing effect. It suppressed, at least for a while, the differences among its leaders, then centring on the question of the powers of the President and the Prime Minister, and their standing with Khomeyni. (See chapter on Iran.) In addition, reacting to the external threat, opposition groups called off strikes and suspended their attacks on the Government, and declared their wholehearted support for the war effort. "The war is very useful for us," President Bani Sadr said in two interviews; "it consolidates our Islamic Republic."[46] As supreme commander of the army (originally not a function of the President, but of the "leader", i.e. Khomeyni), Bani Sadr's domestic position seemed to be strengthening with the army's unexpectedly vigorous performance. (See chapter on Iran.) Nevertheless, the power struggles persisted behind the facade of the nation's rallying around the war time leadership. The clerics, in particular, now faced the dilemma posed by their need for competent field commanders and their distrust of the (present or future) loyalty of successful officers. They sought to resolve the dilemma, in part, by deploying Revolutionary Guard units at key points along the front.

The pan-Islamic, and perhaps more important, the pan-Arab slogans raised by the two rivals produced little unity in either camp. Iraq's claims that it was fighting for an Arab cause was called into question by some Arab countries joining Iran. In more than one Arab country, Iraq's rallying call was regarded as no more than a propaganda device which proved to be of limited effectiveness.

Taken all in all, the war failed to change the direction of major inter-Arab developments. In the Islamic arena the appeal to Islamic sentiment was soon complemented by evocations of plain "old-fashioned" (and, in Khomeyni's earlier view, "un-Islamic") patriotism, and by calls to defend the homeland as well as, or rather than, the Faith.

Ami Ayalon

49

NOTES

1. For a more detailed account see D. Dishon (ed.), *Middle East Record, 1969–70* (Jerusalem: Israel Universities Press, 1977), pp. 651–659.
2. The full text of the agreement and supplementary protocols as ratified on 13 June 1975 is given in *Orient*, Leiden, September 1975, pp. 96–111.
3. *Al-Majalla*, London, 24–30 May 1980; R Baghdad, 17, 25, 28 September, 2 October—US Foreign Broadcast Information Service, Daily Report; Middle East and North Africa (DR), 18, 26, 29 September, 5 October 1980.
4. Husayn's speech over R Baghdad, 28 September—DR, 29 September 1980.
5. Text in R Baghdad, 17 September—British Broadcasting Corporation, Summary of World Broadcasts; the ME and Africa (BBC), 19 September 1980.
6. Agence France Press, Paris, 17 September—DR, 18 September 1980.
7. R Tehran, 18 September—DR, 19 September 1980.
8. Precise details of the military moves have been extremely difficult to establish: Iraqi and Iranian sources have given altogether contradictory accounts and outside observers on both sides were allowed no more than partial and selective coverage. The following account is based mainly on descriptions by Western reporters in the field.
9. R Baghdad, 2 October—BBC, 6 October 1980.
10. *The Times*, London, 10 October 1980.
11. R Baghdad, 18 October—BBC, 20 October 1980.
12. Iraqi News Agency (INA), Baghdad, 25 September—DR, 26 September 1980.
13. INA, 25 September—DR, 26 September 1980.
14. R Tehran, 26 September—DR, 29 September 1980.
15. R Tehran, 27 September—DR, 29 September 1980.
16. R Baghdad, 28 September—DR, 29 September 1980.
17. R Baghdad, 29 September—BBC, 29 September 1980.
18. R Tehran, 30 September—DR, 1 October 1980.
19. *International Herald Tribune (IHT)*, Paris, 2 October; R Tehran, 2 October—DR, 3 October 1980.
20. R Baghdad, 5 October—DR, 6 October 1980.
21. *Le Monde*, Paris, 8 October 1980.
22. *Le Monde*, 10–11 October; *IHT, The Guardian*, London, 10 October 1980.
23. R Tehran, 19 October—BBC, 21 October; *The Guardian*, 20 October 1980.
24. E.g. R Tehran, 24, 27, 30 September—DR, 25, 29 September, 1 October 1980.
25. The battle of Badr (624 A.D.)—the first major battle of the Prophet Muhammad and his followers against the non-believers of Mecca. Al-Qādisiyya (637 A.D.)—the first and most important battle of the Islamic army under Saʻd Ibn Abī Waqqās against the Persians. Al-Yarmūk (636 A.D.)—the Muslim battle against the Byzantine army, which opened the road to the Muslim conquest of Syria and Palestine. Ḥittīn (1187 A.D.)—Saladin's decisive victory over the Crusaders.
26. E.g. R Baghdad, 23, 25, 28 September—DR, 25, 26, 29 September 1980.
27. E.g. R Baghdad, 17, 23, 25, 28 September—DR, 19, 25, 26, 29 September 1980.
28. R Amman, 23, 29 September, 5 October—DR, 25, 30 September, 6 October 1980.
29. R Amman, 5 October—DR, 6 October 1980.
30. *Al-Ḥawādith*, London, 26 September; *The Jerusalem Post, (JP)*, 14 October 1980.
31. *Al-Qabas*, Kuwait, 7 October; R Amman, 9 October 1980.
32. *Daily Telegraph*, London, 9 October; *The Times*, 11 October; *JP*, 14 October 1980.
33. R Baghdad, 25 September—DR, 30 September 1980.
34. R Cairo, Voice of the Arabs, 12 October 1980.
35. TV interview with Columbia Broadcasting System, 5 October 1980.
36. R Damascus, 19 September 1980.
37. R Damascus, 13 October 1980.
38. Kuwaiti News Agency, 28 September; R Baghdad, 28 September, 5 October—DR, 1 October; *The Guardian*, 9 October; INA, 11, 16 October; *IHT*, 11–12 October 1980.
39. INA, 4 October—BBC, 6 October; *IHT*, 11–12 October 1980.
40. R Tripoli, 9 October—DR, 10 October 1980.
41. E.g. the Kuwaiti dailies *al-Anbā*, 18 September; *al-Siyāsa*, 23 September; *al-Ra'y al-ʻĀmm*, 28 September 1980.

42. Middle East News Agency (MENA), Cairo, 22 September—DR, 23 September 1980.
43. R Cairo, 24 September—DR, 25 September; MENA, 25 September—DR, 26 September 1980.
44. *October*, Cairo, 12 October 1980.
45. *The New York Times*, 24 October 1980.
46. *Newsweek*, New York, 6 October; *Le Monde*, 8 October 1980.

Libya's Intervention in Chad

It was not just Col Muammar Gaddafy's bold and successful military intervention in Chad which created a new climate of uncertainty in West Africa towards the end of 1980; it was no less his support for Islamic opposition groups to the established regimes in, and close to, the Sahel region. Not since the late Dr Kwame Nkrumah's heyday in the early 1960s has an African leader embarked so openly on a campaign of subverting governments in the name of 'revolution and anti-imperialism' as has the Libyan leader; but, unlike Nkrumah, Gaddafy has immense riches to promote his aims and a religious cause more directly appealing to masses of people than the more abstract ideal of Pan-Africanism.

However, Gaddafy is more of a maverick than was Ghana's first President; and he has powerful enemies within the Islam camp itself. One such enemy, President Seyni Kountche of Niger, complained to the Islamic summit conference held in Taif (Saudi Arabia) in January 1981:

> We sincerely deplore the behavior of a certain Head of State in our region who continues to indulge in activities lacking all wisdom under the cover of a faith of the Islamic foundations. . . . We see a man who has become a prisoner of a hegemonic vision that undermines the very existence of our region. . . . We are trying not to consider the abominably racist nature of his dream, by which he makes a shameless call on some ethnic groups of Semitic origin in some of our states to join a so-called Islamic Legion to crush us.[1]

Other African leaders, mostly Left-wing radicals, take a different view of Gaddafy's role and ambitions. Rahman Mohamed Babu, a prominent figure in the Zanzibar revolution of 1964, sees 'this sudden Western outcry (echoed by its allies in Africa) about the so-called Libyan "intervention" as nothing but a desperate public expression of (the) fear of Africa adopting diplomatic and economic policies independent of Europe. . . . France is especially a pastmaster in these kinds of manoeuvres'.[2] He also sees Chad as being 'strategically crucial for a genuine revolution in the continent.'

A similar attitude was expressed by Dr Yusufu Bala Usman, adviser to the Governor of Kaduna State in an Open Letter addressed to parliamentarians in which he warned against 'Nigeria being drawn into a war, primarily pitted against Libya, fighting basically to preserve France's military, political and economic system in Africa'.[3]

What Babu, Usman and other critics like them ignore is that the 'outcry' over Libya's policy in Chad comes not just from a few pro-French African leaders, or those they would describe as 'Western stooges'; it comes from the great majority of the member-states of the Organization of African Unity (OAU). It was not French policy but the OAU's own policy in Chad (however feebly and ineffectively it was applied) that was challenged by Libya's military intervention. Those who criticize Gaddafy's action include radicals like President Sékou Touré of Guinea and, though more reluctantly, President Kerekou of Benin. Nor does Babu, with his strong faith in 'revolutionary action', address himself to the question of what kind of revolution he expects to see come out of Tripoli. Gaddafy is indeed a revolutionary–a messianic Islamic revolutionary. But what are his aims and ambitions for the Sahel and its neighbours?

COL GADDAFY'S AIMS AND POLICIES

While Gaddafy's philosophy of revolution is clearly set out in his Green Books[4], the central thrust of his strategy is towards the Arab world and other Islamic countries. What is less clear are his aims and interests in Black Africa–to which Chad belongs as much (or, measured in population terms, even more) than it does to the Arab world. According to ex-President Senghor of Senegal, Gaddafy wants to create a 'Republic of the Sahara', or 'A United States of the Sahel'.[5] A Malian political ally of Gaddafy's, Didi Demba Medina Soumbounou, said in an interview in 1979 in Tripoli (where he was negotiating with the regime to overthrow President Moussa Traoré) their aim was to create an 'Islamic State of the Sahara', which would include Libya, Chad, Mali and Niger.[6] Gaddafy himself told the Arab People's Congress in Tripoli in January 1981 that 'the main and most pressing issue is to achieve Arab unity from the Atlantic to the Gulf, or, at least, unity between several Arab countries such as Algeria, Libya, Egypt and Sudan. Then, work can be done to achieve unity with Chad.' He went on to say:

> The Africans who objected to the unity between the Jamahiriyah and Chad did not look at it from the point of view of *Arab nationalism*, but rather from a racist view. What prevents the unity between two African peoples? And how can we make a distinction between Zanzibar and Tanganyika's unity from unity between the Libyan and Chadian peoples? This is a racist view dictated by imperialism. . . . We fight alongside Africa because we are Africans and members of the OAU which calls for unity in Africa.[7]

(The OAU member-states' objections to the proposed Libyan–Chad unity was that it was announced without the Chadian people being consulted; they did not object to the idea of mergers between countries, but called for elections to test opinion.[8])

Gaddafy's interest in Chad, Mali and Niger goes back to the 1960s when he first backed the Front for the National Liberation of Chad (Frolinat), whose exile leader, Dr Abbas Siddick, had his headquarters in Tripoli.[9] (Siddick later quarreled with Tripoli, which transferred its patronage first to Hissene Habre–now denounced as a traitor, and then to Weddeye Goukouny who also briefly quarreled with Tripoli in 1979 and invited French military support.[10]) During the period of this break, Tripoli made an alliance with the non-Muslim, Southern leader, Col Wadal Abdelkader Kamougue;[11] even though Tripoli's original justification for backing Frolinat was that it had developed as a Muslim struggle to win their rights against the South-dominated Tombalbaye Government. Gaddafy's choice of Chadian allies can therefore be seen to have been determined by which of its leaders was willing, at any particular time, to accept Tripoli's support in exchange for accepting its line. (For example, when Goukouny briefly turned against Gaddafy, he accused him of having annexed the Aouzou Strip.)

Quite apart from any possible 'revolutionary' interest in Chad, Libya has also displayed a keen national interest. In June 1973 it occupied the Aouzou Strip in the north, which is supposed to be rich in minerals, especially uranium. Mussolini, when he occupied Libya, drew its border line to include Aouzou, and persuaded the French traitor, Laval, to endorse it in a treaty. Gaddafy based his own claims to the Strip on the Mussolini–Laval treaty.

Libya has also long supported opposition groups in two of its neighbouring states, Mali and Niger; there his chosen allies are the nomadic Touaregs–a Berber

53

people speaking Tamachagh, although Gaddafy claims them as Arabs. Relations with Niger thrived for a time after 1974 when Col Seyni Kountche (see above) staged a military coup. But relations cooled in 1976 when a map was published in Tripoli showing that Libya had moved its borders to include not only the Aouzou Strip but also a chunk of Niger which has considerable uranium deposits.

In the late 1970s, Libya's interests shifted to include support not only for Polisario in Western Sahara, but also to opposition elements in Senegal and The Gambia. In late 1979 Libya gave its support to an Islamic fundamentalist group in Senegal whose leader, Ahmad Niasse, formed the *Hizboulahi* (God's Party) before going into exile in Tripoli. Senegal accused Libya of training a force of 5,000 men recruited from the Sahelian countries for his Islamic Legion. Niasse was also accused by the Gambian Government of having recruited 40 political dissidents to join his Islamic Legion.[12]

Senegal, The Gambia and Niger broke their diplomatic ties with Tripoli in 1980, while Mali expelled Libya's diplomats without, however, breaking off relations completely. During 1980, too, Libya's media began to mention the Front for the Liberation of Eastern Sahara, an entirely unknown organization.

The number of Sahelians recruited for Gaddafy's Islamic Legion (which also comprises Palestinians and dissident Egyptians and Sudanese) was variously estimated at 4,000–5,000. Syria agreed in early 1981 to provide officers to train the Islamic Legion.[13]

THE ROLE OF THE ORGANIZATION OF AFRICAN UNITY IN CHAD
NEGOTIATIONS FROM 1977 TO DECEMBER 1980
The OAU first addressed itself to the question of Chad at its 1977 Libreville summit, when it appointed an *ad hoc* Committee (Gabon, Algeria, Mozambique, Nigeria, Senegal and Cameroon) to negotiate in the dispute between the Malloum regime and Libya over its support for Frolinat.[14] With the dispute still unresolved, the next OAU summit, held in Khartoum in 1978, appointed a new *ad hoc* committee (Sudan, Cameroon, Niger and Nigeria) to mediate in the conflict.[15] Their efforts produced the first ceasefire between the Chad Government and Frolinat, which was signed on 27 March 1978 at conferences in Sebha and Benghazi. Libya was actively associated with Sudan and Niger in securing this agreement.[16] But the ceasefire never took effect.

However, the Chad situation was completely transformed in February 1979 with the defeat of Gen Felix Malloum's regime by the forces of Hissène Habré.[17] This new situation spelt the end of Southern domination over the Muslim North; but it also intensified the struggle for power among the Muslim leaders themselves. In this situation Habre was challenged by not only the new Southern leader, Lt-Col Wadal Abdelkader Kamougue, but also by his long-standing Northern rival, Weddeye Goukouny. Therefore, the OAU summit in Monrovia (July 1979) concentrated on ending the fighting, encouraging the formation of an effective national government of unity, and eliminating both French and Libyan intervention. In place of Sudan, Nigeria now took the leading role in trying to implement OAU decisions. It succeeded in getting all eleven Chadian factions to sign the Lagos Agreement of 21 August 1979[18], which provided for the creation of a Transitional Government (the GUNT) representative of all the factions; a ceasefire; the introduction of a three-nation African peacekeeping force (Guinea, Congo and Benin); and the withdrawal of France's military forces. The French withdrew all their forces in May 1980. But the peacekeeping force did not eventuate. Only Congo provided its quota; Guinea and Benin announced that they could not meet the costs involved. Of the OAU's promised contribution of $6m, only $600,000 was raised. By the time of the next OAU summit in Freetown (July 1979) the GUNT had broken up into warring parties and the civil war had reached a new pitch of intensity. The OAU secretary-general reported to the Heads of State:

> We are watching with impotence the expansion of a relentless civil war, with all its paraphernalia of destruction and misery. . . . Chad is being destroyed and the warring parties will soon arrive at that gruesome result if they continue to act as they are doing. . . . Intransigency has supremacy over conciliation. At any rate, the situation today is even more dangerous, and no amount of recantation, tact or anaesthetic manoeuvre can settle the problem. . . . The Chadian affair is presently clearly revealing the limitations of our Organization, and the restricted scope of our action. It glaringly reveals the growing discrepancy between what is said and what is believed, between absolute 'will' and relative 'ability', between declared intentions and actual results. It therefore dictates a change of conception of our machinery, a renovation of principles and action.

The Freetown summit resolved to 'make one further attempt to find an African solution to the crisis', particularly in providing a neutral Peacekeeping Force by requesting African States in a position to provide forces at their own expense to do so in accordance with conditions to be determined at the summit. It also decided that if the OAU failed to raise the necessary funds for its own peacekeeping effort after a period of two months, the UN Security Council should be asked for assistance–particularly for the necessary financial means to enable peace to be restored in Chad.[19]

The OAU subcommittee on Chad held two meetings in Lomé on 13 October and 28 November 1980 under the joint chairmanship of its current chairman, President Siaka Stevens of Sierra Leone, and President Eyadema of Togo. After the October meeting a mission went to Ndjamena for talks with the Chadian leaders. While Weddeye Goukouny received the mission, the army commander, Hissène Habré, made himself unavailable.[20] Nor did Habré attend the subcommittee's next meeting in Lomé on 28 November; only Goukouny arrived for the discussions with the Presidents of Sierra Leone, Togo, Guinea, Benin and the OAU secretary-general, Edem Kodjo. The four Presidents and Goukouny signed a five-point agreement providing for a ceasefire to become effective by 15 December; a commission to supervise the ceasefire made up of representatives from Benin, Congo, Guinea, Togo, Sierra Leone and the OAU secretary-general; a neutral peacekeeping force to be provided by Benin, Congo, Guinea and Togo; if necessary the UN to be consulted to provide assistance for this force; Ndjamena to be demilitarized, its inhabitants disarmed and all military forces withdrawn to points 5 km beyond the capital; and appropriate action to be taken against any party violating the ceasefire.

At the same time, the signatories to the agreement (with Goukouny signing on behalf of GUNT) adopted a second document calling on the Heads of State of the members of the subcommittee to monitor the agreement's implementation; invited Nigeria to convene a conference of the signatory members of the 1979 Lagos Agreement; demanded the withdrawal of all foreign forces currently in Chad; and urged all countries to abstain from intervening in any way in Chad's internal affairs.[21] Hissène Habré, having refused to attend the Lomé talks, went instead to explain his position to President Ahidjo in Yaoundé, where he said he refused to sign a ceasefire so long as Libyan troops remained in Chad. It was not until 16 December that Habre finally signed the ceasefire agreement in Yaoundé, while still insisting that GUNT was illegal and vowing that he would continue the struggle.[22] He accused Benin of acting as an agent for Libya in Chad.

Hissène Habré–whose stiff-necked and uncooperative policies were perhaps the major reason for the failure to implement the Lagos Agreement[23]–was nevertheless right about Libya's growing military presence. For even when Goukouny was putting his signature to the OAU statement in Lomé on 28 November–accepting, *inter alia*, the withdrawal of all foreign troops from his country–he was already heavily engaged with the Libyans in planning the final onslaught on the embattled capital of Ndjamena. Goukouny's Foreign Minister, Ahmat Acyl, disclosed that Gaddafy had been in Libya in the first week of November; but in the same statement he denied the presence of any Libyan troops in Chad.[24] As late as 3 December, Chad's Information Minister, Boukar Nanasbaye, was still busy travelling round African capitals, reassuring them that 'Libya is not intervening in the Chad conflict.'[25] Yet, just over a week later, 4,000–5,000 Libyan troops were storming Ndjamena.

RESPONSE TO LIBYA'S MILITARY INTERVENTION
The Libyan build-up had, in fact, been carefully monitored since August (three months after the French forces' withdrawal) by African intelligence services as well as by the French. However, the African leaders who met in Lomé and Lagos seemed to have relied on their ability to persuade the Libyans to withdraw once a new OAU agreement had been worked out with Chad's leaders; at any rate they did not appreciate the seriousness of Libya's new military and political commitments in Chad.

The further conference decided upon at the Lomé meeting was convened by Nigeria on 23 December–but by then Ndjamena had already fallen. It was attended by the Presidents of Nigeria, Niger, Sudan, Central African Republic, Cameroon, Togo, Guinea, Benin, Congo and Sierra Leone and the Foreign Minister of Libya. Prior to and during this meeting, Nigeria came in for strong criticism from several Francophone countries over what they felt was its vacillation in refusing to condemn Libya outright. President Shehu Shagari's spokesman later explained that his refusal to do so was because he did not wish to drive Weddeye Goukouny out of the fold, which would have happened if Tripoli were openly criticized.[26] As it was, Goukouny had at first refused to attend the Lagos talks; even when he was finally persuaded to fly to Lagos it needed hours of talks between him and Shagari before he finally agreed to enter the meeting. Meanwhile, Hissene Habre was told by Nigeria's Foreign Minister that he would not be welcome in Lagos. He stayed away. (At this point Nigeria used the transformation of the Libyan embassy into a People's Bureau to expel Tripoli's diplomatic staff; its ambassador's activities, especially in Borno state, had already been troubling the Nigerian authorities.)

The Lagos summit was a stormy affair, with its participants sharply divided over how to handle Libya's intervention. Seven of the Presidents (Cameroon, Central African Republic, Guinea, Niger, Sudan, Senegal and Togo) proposed a resolution demanding the immediate withdrawal of all Libyan troops and an end to its interference in Chad's internal affairs. An amendment–supported by Nigeria, Sierra Leone, Congo and Benin–sought to tone down criticism of Libya, a move supported by its own Foreign Minister. Goukouny came under attack because of his claim that he had a 'sovereign right to invite Libyan intervention without consulting the OAU, even though his Presidency at the head of the Transitional Government was legitimized by the OAU. Unanimity was finally reached on a compromise resolution which, without mentioning Libya by name, 'urged that no foreign troops be stationed in the national territory of Chad, except in accordance with the 1979 Lagos Accord'. The Presidents added that they were convinced that any interference in the internal affairs of Chad would undermine the relative peace established through the recent developments on the military front.' Finally, they called on Goukouny to arrange for general elections to be held in 1982, and instructed the OAU general-secretary to convene a special conference to assess Chad's needs for reconstruction and rehabilitation of refugees.[27]

Nigeria's policy of quiet diplomacy might have brought results had it not been for the announcement immediately after the Lagos meeting of the Chad–Libya merger. This bombshell and Tripoli's announced intention of sending even more troops into Chad, because of French military moves in Central Africa, added a new dimension to the affair. The Presidents of twelve African countries–Togo, Ivory Coast, Niger, Benin, Sierra Leone, Nigeria, Guinea, Central African Republic, Senegal, Congo, Ghana and Cameroon–came together in Lomé on 14 January 1981. They unanimously condemned the proposed Libya–Chad merger as violating the 'spirit and letter' of the 1979 Lagos Accord; reaffirmed their intention to send a peacekeeping force to Chad, with UN support if necessary; called on Libya to withdraw its forces; proposed elections in Chad in April 1982; and urged Chad's six neighbours not to allow Chadian dissident forces to operate from their territories. (This was the first time that Benin had joined in the criticism of Libya's role.)

The OAU secretary-general later explained that the organization's stand was not against the Chad–Libyan merger itself, but over the manner in which it was carried out. He put special emphasis on the need for elections to put the merger proposal to the people; but he insisted that it was indispensable for the Libyan troops to withdraw in favour of a neutral OAU Peacekeeping Force, and to allay Goukouny's fears over continued attacks by dissidents. He concluded: 'Of course our objective is not to throw African forces against other African forces. The Libyans must leave Chad.'[28]

The crisis was then moved to the OAU Council of Ministers meeting in Addis Ababa in late February 1981. They confirmed the Lomé decisions for elections to be held in April, withdrawal of Libyan forces, and the despatch of the OAU Peacekeeping Force. But a final decision on Libya's intervention was put off until the next OAU summit in Nairobi in June 1981.

THE PROPOSED LIBYA–CHAD MERGER: WHAT REALLY HAPPENED

The proposed merger was not at all as Gaddafy had described it: a voluntary agreement to give substance to the historic ties between the two countries. The reality was quite different. Before putting his signature to the merger agreement, Goukouny had communicated with President Shehu Shagari of Nigeria saying that he had been summoned to Tripoli but that he was reluctant to go because two of his senior military commanders, who had gone as his emissaries when he begged off, had not returned from Tripoli. He had reason to believe they had been murdered. Goukouny went on to explain that he had no alternative other than to go to Tripoli, but he wanted a formal invitation from President Shagari asking him to come to Lagos on an agreed date. This, he believed, would make it difficult for Gaddafy to detain him in Tripoli for any length of time. Nigeria agreed to his proposal and a date for his visit was set. In Tripoli, Goukouny was told that his two military commanders had been murdered by Chadian dissidents; just how they were able to kill the two commanders in Libya was never properly explained. Obviously, Goukouny did not believe the story. But he felt he had a gun behind his back when he was presented with the merger proposal. These facts became well known in OAU circles.

57

When Goukouny arrived in Lagos he explained that he had no alternative but to agree to the merger in view of the present situation in Chad and the threat of renewed attacks coming from Hissène Habré and other of his opponents. He accepted the Lomé decisions to hold elections, but argued that the four nations proposed for the peacekeeping force were not balanced; instead, he suggested that the Nigerians should themselves provided the forces for peacekeeping–a proposal Shagari rejected on the grounds that the OAU decision had been that none of Chad's immediate neighbours should be involved in the peacekeeping operation.[29]

LIBYA'S STAND ON CHAD: SELF-DEFENCE AND HISTORIC ETHNICITY
Col Gaddafy told the Arab People's Congress in Tripoli on 20 January 1981 that:

> Libya has intervened militarily in Chad in response to Frolinat, ending the war which lasted many years and resolving the conflict in Chad in the interests of the friendly forces and the People's Forces represented by Frolinat which led the armed struggle for 20 years and defeated the racist and reactionary forces and imperialism backing them. For the secession led by Habré had behind it Sadat, his stooge Numeiry, and the French agents in Africa. . . . The war in Chad was against the Jamahiriya. . . . We have crossed the border in self-defence when an act of force was used to impose a pro-imperialism regime hostile to the Chadian people.

He did not refer to the OAU attempts to introduce a neutral peacekeeping force of its own, or to Libya's own support for the 1979 Lagos accords which ruled out any foreign military intervention in Chad. Instead, he sought to justify his action as 'being purely an act of self-defence' and on grounds of historic ethnic links:

> The complete mass unity between the two countries, based on people's power as stipulated in the joint Libyan–Chadian statement, is not like the familiar constitutional political unity. For there is a very old historical interaction between the Libyan and Chadian peoples, and between the Chadian people and the Arab nation, and the borders are open between the two countries.
> The Chadian people are similar to the Sudanese people in make-up. For there is a large proportion of Arabs among the Chadian people. Eastern and south-eastern Chad is entirely Arab and a large section of the Chadian people are Arab by origin and race, while the *overwhelming number* are Muslim and Arab culture is the prevailing culture in Chad. The Chadian people have a specificity very different from all Black African peoples. A very large number of Libyans emigrated to Chad, settled there and became Chadians. Similarly a very large number of Chadian people are at present in Libya. (Italics added.)

The Libyan case also rests on its role in helping to free Chad, and the rest of Francophone Africa, from French 'imperialism'. In a speech on 8 February 1981, Gaddafy told students:

> Chad's security is linked to Libya's security. We say to all those fearful minds in Sudan, Niger and other African countries that Libyan troops only intervened after urgent and recurrent appeals. The Libyans have no intention of sending their troops abroad or engaging in anything but defensive battles.[30]

The danger to 'untrusting governments', he went on, comes not from Libya but from

> French forces who installed Bokassa, overthrew him and reinstated Dacko in the Central African Republic. France has no friends. It has colonial interests. Other African regimes all face rebellion. The presence of French forces is in itself a factor that both threatens peace and stability because these forces are behind the coups carried out in Africa to secure colonialist interests.

Libya's Foreign Minister, Abdul Obeidi, agreed that while his country's policy was generally directed against parliamentary rule it favoured a general election in Chad as soon as possible.[31] But, he insisted, Libyan troops would remain in Chad until they were asked to leave by its Government.

FRANCE'S ROLE IN CHAD
Just as in the case of Libya, France has supported each of the Chadian leaders in turn, although it never looked with much favour of Hissène Habré because of his role in taking French hostages and shooting some of them. Paris had military agreements with both Goukouny and Kamougue at times when each felt the Libyans were supporting his rival. The withdrawal of the French military factor in May 1980 and the OAU's subsequent failure to replace it with its own peacekeeping force created a military vacuum which came to be filled by Libya.[32]

The French began to monitor the build-up of Libyan forces in Chad from August 1980 and alerted OAU countries about what was happening, hoping for some positive reaction. By mid-December, the French stood poised to intervene directly in the fighting, and had three battalions standing by in readiness.[33] However, Paris informed Tripoli on 23 December that it had no intention of itself intervening, but called on the Libyans to respect Chad's independence.[34]

When the Chad–Libya merger was announced in January 1981, France formally condemned the move as an act of *force majeure*. Paris came under strong pressure from a number of its Francophone African allies to demonstrate positively that others who felt themselves threatened by Libya would not find themselves abandoned in time of crisis. Responding to these demands, the French Foreign Minister, François Poncet, while on a visit to Abidjan on 10 January 1981, said: 'Our African friends can count on us. France's solidarity will not be lacking when they appeal for it.'[35] A few days later, French military units were sent to the Central African Republic at President Dacko's request to complement the 1,400 troops already there. France was reported to have asked Niger for permission to send in more troops to help protect the 2,000 Frenchmen working on its uranium mines. Talks were also held in Khartoum to discuss French military support for Sudan, and possible aid to Hissène Habré's forces who had withdrawn to that country after their defeat. France also declared its readiness to increase the number of Jaguar fighter bombers in Gabon from four to twelve. France has c. 12,000 soldiers in West Africa, and c. 3,000 in Djibouti. It also has an Indian Ocean naval force based in Mayotte and the smaller islands off Madagascar and Mauritius.[36]

While Libya reacted strongly to France's criticisms of the proposed merger and to its military moves, it nevertheless insisted, at the same time, that it was anxious to maintain good relations with Paris. When the French refused to hand over ten gunboats on order from Libya in March 1981, Gaddafy expressed his wish to restore good relations with France.[37] 'We did not wish a clash with Paris,' he said, 'It is Paris which is attacking us.'

This ambiguity in Gaddafy's attitude towards France has characterized his policies over the years, casting some doubt on the vigour with which he proposes to combat 'French imperialism'.[38]

NIGERIA'S POLICIES TOWARDS THE CHAD CRISIS
Although Nigerian leaders were at some pains to mute their criticisms over Libya's behaviour in Chad and in other West African countries, this was not because they felt any less concern than other governments in the region; their approach was based on the belief that quiet diplomacy might be the best means of extricating Chad from the Libyans' web. With its massive Muslim population and

its common border with Chad, Nigeria left itself vulnerable to pressures from Islamic radicalism. They suspiciously looked for Tripoli's hand in the violent riots in Kano in January 1981.[39] There was more positive evidence, though, of Libyan activities in Borno. Nigeria's External Affairs Minister, Dr Ishaya Audu, said that without his Government's knowledge, Libyans were engaged in buying massive supplies of food for Chad in Borno State.[40] He also revealed that two Libyan aircraft, allegedly looking for a missing third plane, had been detained for a week in Maiduguri. 'I sincerely hope they will keep out of this country,' Dr Audu said. 'But if they continue we will have to take drastic action.'

Dr Audu held two days of talks in Paris in January 1981 where he emphasized that Nigeria would not intervene unilaterally in Chad, but would go in only as part of an OAU force if asked to do so. He did not comment on a French proposal of assistance for such an African peacekeeping force.[41] After ordering the closure of the Libyan embassy in Lagos in January 1981, Dr Audu commented critically of Libya's 'error' in informing Nigeria about the change of name of its diplomatic representation to the People's Bureau. 'There is a limit to the extent you can allow the sovereignty and authority of any country to be flouted,' he said.

Nigerian public opinion, as reflected in the mass media, was inflamed by Libya's policies in Chad and West Africa. The well-known columnist, Layi Ogunsola, wrote:

> War with Libya is inevitable; about that let there be no kidding. Our armed forces must be strengthened and modern sophisticated equipment purchased, if need be at the expense of our development plans.[42]

The influential *New Nigerian* (Kaduna, 17 January 1981) editorialized:

> Col Gaddafy's irredentist policy that has resulted in Chad and Libya entering into some kind of *entente cordiale* aimed at merging the two countries must dictate to us the importance of preparedness and making material commitments to matters of defence and national security . . . a financially weak Federal Government will have serious problems defending its borders and maintaining internal security.

OTHER AFRICAN REACTIONS TO LIBYA'S INTERVENTION

Egypt and Sudan–with their well-known antipathy to Libyan policies–took a prominent place alongside the Francophone African community in drawing attention to what they saw as the sinister implications of Gadaffy's moves. An Egyptian Foreign Ministry statement on 8 January 1981 called for a firm African stand:

> Against the plots of Libya's Gaddafy . . . to fulfill dreams of controlling independent states neighbouring him, at the expense of the stability, security and freedom of peoples in this sensitive part of the world.

Taking a similar line, Sudan's Minister of State for Foreign Affairs, Mohammed Mirghani Mubarak, said:

> The Libyan intervention in Chad is not restricted to the geography of that country, but represents an intricate regional problem having dangerous repercussions harmful to Afro–Arab solidarity.[43]

Gabon's President Bongo declared that if Libya felt it had some claim over Chad simply because of helping it, 'I think we should simply say that Libya is playing the role of an imperialist.'[44] Upper Volta's Foreign Minister, Lt-Col Felix Tiemtarboum, rejecting Tripoli's proposal to change its embassy in Ouagadougou to a People's Bureau, declared that this move constituted only a part of the country's problems with Libya. He added:

The threats of destabilization which are weighing down on countries that have common borders with the Libyan Arab Jamahiriya–some of whom are our direct neighbours–concerns us in many ways. What we may call the Chadian tragedy cannot leave us indifferent.[45]

The Mali Government also refused to accept the change in the status of Libya's embassy, but it did not break off diplomatic relations. President Moussa Traoré said in Paris in November 1980 that Mali was prepared for any aggression from Libya.[46] Senegal's former President, Leopold Senghor, accused Gaddafy of wishing to stir up trouble in Chad, Niger, Mali and Senegal, for which purpose he had trained 5,000 men to create a 'Republic of the Sahara' under his control.[47] He added that the reported abortive coup in The Gambia was the 'beginning of the plot', and added that Libya's intentions amounted to 'racism against Negro-African countries.' Guinea's President Sékou Touré said:

If the Libyan troops were able to break the Lagos agreement by going into Chad with arms to take part in a fratricidal war on the side of one faction, then Sudan, a well-armed neighbouring country, the Nigerian Federation, another well-armed neighbour, as well as Cameroon, the Central African Republic and Niger could also have acted in favour of other Chadian factions; this would have been a marked violation of the Lagos agreement on the part of everybody.[48]

The Central African Republic's President, David Dacko, also accused Libya of violating the Lagos Agreement. He described developments in Chad as disquieting to the CAR, which borders on it, and added:

Libya's dream of creating a vast community subject to Islam, and about which an agreement was signed by Bokassa in December 1976, would come about and would create problems for all states which do not share the same religious faith.[49]

Mauritania, another of Libya's neighbours, described it as 'most regrettable that a fraternal and friendly state should adopt such a misconceived attitude towards us and arrogantly embark on political subversion against our people at a time when they need every help and encouragement.'[50]

The Gambia severed its relations with Libya after alleging the discovery of an attempted coup engineered from Tripoli.[51] One of the toughest attacks against Gaddafy's policies came from Niger's President, Seyni Kountche (see above).

THE MAJOR POWERS AND CHAD

The NATO powers have for a number of years shown growing concern about the developing military relationship between the Russians and Libyans–but more particularly over the possible use by the Russians of naval and air bases in the Mediterranean. According to the CIA, there are 81 usable airfields in Libya, including 19 with hard surface runways.[52] But it was not until the remarkably efficient Libyan military operation in Chad that NATO planners began to see a possible new dimension in Gaddafy's role. While hardliners in Western defence establishments believe that Gaddafy is willing to act as a Russian surrogate,–a view promoted by Egypt–this is not taken seriously among most Western political and military strategists. Nevertheless, they don't rule out the possibility of Moscow and Tripoli cooperating in areas where their interests happen to coincide.

Gaddafy was at great pains to deny any Russian involvement in Chad–'not even with a transport plane inside Libyan territory. All the war and administrative effort was by the Libyan armed forces and the Libyan people.'[53] On another occasion he said that not even Washington seriously believed that there had been Russian involvement. But while Gaddafy praised the Russians for remaining neutral over Libya's role in Chad, this was very far from being the case.

So far as I am able to ascertain, for the first time ever, a leading Soviet commentator, Yuriy Ulyanovskiy[54] directly criticized the OAU, something the Russians have always been careful to avoid doing. 'The strident campaign against Chad and its Government, set up with the participation of the OAU, might seem strange at first', he wrote, but he went on to explain it by referring to the role of 'certain African regimes' working with French interests. He omitted any reference to the role of countries like Nigeria, Guinea and, even, Benin. Other Russian commentators, like Valentin Korovikov, sought to explain that the OAU subcommittee's decision taken in Lagos in December had 'undoubtedly strengthened the position of GUNT.'[55] But GUNT had already ceased to exist, while the Lagos statement was aimed specifically at removing Libya's forces. All the Soviet bloc media gave their support to Libya's intervention in Chad as a positive contribution to restoring peace in the country. The proposed merger of the two countries was sympathetically reported. No African criticisms of either Libya's intervention or of the proposed merger was published in the Soviet media.

© copyright *Africa Contemporary Record*, 1981

Colin Legum

NOTES

1. Radio Niamey, 28 January 1981.
2. *New African*, London, March 1981.
3. *West Africa*, London, 2 March 1981.
4. See *Africa Contemporary Record (ACR)* 1977–78, p B65; 1978–79, p B62.
5. *Le Soleil*, Dakar, January 1981.
6. See *New African*, December 1980. Soumbounou later denied his own interview after intervention by the Libyan authorities.
7. *Jamahiriyah Arab News Agency (JANA)*, Tripoli, 20 January 1981.
8. See essay on the OAU.
9. See *ACR* 1968–69, 1969–70, 1970–71, 1971–72, 1972–73, 1973–74, 1974–75, 1975–76, 1976–77, 1977–78, 1978–79, 1979–80.
10. See *ACR* 1979–80, p B415.
11. See *ACR* 1978–79, 1979–80 and chapter on Chad in this volume.
12. See chapters on The Gambia and Senegal.
13. See Colin Legum in *The Observer* London, 22 February 1981.
14. See *ACR* 1977–80, p C5.
15. See *ACR* 1978–79, p C36.
16. *Ibid*, p C87.
17. *Ibid*, pp B528ff.
18. See *ACR* 1979–80, pp B409–11.
19. See Documents Section in this volume for resolution.
20. Radio Lomé, 16 November 1980.
21. *Ibid*, 29 November 1980.
22. *The Times*, London, 17 December 1980.
23. See chapter on Chad.
24. *Financial Times (FT)*, London, 10 November 1980.
25. Radio Bangui, 3 December 1980.
26. *West Africa*, 23 February 1981.
27. *The Times*, 24, 27 December 1980; *West Africa*, 5 January 1981.
28. *The Times*, 23 January 1981.
29. *Le Monde*, Paris, 30 January 1981.
30. *JANA*, 8 February 1981.
31. *Observer Foreign News Service*, 2 March 1981.
32. See essay on *France's Role In Africa*.
33. *The Guardian*, Manchester, 15 December 1980; *Daily Telegraph*, London, 15 December 1980.
34. *Financial Times*, 24 December 1980.
35. *The Times*, 12 January 1981.
36. *The Guardian*, 13 January 1981; *Daily Telegraph*, 10 January 1981; *Financial Times*, 19 February 1981.
37. *The Times*, 4 March 1981.
38. Also see essay, 'France and Africa' and chapter on Libya.
39. See chapter on Nigeria.
40. Interview with *The Times*, quoted in *West Africa*, 1 December 1980.
41. *Financial Times*, 28 January 1981.
42. *Sunday Tribune*, Ibadan, 11 January 1981.
43. Sudan News Agency, 8 February 1981.
44. Radio Libreville, 8 January 1981.

45. Radio Ouagadougou, 16 January 1981.
46. *West Africa,* 24 November 1980.
47. *Ibid*
48. Quoted in *Horoya,* Conakry, 27 January 1981.
49. Radio Bangui, 13 January 1981.
50. Radio Nouakchott, 30 December 1980.
51. See chapter on The Gambia.
52. See Drew Middleton in *International Herald Tribune,* Paris, 4 March 1981.
53. Radio Tripoli, 8 February 1981.
54. *Tass,* Moscow, 26 December 1980.
55. *Pravda,* Moscow, 27 December 1980.

PART II
The Middle East and World Affairs

The United States and the Middle East

In 1979 and 1980, for the first time in many years, the Arab-Israel conflict was not at the centre of American thinking and policies concerning the Middle East. That geographical term began to give way, in official and Press parlance, to "Southwest Asia", perhaps to be sure that Afghanistan was included. It was a surface indication of a shift in attention from the Eastern Mediterranean to the region of the Persian Gulf, not surprising in view of the spectacular changes made in the political map by the revolution in Iran and the Soviet takeover of Afghanistan. It reflected also a conscious effort on the part of Washington to work out new and consistent policies responsive to those changes and adequate to protect its interests in the face of threats to the global and regional balance of power and to the Western world's access to Persian Gulf oil.

The Arab-Israel conflict did not, of course, disappear from Washington's view. It had been the occasion of President Carter's most notable diplomatic successes, the Camp David accords of September 1978 and the Israeli-Egyptian peace treaty of March 1979. America remained deeply committed to Israel and to Egypt and to the continuation of the Camp David process by which they were to move toward negotiated settlement of other aspects of the Arab-Israel dispute, notably the status of the remaining occupied areas and of the Palestinian Arabs and the normalization of relations. The way in which the process was unfolding, however, bore little resemblance to the hopes of Camp David. No Arab party other than Egypt was prepared to join the negotiations; Egypt and Israel took widely divergent positions on what Palestinian autonomy in the West Bank and Gaza should mean; and the Carter Administration, after its earlier herculean efforts at mediation, did not have much capital to expend in new mediatory endeavours although keeping at the task with exemplary persistence.

The American presidential campaign of 1980, moreover, began well before that year opened, and it was a recognized fact that election years have not been noted for bold American initiatives in the field of Arab-Israel relations. President Carter, engaged first in a primary struggle with Senator Kennedy and then in the main event with Ronald Reagan, both of whom took stronger pro-Israel positions than he did or could, was hardly in a position to repeat the tactics of persuasion on both sides that had worked at Camp David. Not that the Administration could feel satisfied or unconcerned with the lack of progress in negotiation, with Israel's policies that put obstacles in the way, or with Sādāt's embarrassing isolation in the Arab world. But its attention was inevitably directed to events farther to the East. Without any basic change in the American commitment to Israel and the aim of promoting an Arab-Israel settlement, they would be seen in a broader context, for there was no doubt that policy in the Gulf and policy in the Eastern Mediterranean were interdependent, useful as it had been at times to keep them apart. The question was how they would be related in the minds of policymakers in Washington. We shall return to that question after looking first at the issues which arose in Iran and Afghanistan.

IRAN AND THE HOSTAGE QUESTION

Strategic positions were not all the US lost when the victorious revolutionary forces of Iran dethroned the Shah. Those events were a blow to American prestige and influence in the region and also to America's own confidence in its ability to defend vital national interests and those of friends and allies. During the course of 1979 the Administration was doing what it could to adjust to the new Iran, accepting the fact that the new regime would be nonaligned and unco-operative, as long as it did not lend itself to the strategic designs of the Soviet Union or deny its oil to the West. The difficulty was that, with the fragmentation of authority, it was not clear what was happening or would happen in Iran, what kind of regime the "Islamic Republic" would be, or whether the country would hold together as political factions and ethnic groups pulled this way and that. Despite the continuance of high-pitched denunciations of America as "the great Satan", Washington saw Iran's obvious need for a minimum of public order, a reconstituted army, a functioning economy, and ties with the West to balance Soviet power—and hoped the Iranians would see it too. The presence of secular elements in the Government, notably Prime Minister Mehdi Bazargan, seemed to justify that hope.[1]

The revolution, however, did not settle down. Islamic fervour and anti-American hysteria were still powerful factors in the struggle for dominance. Bazargan was a victim of that struggle, and so was the entire staff of the American embassy, seized by militant students on 4 November 1979. Their seizure and detention was to dominate US-Iranian relations, and affect American policy in the entire region, for more than a year.

The action was unprecedented and the remedy not easy to find. No power, great or small, could accept such a flagrant violation of the rights of its representatives and of international law and comity. The Security Council (SC) condemned the Iranian action (4 December) and the International Court of Justice found it illegal (15 December); but their decisions did not prevail upon Iran to release the hostages. Washington decided against the use of force, at least initially, as it would risk the death of the hostages and would turn to hostility much of the sympathy that had been gained throughout the world, especially in the ME region itself. And so began the long months of frustration in which Washington tried in vain—by unilateral punitive measures such as freezing Iranian funds and cutting off trade, by efforts to persuade allies to join in sanctions (with only partial success), and by attempts to negotiate through any available channels, especially the machinery of the United Nations (UN)—to get the hostages home.

It is not possible or necessary to chronicle those efforts here. They had some effect but they failed in their main purpose because the sanctions were not universal, because Iran's Revolutionary Council was willing to let the economy run downhill, and because the issue was intertwined with the struggles for power going on within Iran. Those politicians, like President Bani Sadr, who might be willing to make a deal and be rid of the hostage problem, were unable to stand up to the more intransigent clerical factions, and no one could make a decisive move without the approval of Ayatollah Khomeyni, whose periodic pronouncements used the issue to rally the nation behind his leadership and served to postpone a solution. When in April 1980 the US finally resorted to a desperate attempt to rescue the hostages by direct action, it was because nothing else had worked; and when that mission ended in failure and humiliation in the blaze of American aircraft in the Iranian desert, the result was further humiliation, more hostility and vituperation from Iran, and a fading of what little hope remained.

The President, the news media and the American public were mesmerized by the hostage question. It ate into the national consciousness and into domestic politics, for it was obvious that its resolution or non-resolution would have an effect on President Carter's chances for re-election. Concentration on the problem, however, did not help to solve it. No American Government could have returned the former Shah's assets or issued an apology for its policies of the past quarter century, two points which appeared in most Iranian lists of demands. Washington did not rule out an international inquiry, but the experience of UN Secretary-General, Dr Kurt Waldheim and of the special UN commission he sent to Iran revealed the inability or unwillingness of Iranian political leaders to negotiate a compromise.

The matter was particularly galling to Washington because it interfered with the larger task the President and his advisers were trying to address: how to shore up a political and military position in the region which had been greatly weakened not only by the fall of the Shah and the hostility of the new regime in Iran, but by a series of developments elsewhere favouring the Soviet Union at America's expense. The consolidation of Soviet influence in Ethiopia and in South Yemen (PDRY) had alarmed the Yemeni Arab Republic (YAR), Saudi Arabia, Sudan and Egypt, all of which looked to America for help. They were already receiving American arms, but that did not prevent their questioning the capacity of America to protect their security, or even its own interests.

In estimating the international consequences of the revolution in Iran, the US had to consider several contingencies, all of them ominous: that the Iranian pattern of revolution, encouraged by Khomeyni's success and the impact of his propaganda, might be repeated in Saudi Arabia, Egypt or other states with economic and social tensions; that conflicts within the region might interrupt vital oil supplies; that the confusion and internal strife in Iran might offer opportunities for the Soviets to intervene in that country, either by invitation or "to restore order" on their frontiers; and that local States would seek to adjust to the apparent shift in the balance of power, revising their relations with the US and the USSR accordingly.

The adverse trends were apparent to the Carter Administration and to the influential sectors of public opinion from the time of the fall of the Shah in early 1979. What to do about it remained a topic of discussion throughout that year.[2] The simplest conclusion to be reached was that America would have to hold a stronger military posture, partly as a means of meeting new emergencies but, above all, as a demonstration to the Soviets and to the local States that America was not in retreat and intended to defend its friends and its interests. The Government decided (a) to increase US naval power in the Indian Ocean; (b) to create a Rapid Deployment Force (RDF) by which effective air and ground forces could be brought into action in the ME and Gulf area at short notice; and (c) to work toward creating a structure of base facilities in, or near, the region that would be available for use by US forces.[3]

The naval build-up required moving ships from the Mediterranean and Pacific fleets into the Indian Ocean. The need for facilities could be partially met by expanding the installations at Diego Garcia in the middle of the Indian Ocean, but that was a long distance from the Gulf; hence, the intention to negotiate with States willing to permit use of their facilities. That Kenya, Somalia and Oman (and possibly Egypt) were the only States willing to engage in such negotiations was an indication of how difficult the political problems were. While Saudi Arabia and other Arab States may have wanted America to show more strength and resolution, they wanted the American military presence over the horizon, not on their territory.[4]

THE IMPACT OF AFGHANISTAN

The Carter Administration was just beginning to tackle these military and diplomatic tasks when, in the final week of 1979, Soviet forces invaded Afghanistan, already a satellite state but one with a Government which Moscow found insufficiently subservient, ineffective, and in danger of being overthrown by a popular rebellion inspired by nationalism and by Islam. With that one Soviet move and the American reaction to it, Soviet-American relations underwent a major change, both objectively and, no less important, in the mind of President Carter. True, the super-power détente had already suffered serious erosion, and the Soviet leaders may have calculated that Afghanistan was worth risking what was left of it. On the American side, the balance of co-operation and competition, a theme of the President's earlier speeches, was sharply tipped to the latter side and the new theme was an old one: containment of Soviet expansion.

The return to something like the Cold War, of course, had its impact everywhere in the world, but the focal area was the ME. The Afghanistan affair was a new phase of the centuries-old "Eastern Question", the confrontation of Russian and Western power in the lands of Islam, with the stakes now higher than ever because of the West's critical dependence on the area's oil.

Americans and Europeans debated whether the Russian move into Afghanistan was essentially offensive, a strategic advance toward the Indian Ocean and the oilfields of the Gulf; or defensive, a rescue operation to save a client regime on the Soviet border in danger of being overthrown by anti-communist and anti-Soviet forces.[5] The Carter Administration did not give out an official interpretation. Yet there was no doubt that it saw the move against the backdrop of recent Soviet gains in the Horn of Africa and on the rim of the Arabian Peninsula; of events in Iran, the hostage issue, and the evident vulnerability of that country; of the weakness of Pakistan; and of the West's absolute need for ME oil. Offensive or defensive, the occupation of Afghanistan brought Soviet military power closer to the vital interests of the West and increased the potential for Soviet pressure on Iran, Pakistan and other States of the region. And so, in reacting strongly—overreacting, some of the President's critics said—he and his Administration were not only protesting a blatant act of aggression and "punishing" the Soviets for it with economic sanctions; they had their eyes on the Gulf and its oil. They could not do anything in a military way to get the Russians out of Afghanistan, but felt they had to do something to prevent their going further.[6]

President Carter, in his State-of-the-Union message to the Congress on 23 January 1980, uttered the following well chosen words: "Let our position be absolutely clear: An attempt by any outside force to gain control of the Persian Gulf region will be regarded as an assault on the vital interests of the United States of America. And such an assault will be repelled by any means necessary, including military force."[7]

A statement made on the President's own authority, it was generally supported in the Congress and in the public print, although not immune to criticism. The principal critique was that it was an empty warning, since the US did not have the military capability of stopping Soviet troops if they chose to march on beyond Afghanistan. Pentagon officials conceded that large conventional forces capable of swift and effective action in Southwest Asia were not yet in being, although "tripwire" forces could be brought there very quickly.[8] The purpose of deterrence, however, would hardly be served if the US Government delayed its warning until it had forces capable of defending all the borders of Iran or Pakistan. The important point to drive home, as Zbigniew Brzezinski noted later, was that a

70

military move into the Gulf area would bring the Soviet Union into conflict with the US; that conflict would not necessarily be confined to the geographical point of the aggression, nor would it necessarily be confined to conventional weapons.[9]

Another criticism was that the new policy, dubbed the "Carter doctrine" by the Press, was a unilateral statement not co-ordinated with America's European and Asian allies, whose interest in ME oil was even greater, nor with the States in the region the policy was intended to protect. More consultation with the Europeans and Japanese would have been desirable, but they were not of a mind to join such a commitment or in a position to make a major contribution to the military force needed to make it credible. As for the States of the region, how they would be affected and what co-operation they might provide were indeed key questions for the success of American policy. But it was obvious that these questions could not be negotiated with them at the time. Iran was holding Americans hostage and breathing defiance; Iraq was linked to the USSR by a security treaty and had no diplomatic relations with the US; Saudi Arabia was carefully avoiding the appearance of alignment with America in military policy. The Central Treaty Organization was dead, and nothing like it could be revived. What the situation demanded, in Washington's view, was the US itself take a position and let the Russians and the world know it. How to bring others into the picture was something to be worked out later.

That was one of the major tasks for 1980. The other was to build up the necessary military forces as rapidly as possible. The first step was to send two aircraft carriers, with accompanying vessels, to the Arabian Sea. US naval forces in the Indian Ocean were brought up to a total of about 30 ships and kept at that level. The Pentagon went ahead with the projected RDF, but it could not be done overnight. It required new airlift and sealift, not yet available, and facilities in the region beyond those already in existence in Diego Garcia and, on a limited basis, in Bahrain. The former was too far away and the latter was a bit too close—the Gulf itself was not a good place for more than a small but visible naval presence, which was what the US had maintained there for some years. For the planned RDF, access to other facilities would be necessary. "We seek no bases," Assistant Secretary of State Harold Saunders told the House Foreign Affairs Committee, but "selective and limited access to air and naval facilities."[10] Kenya, Somalia and Oman were prepared to negotiate.

At a time when so few ME states were willing to accept an American military presence, even if designated "limited access", inevitably eyes turned to the two relatively powerful and important states with which the US already had close and friendly relations, namely Egypt and Israel. Sādāt was doing all he could to expand military co-operation with the Americans, as a means of arming and training his forces. In public statements he offered the use of Egyptian territory if necessary to meet Soviet aggression in the Gulf; he welcomed military visits, joint training exercises, and the build-up of facilities at Ra's Banās on the Red Sea. As for Israel, the Begin Government was desirous of playing the role of military partner and seemed prepared to offer facilities if they were wanted.

The State Department, however, was acutely aware of the political problems involved in tying the American military presence and strategy for the Gulf to the "special" relations with Israel or Egypt, or to the two in combination. Israel was still the enemy so far as the other Arabs were concerned; an American base in Israel for the purpose of protecting, for example, Saudi Arabia would hardly appeal to Riyadh or help Saudi-American relations. Egypt had already spoiled its relations with the other Arab States by its peace with Israel and its close ties with

71

the Americans; even Sādāt held back from inviting American use of the Sinai bases Israel was to give up under the peace treaty. Friends of Israel and Egypt in the US Congress might see logic in building a regional military position on those States, but the Administration had to consider the politics of it and was not writing off the rest of the Arab world.

POLITICS AND REGIONAL SECURITY

The military posture envisaged for deterrence could not be effective by itself. The local States had to do something about their own defence, even if they could not be expected to put up successful resistance to a Soviet attack. They had to want Western power to be in a position where it could balance Soviet power. They had to be aware of their own weaknesses and of Soviet ability to exploit them. Even if they accepted these considerations, moreover, no one state was likely to interpret them in the same way as the others, or as the Americans did. Each State had interests and concerns of its own, related to the Soviet threat only marginally or not at all. Harold Saunders spoke of the need for a defence posture "finely tuned to the sensitivity and sovereignty of the States in the area", and for a policy involving "a complex of military, economic and political actions, and working in close co-operation with our allies, our friends in the Gulf, and key States in the broader region."[11]

That was a tall order. Neither the politics of the ME nor the domestic factors in Washington were easily made subject to fine-tuning by the State Department or the White House. The Pentagon went ahead with its plans for a stronger posture, calculating the military contingencies and impatient with political obstacles. The diplomats tried to take account of local sensibilities. But when they were up against such touchy matters as Palestine, Iraqi-Iranian hostility, America and the Shah, and Pakistan's relations with India, no comprehensive approach by Washington had much chance of success.

Most of the ME States wanted to be shielded from super-power competition. But they were not ready or able to put together a regional security system of their own. They wanted arms, but not for the common defence. As it turned out, the American effort of fine-tuning had to be applied separately to individual States, of which the most important were Turkey, Pakistan, and the two erstwhile "pillars of security" in the Gulf in the era of the "Nixon doctrine", Iran and Saudi Arabia.

TURKEY'S ROLE

Turkey looks West as a member of NATO and in American eyes presents problems of security and diplomacy primarily related to the defence of Europe. Pakistan is part of the Indian subcontinent and is transfixed by its relations with India. Yet both Turkey and Pakistan are geographically and strategically attached to the ME. From the early 1950s, when John Foster Dulles was trying through the Baghdad Pact to extend the barrier of containment Eastward from the North Atlantic Treaty Organization (NATO), American policy saw Turkey and Pakistan as the abutments of a ME defence system to be completed by alliances and other arrangements with States lying in between. Thirty years later, in the face of growing Soviet power, they were just as important, but more questionable than ever. To the Carter Administration, struggling to cope with a situation of uncertainty and potential disaster in Iran, it was evident that something had to be done to reduce the vulnerability of the remaining States of the "Northern Tier", which had so long served as a physical barrier separating the USSR from the Arab world.

Turkey, by 1980, was in dire economic straits and prey to a crisis of political violence by extremists of Right and Left which elected governments under the

72

established parliamentary system could not control. The US could not do anything about the latter problem, but might help to make it more manageable by acting decisively on the former. Washington moved to mobilize an aid package for Turkey which included $1.6 bn from the International Monetary Fund (IMF) and $1.2 bn in loans and grants from major Western countries. The Government of Süleyman Demirel, to meet the requirements of the aid-givers and of the situation, undertook in January 1980 a stringent programme of economic retrenchment. Yet, while the economic prospects improved, the political did not, and the growing disorder ultimately provoked the military chiefs to take political power in August 1980.

In the American view, Turkey's politics were the Turks' affair. The important thing was that Turkey should continue to maintain its strength as a member of NATO, stand firm in control of the Straits, and block the Soviet road to the Mediterranean and the ME. With its dedication to the cause of human rights and political liberty, the US Government did not find it appropriate to express approval of the military's takeover of power from an elected civilian administration. But it could not be other than relieved by the knowledge of the generals' loyalty to NATO, the announcement that the economic reform would go on as planned, and the promise of a drastic reduction of civil violence.

That Turkey would draw closer to Arab States, a trend begun under the preceding civilian governments, was inevitable in view of its need for oil, its sensitivity to the new emphasis on Islam, and its desire to find new friends and allies beyond the confines of the super-power rivalry. These factors induced the new Turkish regime to reduce relations with Israel to the lowest possible level without a formal break. America could not be pleased with this contribution to the increasing isolation of Israel, but Turkish *rapprochement* with Iraq and other Arab States, whether the theme was Islamic solidarity or mutual support for national independence, tended to strengthen the region against Soviet pressures and therefore to serve long-term American interests.

In the aftermath of Afghanistan, Turkey could best serve itself and the security of the ME by maintaining domestic order while preparing for eventual return to democracy, by revitalizing its economy, by strengthening its armed forces, and by maintaining the NATO connection. The military regime appeared to have a better chance of doing those things than its predecessors. It could therefore count on benevolent support from Washington.

PAKISTAN'S ROLE

With Turkey the American course, although expensive and uncertain of success, was fairly clear. At the other end of the Northern Tier, the situation in Pakistan was complex and the indicated policies not clear at all. With Soviet military power deployed along the length of Pakistan's Northern border, troubled relations and difficult decisions were predictable. The frontier was no barrier either to refugees coming out of Afghanistan, or to Afghan fighters and a trickle of arms going in. The Soviet Union was charging Pakistan and its great-power allies (America and China) with inciting and supporting rebellion in Afghanistan. The old Afghan claims to Pakistan's Northwest territory was there to be used by the puppet regime in Kabul if the Soviets should so choose. Pakistan, moreover, was weak, shaken by the recent execution of Zulfiqar 'Ali Bhutto and threatened with tribal dissidence or separatism in Baluchistan.

The situation was beyond any possibility of management by the Americans. Pakistan had long since become disillusioned with its ties of alliance with the US, never having received the desired levels of military aid and political support

73

against India. With the Soviet incursion into Afghanistan, and only a few hundred miles of Pakistani territory separating Soviet forces from the Indian Ocean, America was reassessing the importance of Pakistan and presumed that the Pakistanis might be re-evaluating their own position. Zbigniew Brzezinski's melodramatic visit to the Khyber Pass in February 1980 was intended to demonstrate America's purpose and commitment. The proposed instruments of policy, however, were those of an earlier era, the shipment of arms and the refurbishing of a security agreement signed in 1959. In the ensuing negotiations nothing was accomplished. Pakistan's President, Muḥammad Ziya al-Ḥaqq, hesitant to offend the Russians without massive aid and clear assurances from America, dismissed Washington's offer of $400m in arms as ''peanuts'', and no new or revised security agreement was signed. Each side decided to wait until further light dawned on the other.

IRAN AND THE CONFLICT WITH IRAQ

In the American picture of a relatively stable and defensible ME, a united and independent Iran was a central and necessary part. The difficulty in 1980 was that Iranians seemed to be concentrating only on the past—the American role in the Iran of the Shah; while Americans were concentrating only on the present, the fate of the hostages. Washington took due note of statements of Khomeyni and of Tehran officials condemning the Soviet action in Afghanistan and rejecting any Soviet meddling in Iran. But if there were parallel American and Iranian interests to be cultivated in the future, the two Governments could not even communicate with each other on the subject.

Carter's desperate attempt in April to rescue the hostages by military means was a result of the pressure he felt, and which all US officials felt, to get them home—even though the consequences for relations with Iran and for policy in the region, whether the venture succeeded or failed, were likely to be adverse. Cyrus Vance gave as a major reason for resigning as Secretary of State over the affair the inevitable driving of Iran toward the USSR and the harm that would be done to a broader ME policy.[12] Actually, the US was lucky that the results of the fiasco were no worse than they were.

In time the situation changed, not through any initiative of Washington, but because war broke out in late September 1980 between Iran and Iraq. That war raised in more acute form issues which had been partially lost from view because of the hostage question, issues affecting the structure of power in the region and the supply of oil. Yet what the war would mean and how to react to it were questions to which America had no ready answers.[13]

Iraq was striking out for a position of dominance among local states in the Gulf, taking advantage of Iran's weakness and disarray. Iran was fighting for its territorial integrity and also to save ''the revolution'', for this war, although fought on the frontiers, became one in which each side declared its aim of overthrowing the regime of the other. For the US, as for the Soviet Union, the war opened up possibilities for advantage, but also for loss, and neither could be identified in advance. The USSR was the friend and supplier of arms to Iraq, but also the potential friend (and minor and indirect supplier) of Iran. America had no diplomatic relations with either party and, indeed, was blamed by both for backing the enemy.

As long as the war went on, the drop in oil exports from the two countries (in the neighbourhood of 4m barrels per day) would have its effect on the supply, and probably the price, of oil available to the West, if not immediately then within a matter of months. And the longer it went on, the danger remained that it would spread, affect other oil producers, and perhaps draw in the Super Powers. But neither Super Power was prepared to take an active initiative to bring the war to an end, nothing more than to vote for a mild and toothless resolution in the SC.

The war scrambled alignments in the region, as Syria and Libya favoured Iran while Jordan supported Iraq, and Saudi Arabia, as usual, preached Arab solidarity without taking a clear stand on anything. The line-up showed in clear relief how difficult it would be for American diplomacy, having little or no influence on most of the local States, to focus their attention on the Soviet threat. Nevertheless, the concern of the Saudis that their neighbours' war was too close for comfort led them to accept the presence of American AWACS aircraft to provide intelligence and warning.

A disorganized Iran was having a hard enough time fighting the war without the added handicaps of being subject to US economic sanctions and semi-isolated in the international community. Substantial quantities of US arms, already paid for, remained undelivered; billions of dollars remained blocked by the US, unavailable for buying arms in the world market; European countries had restricted trade; and no support would come from the UN, even though Iraq was the aggressor. These factors seemed to have some weight in the counsels of Tehran, indicating a new look at the costs of holding the hostages. The four demands stated by Ayatollah Khomeyni in September 1980 as the price of their release (leaving out apologies for past sins), later adopted by the *Majlis* in October, provided a basis for intensive negotiations with Washington, through Algeria, in November and December. But by year's end the minimum position of each side was still unacceptable to the other.

Iran's strange regime, although shaky at home and losing a war, was still trapped—or still inspired—by its complex about "the great Satan". And America was still trapped by its hostage complex. Only when the two nations were at least partially freed of these complexes, apparently, could an American Government begin to work out a national policy for the area. But some matters could not wait, including relations with America's now principal partner there, Saudi Arabia.

SAUDI ARABIA'S ROLE
The American view of Saudi Arabia as a partner, a special friend if not a formal ally, had to be interpreted in practice in the light of what the Saudi ruling family thought its own interests to be. Their foreign policies were pointed in five general directions: (a) to maintain the security of Saudi Arabia itself and of the regime at home; (b) to exert leadership among the smaller Arab States of the Peninsula and the Gulf; (c) to play an active role in the Arab world, using financial power and diplomacy to promote solidarity and appease conflicts; (d) to translate oil power into longer-term development in co-operation with advanced countries; and (e) to support the Arab cause in Palestine and Arab (and Muslim) rights in East Jerusalem.

America was generally sympathetic with all of those aims except the last, and even there the gulf was not as wide as it often appeared from statements made in absolute terms. In several respects, moreover, the international role the Saudis envisaged for themselves fitted in with what was expected of them by the US. They were moderate in oil matters, keeping their prices at the bottom of the Organization of Petroleum Exporting Countries (OPEC) range and maintaining, or increasing, output when extraordinary events like the Iranian revolution or the Iran-Iraq war reduced total OPEC production. The Saudis wanted arms, and the Americans sold them in quantity. The Saudis wished to protect the YAR and Oman against incursions or invasion from neighbouring PDRY, and US arms went to both. American military missions and private contractors were advising and training the Saudi armed forces. American construction firms held the big contracts for building the new cities and industries which were the promise of Saudi Arabia's future. American oil companies, although losing ownership of Aramco, remained in the picture through their contractual role in exploration, operations and transport.[14]

The American premise of co-operation and mutual interest, however, ran athwart fixed ideas on what, to Saudis, were inescapable realities of the ME: inter-Arab politics and the question of the Palestinians and Israel. The Americans, told again and again of Saudi Arabia's hatred for communism and fear of the Soviet Union, and seeing the country's military weakness, found hard to understand Saudi reluctance to engage in close military co-operation and Saudi insistence on Arab solidarity when it scarcely existed and on keeping clear of *both* Super Powers. They did not easily adjust to seeing Saudi Arabia, a traditional state fearful of radicalism, helping radical regimes and subsidizing the Palestine Liberation Organization (PLO). They asked why, if Saudi Arabia wanted a settlement of the Palestine problem, it did not urge Palestinians to join Egypt and Israel in the Camp David process.

Saudi officials did not hesitate to point out that their policies on oil were beneficial to America, and that they did not have to produce as much oil as they did, or to be moderate in pricing; but that America, in contrast, did not appear to show similar solicitude for Saudi interests. They always mentioned Palestine, and whether the concern was about Palestinians in the Gulf region and in Saudi Arabia itself, or about those in the West Bank, it was real.[15] They would sometimes designate a particular issue, on which they felt strongly, as a test of America's friendship. So it was with the Saudi request for F-15 aircraft. The US passed the first test in 1979 by agreeing to provide them. But then came a second test in 1980, when Riyadh asked for additional equipment to increase the range and bombing capabilities of those planes, which would make them a greater potential menace to Israel. This time Carter's answer, in the midst of his campaign for re-election, was negative. But the question remained on the agenda of US-Saudi relations.

Thus, there was an Israeli angle even to the question of arming Saudi Arabia, just as there was to policy on oil. The Saudis were not brandishing or using the "oil weapon" in 1980 as they did in 1973, but that experience had not been forgotten by either side; and short of such drastic action there were policies on production and other matters the Saudis could easily modify to America's disadvantage, should they choose to do so. This uneasy atmosphere in the bilateral relationship could hardly change in the absence of other changes not on the horizon—in the American commitment to the Camp David process, in Egypt's place in the Arab world, in the declared positions of the PLO, or in American relations with Israel.

Scarcely hidden beneath the surface, and capable of erupting as in the episode of the seizure of the Great Mosque of Mecca in November 1979, were the cultural shocks and social changes wrought by the rapid pace of Saudi Arabia's modernization. The ruling family was well aware that the close association of America with that process, as in the case of Iran, might be more harmful than helpful to its security, and that neither American arms deliveries nor American military deployments in the area provided any answer to that danger.

THE UNITED STATES AND THE ISRAEL-EGYPT NEGOTIATIONS

Amid all the furore over Afghanistan, oil and the affairs of the Gulf, the continuing Camp David negotiating process kept its share of attention in America's view of the ME. Aside from the President's commitment to the process and to the goal of negotiated peace between Arabs and Israel, it was important to keep both Israel and Egypt co-operating with America and with each other. They held, beside a promise for the future, a substantial weight in the military balance of the present, especially significant when developments in the rest of the region were adverse. The heavy flow of US arms to both countries, while part of the price to be paid for the peace agreements and a means of maintaining a certain balance between them, had a wider influence too. Finally, because much of the Arab world, including states important to American interests, rejected the Camp David process and did not let the Americans forget it, they were challenging Washington to demonstrate that Camp David was not what they condemned it as being: a separate peace. If the Carter Administration and its Israeli and Egyptian friends could not bring Jordan into the autonomy talks or get King Husayn's and the Saudis' benevolent support—and that seemed a very thin hope—then they would have to show real progress in their own efforts to make Camp David work.

How great was the urgency? Not so great in 1980, apparently, as before. President Sādāt seemed pleased with the success of his strategy. He was surviving the contumely of his fellow Arab rulers, taking comfort in their disagreements among themselves, still in firm control at home, and counting on the flow of American arms and economic aid. In Israel the Begin Government held to its restricted view of what autonomy should be permitted to the Palestinians, meanwhile insisting that security measures taken in the occupied territories and the establishment of Jewish settlements there were matters for Israel alone to decide.

For Carter, too, as Egypt and Israel went forward to normal relations, the sense of urgency diminished. At home he was under no great pressure to push the parties into agreement on the terms of Palestinian autonomy. In an election year the strongest pressure came from the partisans of Israel, whom he had no wish to' antagonize at a time when his political opponents were asserting their own strong support of Israel. Externally, the only serious pressure came from the Saudis, who did not lack the means to impress Carter with their support of the Palestinian cause; but they did not choose to throw their relations with America into a crisis on that issue. Like Sādāt and others, they were prepared to make certain allowances for the fact that in America it was an election year.

It was against this background that the negotiations proceeded. By September 1979, the first anniversary of the Camp David accords, Washington had decided to leave the initiative largely in the hands of Sādāt and Begin. The President's chief ME negotiator, Robert Strauss, recommended that the US cease pushing the issue of Palestinian participation in the talks. American attempts to bring about a compromise UN resolution modifying Resolution 242 and making possible contacts with the PLO had resulted only in angering Israel, disappointing the Arabs, and costing Andrew Young his ambassadorial job. Sādāt preferred that the Americans forget about Palestinian involvement for the time being, and let him go ahead directly with Begin.[16]

In the following months, as the negotiations inched forward in bilateral working groups, the two States were also fulfilling their obligations under the peace treaty, with Israel's withdrawal from two-thirds of Sinai, the opening of borders, introduction of American truce supervisors in the demilitarized zones, and various steps toward "normal relations" (which began officially on 26 January 1980)—all this without Egyptian insistence on linkage with the tortoise-paced autonomy talks.

So far apart were the two sides in those talks that by February 1980 the Egyptians were accusing Israel of departing from the Camp David accords and talking of the need for a new tripartite summit meeting. But Carter was not looking for that kind of political risk unless and until the two parties had narrowed the gap between them. Sol Linowitz, who had replaced Strauss, had the task of moving them closer together; but although the US was providing both countries with aid on a vast scale, he could not translate it into diplomatic influence. The talks went forward so slowly that there was no chance of meeting the 26 May deadline for their conclusion.

The lack of progress tended to focus attention less on the issues under discussion—the nature of autonomy—than on what was actually happening in the West Bank and Gaza: on the one hand, Arab protests and demonstrations; and, on the other, the Israeli Government's measures to curb violence and its insistence on the right to establish and maintain Jewish settlements. The settlements question, on which Carter and Begin had conflicting views as to what was agreed at Camp David,[17] was not susceptible to compromise because to Begin and the parties in his coalition Government Israel's right was a fundamental one; it could not even be suspended, put on the shelf as an unagreed matter, but had to be exercised. Thus, a regular pattern developed: Israel would take a decision on a settlement; the Arabs would protest; the US would deplore it as illegal and an obstacle to peace. It was more or less the same when Israel took action seen as necessary to its security, as by reprisals for Palestinian violence, deportation of Arab mayors of West Bank towns, or raids into Lebanon to strike at the PLO.

The US Government made no secret of its annoyance at Israeli actions it deemed unwarranted, illegal, dangerous, or generally unhelpful to the cause of peace. Yet it had no wish to join in one-sided resolutions sponsored by Arab delegations at the UN and backed by Soviet bloc and Third World sympathizers, condemning Israel out of hand, neglecting provocation on the Arab side, and asking for sanctions; any more than it wished to be left in the position of voting as Israel's lone defender. Abstention became a virtue.

The Carter Administration was not above compounding its own difficulties by mismanagement, as was evident when the US Ambassador to the UN voted on 1 March, on instructions, for a SC resolution calling for a stop to Israeli settlements in the occupied territories, and including references to Jerusalem. Within 48 hours the President was announcing publicly that the vote had been a mistake and did not represent his policy. The result was to hold the Administration up to disdain and ridicule from all sides: from Israel, angered by the original vote, and not mollified by lame explanations; from the Arabs, who said the President had backed away from his own policy under pressure from Israel and the Jewish lobby in the US; and from the American public, which saw the episode as a demonstration of incompetence.

American diplomacy was labouring under limitations which Linowitz's tireless efforts could not change. Sādāt broke off the talks in May, and the agreed deadline passed. In July they were resumed, only to be broken off again by Sādāt in August. None of the three parties was hopeful of a breakthrough before the American election; Sādāt, soured by his experience with Begin, talked of waiting for the next election in Israel. The State Department reiterated its objections to Israel's policies in the occupied territories and matched them with refusal to have anything to do with the PLO until it recognized Israel's right to exist. President Carter, his re-election campaign in high gear, made clear that his 1977 commitment to a "homeland" for the Palestinians did not mean that he favoured a Palestinian State.[18]

Needing to preserve at least the appearance of progress and concerned over the possibility that the worsening atmosphere would disrupt the other part of the Camp David accords, peace and normalization of relations between Egypt and Israel, the US worked to put the negotiations on Palestinian autonomy back on the track. Linowitz finally succeeded in September in getting an agreed statement that both Israel and Egypt remained committed to the Camp David accords; they would resume the autonomy talks; and they would consult on the holding of a summit meeting with President Carter. That meeting, however, could be held only after the American election.

When, on 4 November, the American electorate wrote *finis* to Carter's career as President, it put an end as well to any plans for a tripartite summit in 1980 and to the stage in the process of peacemaking on which Carter had put his stamp. Ronald Reagan, after the election, let Egypt and Israel know that he would maintain the Camp David process. But there surely would be reassessment—in Washington, in Cairo and in Jerusalem—of commitment to an approach to the Palestine question which, more than two years after Camp David, seemed to have reached a dead end.

OVERVIEW

The general conclusion on the record of the year has to be a mixed one. If not the dismal chronicle of weakness and failure described by some of President Carter's opponents and detractors, it was hardly a saga of success. American policy continued to serve the cause of peace and reconciliation between Egypt and Israel. It recognized the relation of power to policy, reacting sharply to the Soviet threat to vital Western interest in the oil of the Gulf, and beginning a necessary build-up of American power in the region. Yet, almost everywhere, policy appeared to be captured by events—the hostages in Iran, Turkey's crisis, the Iraqi-Iranian war, chaos in Lebanon, Palestine—and unable to forestall, direct, or even deflect them. The ME was the most critical segment of the "arc of crisis" which Administration spokesmen discovered along about mid-term. At end of term it was more critical than ever.

Henry Kissinger, surveying the problems of American policy after Afghanistan, warned against quick reactions, shifts of course, and the tendency to *"ad hoc it"*. He called for a consistent strategy which would gain respect abroad and bipartisan support at home.[19] It cannot be said that the US, as it wrestled with the diverse and perverse problems across the board from the Western Desert to the Himalayas, had more than isolated parts of such a strategy.

Neither in building the necessary military strength, nor in meeting the more important political and economic challenges, could the US have effective policies without essential co-operation from its European and Japanese allies. The need was recognized by all concerned; much time was devoted to seeking common or parallel lines of action; but, however one may assign the blame, the fact remains that what was achieved in coping with Iran, with the Soviet invasion of Afghanistan, with oil supply, even with the Arab-Israel question (long an American monopoly), was far less than it could have been. Both America and its allies were the losers.

Even more difficult was the related problem of finding a basis, in relations with

THE UNITED STATES AND THE MIDDLE EAST

key nations of the region, for the furtherance of American and allied interests, mainly in security and oil, over the long term. Here the art of dealing with governments of the day has to be married to an ability to adjust to change while holding firmly to essentials. On that score the Carter Administration made no more than a beginning, and the year 1979–80 was singularly barren of achievement.

John C. Campbell

NOTES

1. Amir Taheri, "Iran: Prisoner of Terminology", *International Herald Tribune,* Paris, 6 March 1980.
2. *Oil and Turmoil: Western Choices in the Middle East* (Washington: The Atlantic Council of the United States, 1979.)
3. Richard Burt, "How US Strategy toward Persian Gulf Region Evolved", *The New York Times (NYT),* 25 January 1980; "US Policy toward the Persian Gulf", address by Under Secretary of State David D. Newsom, 11 April 1980 (Department of State, Bureau of Public Affairs, Current Policy No. 160).
4. Ursula Braun, *Saudi Arabien im Spannungsfeld zwischen Nahost, Golf und Rotem Meer unter besonderer Berücksichtigung des saudi-arabisch-amerikanischen Verhältnisses* (Ebenhausen: Stiftung Wissenschaft und Politik, 1980), pp. 36–37, 65; see also interview with Crown Prince Fahd in *Al-Safir* of Beirut (reported in *NYT,* 10 January 1980).
5. *US Security Interests and Policies in Southwest Asia* (Hearings before the Committee on Foreign Relations, US Senate, February-March 1980, Washington: GPO, 1980), *passim;* Jiri Valenta, "From Prague to Kabul: The Soviet Style of Invasion", *International Security,* Cambridge, Ma., Autumn 1980, pp. 114–141.
6. Addresses by Secretary of State, Cyrus Vance, to the Chicago Council on Foreign Relations, 3 March 1980, and by Secretary of Defence, Harold Brown, to the Council on Foreign Relations, New York, 6 March 1980.
7. *NYT,* 24 January 1980.
8. Testimony of Walter Slocombe and of Lt-Gen. P. X. Kelley, *US Security Interests and Policies in Southwest Asia,* cited, pp. 303–322; see also statement of President Carter *NYT,* 30 January 1980).
9. Interviews in *The Washington Post (WP)* and *NYT,* 30 November 1980.
10. Statement of 3 September 1980 (Department of State, Bureau of Public Affairs, Current Policy No. 215), p. 4.
11. *Ibid.,* p. 3.
12. Interview in *NYT,* 3 December 1980.
13. Richard Burt and Bernard Gwertzman, "Role of the US in the Persian Gulf: How it Evolved", *NYT,* 12 October 1980; Claudia Wright, "Implications of the Iraq-Iran War", *Foreign Affairs,* New York, Winter 1980–81, pp. 275–303.
14. For comparison of US and Saudi objectives, see Ursula Braun, *op. cit.,* pp. 57–65; *The Gulf and the Peninsula: American Interests and Policies in the 'Eighties* (Washington: Middle East Institute, 1980), pp. 14–16.
15. Interview with Crown Prince Fahd, *NYT,* 22 June 1979; Karen Elliott House, "The Anger in Saudi Arabia", *The Wall Street Journal,* New York, 11 June 1979; *US Security Interests and Policies in Southwest Asia,* cited, pp. 51–56.
16. *NYT,* 16 September 1979.
17. William B. Quandt, "One Year Later—the Unfulfilled", *WP,* 17 September 1979.
18. Speech to B'nai B'rith Forum, 3 September 1980.
19. Interview with James Reston, *NYT,* 4 January 1980.

The USSR and the Middle East*

In marked contrast to the concerns of earlier years, the agenda of Middle East policy issues for a high level Kremlin review in the Autumn of 1979 would probably have identified Afghanistan and Iran at the first levels of urgency, ahead of Camp David and the Arab-Israel conflict or other questions of Soviet regional involvement. The events of 1979–80 have only accentuated the critical importance of the Persian Gulf and South Asia subregions. Although the Arab-Israel conflict continues to be featured in the Soviet media, the centrality of this issue has clearly declined still further. At the same time, the Red Sea-Horn of Africa is drawing more media attention, for reasons evidently connected with developments in the Persian Gulf.

THE INTERVENTION IN AFGHANISTAN

Dominating the year's events was the Soviet invasion of Afghanistan in late December 1979. The Soviets gradually came to a decision to intervene because the Afghan army, which had shrunk in size from 120,000 to no more than 40–50,000, was in danger of disintegrating completely under the tribal rebellion. The actual timing of the operation may be explained by Moscow's increasing inability to control the Afghan President, Ḥafīzullah Amīn, Prime Minister under President Nūr Muḥammad Taraki and then President after Taraki's death, who was also associated with the most ruthless aspects of the reform programme undertaken by the Khalq faction of the People's Democratic Party of Afghanistan (PDPA). The Soviets decided in the Summer of 1979 that he was a liability and could usefully be made the scapegoat for the PDPA's failings. In early September they conspired in Moscow with Taraki to oust Amīn. But the plot backfired and Amīn, to Moscow's embarrassment, killed Taraki. Amīn demanded the recall of the Soviet Ambassador and, in November, made frantic requests for a meeting with Pakistan's President, Ziya al-Ḥaqq. The Soviets, fearing that a desperate Amīn might be driven to make a deal with the Pakistanis or the Afghan opposition, increased their combat strength in Afghanistan throughout December and began an around-the-clock airlift on the 25–26 December. The following day one of the leading airborne regiments assaulted the Darulaman Palace south of Kabul and executed Ḥafīzullah Amīn. The ex-President was replaced by Babrak Karmal, who denounced Amīn as an agent of "United States imperialism."

Apart from such short-range calculations, Moscow had a variety of other longer-term motives for undertaking the costly operation. Foremost among them was the fact that its Afghan client was a pro-Soviet Marxist-Leninist regime. This set the PDPA apart from Moscow's other nationalist allies in the Third World, such as the Syrian or Iraqi Ba'th bourgeois parties. The importance of "defending the gains of the April revolution" in Afghanistan related to the prestige and security of the socialist commonwealth as a whole, as well as to the disappointing experiences Moscow had had with its noncommunist clients in the 1970s. A second factor was the geographical contiguity of Afghanistan to the Soviet Union. Kabul had fallen within the Soviet sphere of influence ever since the early 1920s

*Views expressed in this paper are the authors' own, and are not necessarily shared by the Rand Corporation or its research sponsors.

when King Amanullah wrested his country's independence from Britain and signed the first of a series of treaties with Moscow. Overthrow of the PDPA government could have led to the removal of Afghanistan from the Soviet sphere of influence and to an extension of Western and Chinese influence up to the borders of the Soviet Union. As Brezhnev stated on 12 January, this would have meant "the origination on our southern border of a threat of serious danger to the security of the Soviet State."[1] Fears of spillover effects of the Islamic revival must be seen in light of the propinquity of the Afghan Turkmen and Tadzhik populations to their co-ethnics in Soviet Central Asia.[2] A third factor was the opportunities that continued direct Soviet control over Afghanistan would provide for the expansion of Moscow's influence in the direction of the Persian Gulf and South Asia. A large part of the Indian Ocean would be in the range of Soviet tactical aviation operating out of bases in southern Afghanistan, while Afghan-supported ethnic separatism in Iran and Pakistan might ultimately lead to the creation of a Baluchi client state, giving the Soviets direct naval access to the Persian Gulf. Finally, the Soviets had been heavily committed to the war effort since 1978; a defeat would reflect badly on their military prestige. This commitment had been underlined by their signature of a Treaty of Friendship and Co-operation with Afghanistan in November 1978.

Afghanistan represents an important watershed in Soviet foreign policy insofar as it marks the first instance in which Moscow was willing to deploy ground forces on a large scale in a Third World country. The move reflects Moscow's disillusionment with détente and lack of regard for Western opinion, as well as an increased determination of the Soviet leadership to retain as much control as possible over the policies of Third World allies. It is less clear, however, whether the intervention signals an increased Soviet willingness to confront the US over countries of greater inherent political importance—for example, Iran. Whatever regional military and political risks they faced, the Soviets had no reason to expect a military response from the US. In the past, fear of super-power confrontation has been an important constraint on Soviet adventurism in the ME and, in spite of Afghanistan, may continue to be a factor.

In contrast to the smooth military operation, Moscow's political preparation of the intervention was poor. As in the 1968 invasion of Czechoslovakia, Moscow sought to justify its move on legal grounds. Accordingly the new Afghanistan Government stated on 28 December that "taking into account the continuing and expanding interference and provocations by Afghanistan's foreign enemies," it "turned to the USSR with an insistent request for urgent, political, moral, and economic help including military help." On this basis "it was decided to send a limited Soviet military contingent to Afghanistan" which will be fully withdrawn "when the cause which necessitated such action no longer exists."[3] The US, Britain, China, Pakistan and Egypt were all blamed for prior interference in internal Afghan affairs.[4]

In response to this unconvincing justification, the United Nations (UN) General Assembly on 14 January 1980 passed a resolution "strongly deplor[ing] the recent armed intervention in Afghanistan" by a margin of 104–18, with countries like Iraq and Iran voting in favour, and others like Syria, India, and Algeria abstaining. Washington reacted in anger: President Carter announced an embargo of grain and technology sales to the Soviet Union and organized a boycott of the Moscow Olympic Games in July. The SALT II treaty was shelved and the Administration showed some intention of increasing defence expenditures. Moscow tried to blunt this reaction by making a number of cosmetic concessions

82

and offering to negotiate a withdrawal of its forces once outside "aggression" against Afghanistan ceased.

Although the Soviet intervention prevented the Afghan Communists from being swept from power, Moscow was unable to break the back of the tribal resistance, or to extend the Central Government's control significantly into the countryside. Ten division equivalents were deployed; but these were overly mechanized and road-bound to be effective against the highly dispersed and elusive guerillas. Soviet sensitivity to casualties was perhaps one factor preventing Moscow from using infantry to conduct an all-out counter-insurgency campaign. Full-scale pacification of the countryside will require a substantially larger troop commitment. On the other hand, the Soviets learned quickly from their initial mistakes and made numerous adjustments in their tactics and force structure. The guerilla opposition was poorly equipped and lacked even the most rudimentary political organization.

At the same time, Moscow's political base in Afghanistan deteriorated steadily. A general strike in Kabul in February was followed by more serious anti-Soviet demonstrations in several Afghan cities in April. The Afghan army continued to disintegrate and had to be disarmed increasingly and replaced in combat by Soviet forces. Afghan administrative cadres were decimated by the continuing Khalq-Percham rivalry. Whatever part of the bureaucratic and military infrastructure that is not already run by the Soviets will probably have to be taken over by them, reducing Afghanistan over the intermediate term, in fact if not in name, to the status of a Soviet Central Asian republic.

The Soviet intervention has serious implications for the security of other countries in the region. Pakistan's North West Frontier Province (NWFP) has become a haven for well over a million Afghan refugees. The Pakistani Government has not assisted the Afghan guerillas or permitted outside nations to do so in a significant way for fear of provoking the Soviets. But the central government has traditionally exercised only weak control over the NWFP, and there is substantial movement of rebels and weapons between the Pathan populations on either side of the border. The Soviets may at some point undertake a systematic campaign to seal the frontier by bombing refugee camps and engaging in "hot pursuit" raids into Pakistani territory. Furthermore, the regime in Kabul has already indicated its determination to support separatist demands of the Pathan and Baluchi populations in Pakistan and Iran. Islamabad's sense of vulnerability *vis à vis* the Soviets was so acute that in March it refused a US offer of $200 m in military aid, saying that the package was large enough to provoke Moscow but insufficient to buy real security. Iran is also too vulnerable to support the Afghan guerillas, being hemmed in on three sides by Soviet forces and Iraq. Moscow's forceful demonstration of its determination to advance its interests had a profound psychological effect on all the nations of the Persian Gulf.

MOSCOW AND THE PERSIAN GULF

Soviet policy towards the Gulf had to contend with the dilemmas posed by the steady deterioration of relations between Iran and Iraq that ultimately led to open war on 22 September 1980. (See essay on Iraqi-Iranian war.) Moscow had interests to protect on both sides: Iraq was one of its oldest regional military clients, a co-signatory with Moscow of a Friendship and Co-operation Treaty, and an increasingly influential power in the Arab world; while Iran has been the object of abiding Russian interest and, under Khomeyni, had turned fanatically anti-

American. The Soviets have not handled conflicts between "clients" or "near-clients" well in the past: witness Moscow's alienation of both 'Abd al-Nāsir and Qassem in 1959–60 during the period of their rivalry.

Its relations with Iraq were generally cool. The Soviets have looked with some disfavour on Baghdad's efforts in recent years to draw closer to the conservative Gulf states, and to purposely exclude the USSR from regional security arrangements. Furthermore, the leaders of the Iraqi Communist Party (ICP), now exiled in Moscow, were given a forum from which to continue their feud with the Iraqi Ba'th. One Arabic-language broadcast from Moscow in April charged that "Iraqi reactionaries (i.e., the Ba'thists) have launched a fierce and extensive campaign to exterminate the Iraqi Communist Party . . . Their fate will be the same as those who preceded them, such as Nūrī al-Sa'īd . . ."[5] Until the war, however, the Soviets lacked the leverage to win better treatment for the ICP. Over the previous 12 months, they had been displaced by the French as Iraq's primary arms supplier by dollar volume.

Soviet policy towards Iran since the revolution has been twofold. On the one hand, it has tried to cultivate good relations with Khomeyni's Islamic Government so as to encourage the breaking of all its ties with the West. The Soviets have praised Khomeyni as "objectively progressive" and muffled criticisms over such issues as natural gas-pricing, while offering moral support against the US over the hostage question.[6] On the other hand, they have sought to protect and reinforce the Marxist-Leninist Tudeh party (and to lesser degrees the two other Leftist parties) against the religiously-inspired anti-Leftist purges that swept the country in September 1979 and April 1980.[7] Moscow has quietly collaborated in the Tudeh's efforts to weaken the authority of the central government by organizing and supporting the ethnic minorities' centrifugal demands. The Soviets have found Khomeyni a frustrating, unreliable, and ideologically suspect interlocutor,[8] and are doubtless sceptical as to the regime's staying power. Many of Moscow's actions have therefore been geared to positioning their ideological allies within Iran for the upcoming power struggle.

Within this context one might have expected the Soviets to surreptitiously encourage an Iraqi attack on Iran so as to hasten the process of disintegration at the centre and to provide an opening for the Iranian Left. As it turned out, the lure of such opportunities was overshadowed by fears of possible pitfalls when the war finally broke out. Far from encouraging Iraq, Moscow did the minimum necessary to honour its obligations towards Baghdad, while tilting, where possible, towards Iran. In accordance with the Friendship Treaty, the Soviets and Iraqis engaged in *pro forma* consultations prior to the war's outbreak when Tāriq Azīz, Iraq's Deputy Prime Minister, became the first high-ranking official to visit Moscow since December 1978. But Azīz evidently failed to receive either Soviet political backing for the war effort, or commitments on increased arms supply. Two Soviet freighters heading for Basra with military supplies contracted for prior to the war turned back to sea at the outbreak of the fighting; but they later made the deliveries (despite Soviet denials) through the Jordanian port of 'Aqaba. At the same time, Moscow discreetly permitted Libyan overflights of its territory to resupply Iran, and gave tacit support to the Syrian-Iranian axis by signing a Friendship Treaty with Damascus in the midst of the conflict. There have also been persistent though unconfirmed reports of Moscow selling small quantities of arms directly to the Iranians.

Moscow's public position was one of strict neutrality. At a State dinner on 30 September, Leonid Brezhnev blamed the war's outbreak on "imperialism" and warned that:

"Neither Iraq nor Iran will gain anything from mutual destruction, bloodshed and undermining each other's economy. It is only the third side [i.e., the US], to which the interests of the peoples in that region are alien, which stands to gain. As far as the Soviet Union is concerned, we are for Iran and Iraq settling disputable issues between themselves at the table of negotiations."[9]

Brezhnev's remarks seemed to reflect several fears. The first was that the war would serve as a pretext to "intervene in this conflict and establish (Western) control over the Persian Gulf countries and their oil wealth."[10] The dispatch of American AWACS aircraft to Saudi Arabia and plans for a multilateral naval task force to patrol the Straits of Hormuz were duly noted and condemned. The second fear was that the Iraqis would succeed in their stated intention of bringing about the overthrow of the Ayatollah Khomeyni and replacing him with a secular military government, which might in time gravitate back into the American orbit. As early as the previous April the Soviet Press had taken note of reports that "Iraq's authorities have allowed Iranian emigrants to form armed groups devoted to the idea of overthrowing the Khomeyni Government."[11] Finally, it was probably not clear to the Kremlin whether a victorious and successful Iraq would serve Soviet interests. Moscow's influence over the independent Iraqi Ba'th Party has always been greatest when the latter was in a weak and vulnerable position *vis à vis* its internal and external enemies, and therefore dependent on Soviet patronage. A grinding and inconclusive war of attrition might persuade Saddām Husayn to conciliate Moscow in search of weapons and spare parts.

At the same time, the Soviets used the threat of instability in the Gulf as an opportunity to wean directly-affected American allies away from Washington. A commentary in February 1980 by Nikolai Portugalov noted the divergent interests of the US and Western Europe, and suggested an all-European conference on energy by which the Soviet Union would, in effect, guarantee European access to Middle Eastern oil. Portugalov asserted that this was a "promising alternative to the adventuristic and hegemonistic policy of the US in the Persian Gulf region."[12] This trial balloon may become an important feature of Soviet European diplomacy in the future.

In a similar vein, Saudi Arabia became the object of Soviet overtures. Suppressing their occasional ideological criticisms, the Soviets congratulated the Kingdom on its national day in September, and sought to encourage the greatest possible distance between Riyadh and Washington. One commentator asserted that "Saudi Arabia and other coastal countries with the exception of Oman, protest the intensification of the US military presence in the Arabian gulf, and refuse to offer military bases to the US."[13] As in the case of the Europeans, the Saudis were portrayed as victims of American adventurism and hegemonism.

THE SOVIET UNION AND THE ARAB-ISRAELI CONFLICT

No significant change occurred in either Soviet policy or Soviet activities in the Arab-Israeli conflict during 1979–80. Arguably, Soviet prospects in this arena were less bright at the close of the year than at its beginning. Not since the aborted US-Soviet declaration of 1 October 1977, has Moscow appeared even briefly to play a significant role in the events and circumstances centred on the Arab-Israeli conflict. Indeed, the limitations on Soviet progress have been in evidence since shortly after the October 1973 war. American-Egyptian *rapprochement* and Sādāt's turn to peace with Israel effectively isolated the USSR from the ME

THE USSR AND THE MIDDLE EAST

negotiating process. It is of course true that the Camp David negotiations on autonomy made little headway this past year. Since Moscow, along with the Rejectionist Arab States, has repeatedly forecast impasse in the negotiations—although not necessarily for the reasons actually responsible—it might have been expected that the meagre results of the autonomy discussions would have revived prospects for putting the Soviet Union back into the picture. However, the Soviet invasion of Afghanistan, the hostage crisis in Iran and, most recently, the outbreak of war between Iraq and Iran all managed to push the Arab-Israeli conflict out of the centre of world attention.

The invasion of Afghanistan initially appeared to unite the Muslim world in denunication of Soviet move, but the fervour of anti-Soviet sentiment has weakened considerably. On the other hand, the Afghan episode has not helped the Soviets in their goal of forging a regional alliance to regain a central role in the settlement of the Arab-Israeli struggle. These difficulties were brought to a head by the Iraq-Iran war, in which the Front of Rejection of Camp David was openly split—with Jordan and Saudi Arabia supporting Iraq, Libya and Syria supporting Iran, and the Palestine Liberation Organization (PLO) dispiritedly caught in between. In the two years since the Baghdad Summit of November 1978, the unity of the participants who had come together to frustrate Egyptian-Israeli reconciliation had not prospered. The open disarray of the Arab world attendant on the Iraq-Iran war was dismaying to the Kremlin. In late May 1980, Brezhnev exclaimed at a State dinner for a visiting South Yemeni delegation: "Is it not time to return the matter of Near East settlement to the only correct course—the path of collective efforts of all interested sides?"[14] In the Autumn of 1980, Moscow seemed little closer to that goal.

The main focus of Moscow's frustration has continued to be Egypt and Anwar Sādāt. Soviet propaganda appeared to be unable to make up its mind about Egypt's precise role: Is Cairo a full partner of Washington; or is Israel still the favourite, with Egypt suffering the consequences? Sometimes, Egypt is pictured as trying to extricate itself from an unwelcome connection, a victim forced to make concessions because of the special relationship between Israel and the US. At other times, in the conspiracy that Moscow inevitably sees in ME developments, Cairo, Washington, and Jerusalem are equally suspect.[15]

With minor variations, and depending on the tactical context, Soviet invective has been almost as rich in castigating Sādāt as in denouncing Begin. Sādāt was traduced as the leader who had turned Egypt from a fighter against imperialism to "its servitor, betraying the interests of the Arab people" (his growing military co-operation with the US), the "unprincipled intriguer grovelling before the enemies of the Arab nation," who enriched the speculators at the national expense (the "open door" economic policy).[16] Sādāt's ultimate crime is what one Soviet writer called the "logic of apostasy": the "betrayal of Arab interests is followed by attacks on those who are their real friends and allies."[17] In September 1980, the 10th anniversary of the death of 'Abd al-Nāsir, Pavel Demchenko mourned "the full destruction of the policy which used to be followed in the time of Jamāl 'Abd al-Nāsir."[18]

In the period that relations between Moscow and Cairo have cooled, those with the PLO have become openly more cordial. In recent years Moscow has come round to generally unqualified support for the PLO as the uniquely legitimate Palestinian representative. The attachment to the PLO and to the radical Arab states also exacted a price since it made more difficult the task of persuading the US to co-operate in securing a "comprehensive" settlement. Accordingly, the

86

Kremlin has pursued—in the ME as in other regions—a multi-track strategy: along with its political and military support of the PLO and the Rejectionists, it has continued to espouse settlement terms calling for "guarantees for the security of all states in the region, including Israel."[19] The elements of this mixture are not always in balance, as was revealed by Moscow's following the PLO lead in its cool reception of the European Community's Venice declaration in June 1980. (See essay on the European Community and the ME.) Although the Europeans endorsed the right of the PLO to a seat at the peace table, the declaration was viewed as flawed by the injection of an Israeli "right to security," failure to reject the Camp David accords, or to acknowledge the PLO as the sole legal Palestinian representative.[20]

Another element of potential instability in the Soviet multi-track structure is the same as that which eventually drove them out of Egypt—the threat of US "subversion" of a Soviet client through the lure of influence with Israel. Whatever the value of those "cards," as Sādāt used to call them, only Washington holds them. In the Autumn of 1979 Moscow showed signs of being worried about American overtures to the PLO; its media carried warnings to the PLO and the Arab world generally against nefarious American designs.[21] That concern abated with the failure of the various moves in the UN to alter Resolutions 242 and 338 to suit both the US and the PLO, and as the US election campaign heated up. The episode may have been partly responsible (although support for the Soviet Union in Afghanistan also was involved) for an apparent partiality shown to Na'if Hawātima, leader of a smaller but more loyal (to Moscow) wing of the PLO (and to a lesser degree even George Habash), over Yāsir Arafāt of al-Fath. Al-Fath's political programme has not grown more moderate: at its Fourth Conference in Damascus in May 1980, the organization reiterated its goal of at least displacing Israel in the whole of Palestine.[22] (See essay on the PLO.) In the kaleidoscopic ME, only time will tell whether Moscow will again be confronted by the challenge of a US-PLO understanding.

However, Moscow's perspective now seems to be that the US-Israeli relationship is likely to be strengthened rather than weakened, quite apart from whether Reagan is likely to be more pro-Israel than Carter. From Moscow's viewpoint, the most important change in the regional context is the increased militancy of the US. "Recently, especially since the collapse of the Shah's regime in Iran and the defeat of reaction's plans in Afghanistan, the US has stepped up military preparations sharply in the Indian Ocean, the Persian Gulf, and the Near East." For this reason, therefore, and for the purposes of its developing military preparations, "Washington still sees Israel not just as its main ally, but as the chief prop-state and base-state in the Near East, whose significance is enhanced in the context of the new American strategy."[23]

It is in this context that the signing of the Soviet-Syrian Friendship Treaty on 8 October must probably be viewed. To maintain his independence, perceived as much as real, Hāfiz al-Asad had resisted Soviet enticement to sign such a treaty for a decade; but with his internal position sharply weakened by the unfinished business in Lebanon, the demise of the short-lived *rapprochement* with Iraq and, particularly, by the rising level of violent dissent in Syria, Asad could less easily afford to snub his Soviet friends. The defection of Egypt left him feeling exposed to Israeli pressure. Iraq was demonstrating hegemonic intentions in the Gulf, and the US showed signs of wanting to become a power again from the Horn of Africa to South Asia. In this environment, Soviet and Syrian perceptions tended to converge, and the Treaty seemed a natural reaction to the "imperialist counter-attack." Soviet encouragement of Syrian-Libyan "unity" moves in September 1980 should probably be viewed in a similar light.

At the ceremony in Moscow after signing the Treaty with Asad, Brezhnev declared: "This treaty does not just sum up the results of the development of our relations to this day. It raises them to a new, higher level."[24] As transmitted the same day by TASS, the Treaty, (the eleventh to be concluded between the USSR and a Third World country), holds no surprises. However, rumours abounded that there were secret military clauses and that the Soviet military presence in Syria, now several thousand strong, would be sharply augmented. Presumably, enhanced supply of weaponry to Syria was also agreed on. In a future crisis between Syria and Israel, the Treaty might be made the basis for a more direct Soviet military involvement in the conflict.

The Kremlin has repeatedly attempted to make clear that peace in the ME cannot be achieved without the Soviet Union or against its will. The military provisions of the Soviet-Syrian Treaty, and the supply agreements that have surely accompanied it, are efforts to guarantee that the Soviet voice will be heard.

THE HORN OF AFRICA

The two Soviet clients in the ME with the best ideological credentials, the People's Democratic Republic of Yemen (South Yemen: PDRY) and Ethiopia, are marginal to the core ME conflicts. In the former, the coup of June 1978 ended tentative efforts to break out of South Yemen's increasing isolation and dependence on the USSR and brought to power the Moscow loyalists. (See chapter on the PDRY.) Relations between Moscow and Aden thereafter seemed close. Kosygin came to Aden in September 1979; the PDRY was given observer status in the Council for Mutual Economic Aid (Comecon) and additional military assistance. 'Abd-al-Fattāḥ Ismā'īl was invited to Moscow where, on 25 October, he signed a Treaty of Friendship and Co-operation.[25] Moscow called the Arab world's attention to Article 5 of the Treaty, dealing with military co-operation between the signatories.[26]

In April 1980, when Ismā'īl was turned out of office by his brother conspirator of 1978, Alī Nāsir Muḥammad Ḥusnī, little seemed to change. Brezhnev congratulated Alī Nāsir on the morrow of the 1980 coup[27] and invited him to Moscow at the end of May; the Soviet Press recorded the "complete unanimity of views" of host and guest.[28] Several South Yemeni delegations subsequently made their way to Moscow. The Soviet Minister of Defence met with his PDRY counterpart while he was in the USSR "on vacation."[29] In the meantime, the Soviet military and naval presence in and around South Yemen has become normal practice.

The Brezhnev-Kosygin greeting to Mengistu Haile Mariam on Ethiopia's national day in September 1980 hailed "socialist Ethiopia" and the solidarity of the tie to its "reliable friend, the USSR."[30] This greeting was as warm as that dispatched the year before. Nevertheless, the Soviet Union was unlikely to forget that "Ethiopia is merely making its first steps on the socialist road."[31] With the history of other Soviet clients in mind, Moscow was undoubtedly sensitive to the problems of long term influence and control. It was largely in response to Soviet pressure that Mengistu created a Commission to Organize the Party of the Working People of Ethiopia—that is, a "vanguard" party in the Soviet image. That effort is still in train and it remains to be seen whether Moscow will be satisfied with the results.

For the USSR and its allies in the Horn, the big issue was the American search for bases to support a more effective presence in the Indian Ocean and Persian Gulf. An intensive campaign was launched against the US-Somalia agreement as well as against the use of Egyptian and Omani territory for US forces. A Soviet broadcast in Somali said that Addis Ababa viewed "the US base at Berbera as a threat to the existence of the Ethiopian state. The Ethiopian leadership see the establishment of the base as a declaration of war against Ethiopia."[32] The Soviets charged Somalia with continuing its war of sabotage against Ethiopia in the Ogaden, encouraged by its new relation with the US. Moscow fanned the suspicions of Somalia's neighbours, particularly Kenya, to drive a wedge between them and Washington.

CONCLUSION

In the Autumn of 1980, the Soviet Union was engaged in an effort to constrain the scope and effectiveness of the US build-up in the region, extending from the Horn of Africa to South Asia. This time Moscow did not have to contort its logic to find connections between Egyptian-American military co-operation, the Somalia base agreement, the reaction to Soviet intervention in Afghanistan, and events in the Gulf. The links were apparent and the Soviet target was clear; Moscow warned that "the metastases of this dangerous disease affect, above all, those regimes which betray their national interests in the quest for American dollars."[33]

The Kremlin's basic strategy for countering the American moves, apart from any responsive regional military build-up of its own, is the tried and true "unity of anti-imperialist forces" under its own leadership. From Moscow's viewpoint, the most important positive development toward this end was the Soviet-Syrian treaty. In addition, relations with the PDRY and Ethiopia were further strengthened; efforts continued to loosen the attachment of Saudi Arabia to the US and to maintain a flexible stance with regard to developments in Iran with an eye to moving quickly at the opportune moment. On the negative side of the balance, Afghanistan has not yet been pacified. The Iraqi-Iranian war demonstrated the inherent difficulty of operating in a highly unstable environment, where there was no easy handle for Soviet policy comparable to anti-Zionism in the Arab-Israeli arena. Thus far, the Soviet attempt to play a neutral role while subtly tilting in Tehran's direction has been relatively costless, but that may not continue to be true.

At the close of 1980, a new US President was elected who had campaigned on a platform of more rapid increases in defence expenditure and a more militant foreign policy. It seemed likely that Moscow could expect a continuation— perhaps even acceleration—of the American build-up in the ME. Soviet ground and air forces of considerably greater magnitude are located much closer to the scene of events, and reports of Soviet troop concentrations on the Iranian border raise fears of Soviet-American military confrontation. The potential of the Soviet-Syrian treaty for activating the "Eastern Front" of the Arab-Israeli conflict may begin to be tested. In the Horn of Africa, US bases in Somalia might embolden Siad Barreh to escalate the low-level border fray in the Ogaden or, conversely, induce Mengistu to heat up the war in order to embarrass the Americans. All in all, 1981 could see an even higher level of tensions in the ME.

Abraham S. Becker and Francis Fukuyama

THE USSR AND THE MIDDLE EAST

NOTES

1. Telegrafnoe Agentstvo Sovetskovo Soiuza (TASS), Moscow, 12 January 1980.
2. Soviet sensitivity to Islamic spillover effects is suggested by an intriguing article which appeared in *Pravda*, Moscow, in July under the byline of one A. Vakhabov. The latter denounced as "imperialist propaganda" the use of the term "Muslim peoples" when referring to Soviet Muslims in an earlier *Pravda* article by Uzbek Party First Secretary and Politburo candidate member, Sharaf Rashidov. Vakhabov charged that "bourgeois ideologists" were trying to incite a "religio-nationalistic mood among certain elements of Soviet citizenry." (*The Soviet Union and the Middle East*, Jerusalem, Vol. V, No. 7, pp. 6–7). On the other hand, one high-ranking Soviet diplomat told *Die Welt:* "The threat by Islamic fundamentalism has been very much exaggerated. The Muslims— these are humble people. We have 40 million of them in our country, and we do not have any trouble with them. . ." *Die Welt*, Bonn, 14 January 1980.
3. Mikhail Mikhailov in *Izvestiia*, Moscow, 1 January 1980. The article quotes the R Kabul statement of December 27 1980, which was evidently written before the coup and broadcast from the Soviet Union.
4. The Central Intelligence Agency (CIA), for example, was charged with "training Afghan rebels in camps in Pakistan," at times under the cover of controlling the narcotics traffic. *Izvestiia*, 1 January 1980.
5. R Moscow in Arabic, 3 April 1980.
6. The Soviet attitude on the hostage question did not change in 1979–80. Moscow paid lip-service to the principle of diplomatic immunity but encouraged Iran to hold the hostages as long as possible. Their return will remove a major irritant to US-Iranian relations and may adversely affect the Soviet position in Iran.
7. The only time the Soviet Press openly criticized Khomeyni was when his regime attempted to suppress the Tudeh and its organ *Mardom*. See, for example, Alexander Bovin's description of Khomeyni as a "disaster," quoted in Shahram Chubin, "Leftist Forces in Iran," in *Problems of Communism*, Washington, July-August 1980, p. 9.
8. This may be seen from the fact that the Soviet Press took no account of the specifically Islamic character of the Iranian revolution or Khomeyni's role in it until very late, i.e., late November-early December 1978. A revealing critique of Iran's Islamic ideology was written by E. Primakov in *Voprosy filosofii*, No. 8, Moscow, August 1980.
9. TASS, 30 September 1980.
10. Lebedeva commentary, R Moscow in Persian, 4 October 1980.
11. TASS, 10 April 1980.
12. TASS, 29 February 1980.
13. R Moscow in Arabic, 23 September 1980.
14. R Moscow, 27 May 1980.
15. Cf., for example, *Izvestiia*, 17 November 1979 or 27 March 1980, and *Pravda*, 10 March 1980.
16. *Krasnaia zvezda*, Moscow, 8 June 1980; *Mirovaia ekonomika i mezhdunarodnye otnosheniia*, No. 5, Moscow, 1980, p. 123; *New Times*, No. 39, Moscow, September 1980, p. 20.
17. *Pravda*, 18 July 1980.
18. R Moscow in Arabic, 23 September 1980.
19. In another formulation, the Declaration of the Warsaw Treaty Member States called for a comprehensive settlement "on the basis of respect for the lawful interests of all states and peoples of the ME, including Israel," and "ensurement of the sovereignty and security of all states of that area." TASS, 15 May 1980.
20. R Moscow in Arabic, 13 June 1980.
21. E.g., *Izvestiia*, 17 November 1979.
22. See the excerpts from the Conference declaration in *Survival* London, September/October 1980, p. 229.
23. *Pravda*, 9 September 1980.
24. TASS, 8 October 1980.
25. *Pravda*, 26 October 1979.
26. R Moscow in Arabic, 26 October 1979.

27. *Pravda*, 23 April 1980.
28. *Pravda*, 29 May 1980.
29. *Pravda*, 29 June 1980.
30. *Pravda*, 12 September 1980.
31. R Moscow in French to Africa, 11 September 1980.
32. R Moscow to East Africa, 6 September 1980.
33. *Izvestiia*, 6 September 1980.

The European Community and the Middle East

Always an area of significant interest to Europe, the Middle East has increasingly become central to European concerns. Recent developments have been particularly important for the Community, notably the impact of a 130% oil-price increase following the fall of the Shah of Iran; the Iranian seizure of the American Embassy with its personnel as hostages; the Mecca mosque incident in Saudi Arabia; the Soviet invasion of Afghanistan; the perception of increased pressure over the Palestinian question and the Arab-Israeli conflict; efforts at co-ordinated European initiatives in the ME; and the outbreak of the war between Iran and Iraq. These developments suggest a growing sense of Europe's vulnerability, particularly because of its oil-import dependence and insufficient diplomatic, economic and military means to influence outcomes in the ME. The Community's response to this situation was to go in for co-ordination of their policies and initiatives in the region. One result of this was to increase tensions with their American ally, even though their own combined leverage in the region remained decidedly constrained.

EUROPE, IRAN AND THE AMERICAN HOSTAGE INCIDENT
European policy toward the hostage incident exemplifies the array of problems and constraints they face in dealing with the ME. It also reflects their internal differences as well as problems in their relations with the US.

The initial response to the seizure of the US Embassy and the taking of 53 American hostages on 4 November 1979, was offers of verbal support by individual European states for the US along with expressions of hope for an early solution to the problem. They also undertook individual diplomatic efforts to influence the outcome.

France and Britain voted for the Security Council (SC) Resolution of 13 January 1980 imposing an embargo of exports to Iran (except for medicine and food); the banning of new contracts for services and new credits; and calling for the reduction of Iran's diplomatic personnel stationed abroad. The Resolution was vetoed by the Soviet Union. Further delays followed, characterized by European hopes for a breakthrough in the hostage problem and by the Carter Administration's inconsistent and even conflicting signals of their intentions and wishes. Finally, on 2 April the European Economic Community (EEC) Heads of Government at their Luxembourg meeting approved a sanctions policy in principle. They reaffirmed their "solidarity with the US at this time of trial," and agreed upon a two-stage procedure for implementation. The first stage, to take effect immediately, consisted of mostly symbolic actions: reduction of European diplomatic personnel stationed in Iran, and of Iranian diplomats in Europe; reinstitution of visa requirements for Iranians wishing to travel to the EEC; and a halt to arms sales to Iran. They also agreed to impose trade sanctions by 17 May unless "decisive progress" toward securing the hostages' release had been made by that time. This second stage was to include the trade embargo proposed in the vetoed United Nations (UN) resolution.

In the absence of further progress, the EEC Foreign Ministers met at Naples on 17–18 May and agreed to implement trade sanctions against Iran. However, since they were to be restricted to contracts signed after the hostage seizure, this represented a step away from both the original UN resolution and the Commu-

92

nity's own position, which had covered all trade with Iran apart from medicine and food. But even this limited agreement was further weakened when the British Parliament rejected the terms proposed at Naples. Despite Mrs Thatcher's Conservative majority in the House of Commons, and the strong verbal support given by her Government for sanctions, the Cabinet did not throw its full weight behind the measure by making the vote a test of party loyalty. The result was to revise the British position: instead of making contracts signed with Iran retroactive to 4 November, they affected only those entered into after the sanctions policy had been decided upon. These sanctions were still further diluted when the Department of Trade announced that new contracts would be forbidden as from 30 May 1980, but that the limitation would apply only to new contracts by new traders; in other words, firms already doing business with Iran would still be able to expand existing contracts, or even agree on new ones, provided these continued "an established course of business dealing between the same parties relating to goods of the same or similar class." Thus, a major contract held by the British Talbot (Chrysler) automobile firm was not to be jeopardized, and no more than 10% of Britain's exports of $1.6 bn per year to Iran would be affected.[1]

Other EEC members, while critical of Britain's position, adopted regulations to implement the Naples decisions.[2] By finally arriving at this position, some seven months after the start of the hostage affair, the Community gave tangible evidence of its position, but protected most of its economic interests including $7 bn in French capital projects, large German business deals, and $3 bn in Italian construction projects (including a port and a steel mill). Even though the EEC's 1979 exports to Iran represented no more than c. 1% of its total exports, and oil imports from Iran had amounted to just 5% of the Community's 1979 total, its members' concern about oil supplies and the need to maintain its employment and industrial base supported by export markets, all worked against tougher policies. Moreover, there was general scepticism about the likelihood of sanctions producing the release of the hostages. The Americans perceived these European policies as foot-dragging and half-hearted, both on the Iran and Afghanistan issues. On their side, the Europeans expressed criticisms of the inconsistencies in the US leadership, and were dismayed at both the idea and the failure of the hostage rescue mission. These different perceptions exacerbated US-European relations.

THE EURO-ARAB DIALOGUE

Particularly due to French initiatives, the European Community had begun a dialogue between its own nine members and the 21 Arab League States in July 1974, following the October 1973 Middle-East War. It gradually became apparent, however, that tangible results from this dialogue would be slow in coming. The two sides spent the first year in disagreement over Palestinian representation, and when working groups were established in June 1975, these were confined to technical topics such as agricultural development, infrastructure projects and technical co-operation.[3]

The dialogue was a means for the Europeans to assert their independent role and involvement in an area which the US and the USSR tended to dominate on the diplomatic level; nevertheless, the impact of the dialogue itself remained limited in scope and achievement. The crucial subjects of the Arab-Israeli dispute and of oil price and supply were explicitly absent from the agenda. Divisions within both camps dictated the omission of the Arab-Israeli conflict from the agenda,[4] while the Arab League's policy of including important non-oil producers and excluding

93

non-Arab producers from its team while major oil consumers like the US and Japan were missing from the European side, also militated against serious discussions of energy questions. Other impediments to positive results were European preferences for bilateral negotiations, the slowness of the Community's political machinery, divisions among the Arab participants and differences over the Palestinian issue.

The signing of the Camp David accords in early 1979 brought the already moribund Euro-Arab dialogue to a halt. Nor was it possible to resuscitate it so long as Egypt remained divided from most of the other Arab States and left out of the Arab League. However, as the 26 May 1980 deadline for Israeli-Egyptian agreement on Palestinian autonomy approached, the Europeans sought to reactivate the dialogue. In order to avoid coming under increased Arab pressures over issues in the Arab-Israeli conflict, they expressed a willingness to include political issues in resumed talks. This gave much of the impetus to the Community's Venice Declaration of 13 June (see below). Nevertheless, the dialogue itself continued to remain limited, with Arab States using it as a means of exerting pressure on the Europeans. At a meeting in Luxembourg on 12–13 November 1980, they demanded European recognition of the Palestine Liberation Organization (PLO). The Europeans responded by reiterating their view of the need for Israel to withdraw from occupied territories, for the Arabs and Palestinians to recognize Israel's right to exist, and for the Palestinians to have the opportunity to express themselves on the issue of self-determination.[5] As before, energy issues were not discussed. The meeting adjourned with only a recommendation that a Euro-Arab conference at Foreign Ministers' level should take place in June or July of 1981. While this represented an effort to move the formal dialogue to a higher level of participation, it also reflected a lack of tangible achievement and a policy of delay. The outbreak of the Iraqi-Iranian war in September 1980 further exacerbated divisions within the Arab League as well as substantially lessening the immediacy of the Palestinian issue.

In short, the Euro-Arab dialogue continued to be of little relevance as a vehicle for EEC involvement in the ME, and the factors impinging upon it reflected the limited ability of the Europeans to shape major events in the region.

EUROPE AND THE ARAB-ISRAELI DISPUTE: THE VENICE DECLARATION

The most clear-cut European initiative on the ME came with the Venice Declaration of 13 June 1980. With the passing of the 26 May deadline on the US-Egyptian-Israeli negotiations over Palestinian autonomy, the Europeans felt it necessary to take steps to prevent the diplomatic momentum from collapsing altogether. One of their initiatives was to propose that the SC Resolution 242 should be amended to provide for Palestinian participation in a comprehensive ME settlement. This move was strongly opposed by the US on the ground that it would interfere with the Camp David process. It also contradicted the American position that the PLO must first accept Resolution 242 and Israel's right to exist before any negotiating role could be accorded to it. When President Carter pledged to veto any such European move within the SC this initiative was abandoned.[6]

The Europeans, however, made a number of moves to reach understandings with the Arab countries. These included such symbolic and tangible steps as President Giscard d'Estaing's trip to the Gulf from 1–9 March, during which he stressed the need for Palestinian self-determination; the statement by the British

Foreign Secretary Lord Carrington on 17 March, that he did not believe the PLO is "a terrorist organization as such;" a series of individual arms export deals, including large French and Italian sales to Saudi Arabia and Iraq, and a contract for the purchase by Jordan of the advanced British Shir II tanks (formerly intended for the Shah's army), equipped with chobham armour and advanced fire control systems, which had not yet been supplied to the British army itself. The Nine also voted for the UN General Assembly resolution on 1 March which condemned Israeli settlements in occupied territories, including Jerusalem. (The US itself initially voted for the same resolution, then reversed its position a few days later with the embarrassing explanation that there had been a misunderstanding.) In late August, the Netherlands decided to move its embassy from Jerusalem to Tel Aviv, joining its other EEC colleagues already established there; this action was taken under threats from Saudi Arabia, Kuwait and the United Arab Emirates to break relations if the Dutch failed to leave Jerusalem. The immediate cause for this pressure was the Knesset's act in formalizing the annexation of East Jerusalem. The Dutch Government explicitly expressed its regrets about the "pressure" to which it had been subjected.[7]

Meanwhile other European efforts to placate Arab Governments went well beyond anything having to do with the Israeli-Arab conflict. Thus, for example, the West German Government applied pressures on the West Berlin city administration to release two Iraqi diplomats detained on charges of preparing a terrorist bomb attack against a group of Kurdish students.[8] In late May, Denmark signed a three-year oil contract with Saudi Arabia, in which it agreed to avoid behaviour that could "discredit" the Saudi monarchy, government or institutions—a condition insisted upon because of Saudi reactions to the British TV film, "Death of a Princess."

The major co-ordinated European initiative came with the meeting of the European Council (i.e. the Heads of State and Government and the Ministers of Foreign Affairs) at Venice on 12–13 June 1980. The Venice Declaration reiterated a number of previous European positions, including support for Resolutions 242 and 338, and their own Declarations of 29 June 1977, 19 September 1978, 26 March and 18 June 1979. It also restated the right to existence and security of all states in the region, including Israel. However, it broke new ground in several key respects, particularly in regard to Palestinian self-determination and the need to associate the PLO with negotiations. In addition, the Nine declared that they were prepared to participate "within the framework of a comprehensive settlement, in a system of concrete and binding international guarantees . . . on the ground." The Declaration was noteworthy for two additional reasons: it constituted the most cohesive European proposal yet presented on the ME, and it called for a specific follow up. The President of the Council of Ministers was directed to make contacts among all the parties concerned and to report back on the form that a further European initiative should take.

The subsequent fate of the Venice Declaration illustrated the limits of the European's room for manoeuvre in the ME. On 15 June, the PLO criticized the statement for failing to recognize it as the "sole legitimate representative" of the Palestinian people, and described it as a response to US pressures and an effort to draw some Arab States into the Camp David process. While the PLO welcomed the Europeans' move, it called on them to "free themselves of the pressure and blackmail of US policy." On the same day, the Israeli Government bitterly denounced the Venice Declaration for attempting "to bring into the peace process that Arab SS which calls itself 'the Palestine Liberation Organization'. . . ." It also characterized the European document as a "Munich-like capitulation to totalitarian blackmail and a spur to all those seeking to undermine the Camp David accords and derail the peace process in the ME. . . ."[9]

In his capacity as President of the Community, Luxembourg's Foreign Minister, Gaston Thorn, made a series of visits to Arab States and to Israel in August and September 1980. Given the response of the PLO and of Israel, it is not surprising that the effort produced little tangible result. The Nine themselves appeared to back away from their own initiative, and the Thorn mission received no substantive discussion at the Foreign Ministers' meeting at Brussels on 15–16 September. Thorn's mission was virtually buried by two subsequent events: his second visit to Israel in late September, which was abruptly ended due to a disagreement with the Begin Government over conditions for his travels to the West Bank, and the outbreak of the Iraqi-Iranian war. The latter event left the Arabs themselves bitterly divided and diverted attention within the region, at least temporarily, from the Israeli-Palestinian conflict while serving as a reminder that other significant sources of instability existed in the ME.

Another voting dispute at the UN illustrated the difficulties in which the Nine found themselves on Middle Eastern issues. An emergency session of the General Assembly on 29 July led to a roll call vote on a largely Arab-sponsored resolution, which called for the establishment of a Palestinian State in the West Bank and Gaza and omitted any reference to Israel's right to exist. Because of this omission, the Nine chose to abstain. The resolution passed by a vote of 112 to 7, with 24 abstentions. It is significant that Norway, the one European country with both enormous oil and gas resources and (unlike Britain) a robust economy, chose to vote against the resolution, along with the US, Israel, Australia and Canada.

EUROPE'S CONSTRAINED ROLE IN THE MIDDLE EAST

There are those who regard Europe's role as positive and constructive in the ME. In June 1980, for example, European policy-makers claimed that the US Secretary of State, Cyrus Vance, and the State Department had privately expressed the view that it was useful for Europe both to exert pressure on Israel (over its position on the West Bank and the role of the Palestinians) and moderate Palestinians (over recognition of Israel). From a related perspective, it was argued that European efforts to establish or expand special relationships in the region—for example, that of France with Iraq—helped to maintain a Western entrée to the region at a time when America's intimate relationship with Israel might otherwise force the Arab States to make a dangerous choice between the US and USSR.

Europeans could also claim that their efforts sought to move the peace process beyond Camp David in order to include the Palestinians, who would otherwise constitute a major destabilizing factor; and that their position had the virtue of insisting upon both Israel's right to existence and security and recognition of the Palestinians' legitimate rights.

The Nine did appear to have moved toward greater internal agreement and co-operation on ME issues than had previously characterized their foreign policies. The gap between the Dutch, the Danes, and to some extent the Germans (all of whom had previously been more sympathetic to Israel) and the French and Irish, who had been more favourably disposed toward the Arab and Palestinian claims, seemed to have narrowed, with the European consensus moving more in the direction of the French position. This was evident at the UN on the question of Palestinian rights. The absention of the Nine in July 1980 represented a shift away from the pattern of previous years when the French had abstained while their partners voted against. At the same time, the policies of the Begin Government over West Bank autonomy, settlements and the Jerusalem annexation may have affected the position of some European Governments previously more favourable toward the Israeli position. The 1977 defeat of the Israeli Labour Government had also weakened a source of support within the Socialist International movement, particularly among the West Germans. Moreover, the European dependence on Arab oil could not fail to become a major factor in determining the political climate in which European policies were made.

President Giscard d'Estaing dismissed as "absurd" criticisms that "our policy is dictated by petroleum considerations," adding that France had been interested in the ME well before oil had become a problem.[10] Nonetheless, the implicit but primordial factor driving Europe's position on Middle Eastern issues was that of energy dependence. Above all, European policies in the region were designed to establish a *modus vivendi* with Arab oil producers in order to buffer themselves against the consequences of the continued Arab-Israeli conflict and especially against any further worsening of the conflict.

What, then, is the balance-sheet on these European efforts, not only in their own terms but also as they affect the Arab-Israeli conflict as well as Europe's energy security? In essence, it is difficult to avoid the conclusion that these policies have not been strikingly successful. The former Israeli Foreign Minister, Abba Eban, criticized the European initiatives as undercutting the Camp David peace process and rewarding intransigence. "If Europe grants recognition to the PLO before any Palestinian organization has accepted the axiom of Israel's statehood," he wrote, "it squanders one of the incentives which . . . might have induced moderate impulses in the Palestinian community."[11] Other Israeli leaders opposed to the Begin Government's policies were no less critical of the European role. The general Israeli resentment about what was felt to be a European tilt toward the Arabs has deprived the Nine of an effective role as an *interlocuteur valable*. Eban, for example, noted the absence of any constructive European contribution to the series of conciliation efforts between 1973 and 1979. As he put it, "Having placed a parochial and mercantile approach above Israel's survival and Western solidarity, Europe could not expect to be taken seriously as a disinterested conciliator in later months."

Ironically, this distancing from Israel undercuts, not only Europe's role as an intermediary, but also its stature in the Arab world since it so clearly lacks the influence with Israel which, by contrast, the US possesses. The attenuated mission by Gaston Thorn clearly reflects this situation. Moreover, the tangible achievements for the Europeans in protecting their energy sources remain decidedly limited. From 1973 to 1979, the Europeans, including the French, received no substantial quantities of oil which would not otherwise have been available to them; and they enjoyed no significant preferential pricing for their supplies. While an increased number of state-to-state oil deals have been negotiated (e.g., between France and Iraq), any major disruption of oil supplies, regardless of the cause, would trigger the emergency oil-sharing system of the International Energy Agency (IEA). Although France is not formally an IEA member, it is indirectly associated through participation in the analogous sharing arrangement of the European Community, all of whose other members do belong to the IEA.

In sum, the efficacy of the EEC's Middle Eastern policies remains limited. While its policy declarations may have provided a certain degree of symbolic positioning *vis-à-vis* the Arab participants in the dialogue, Europe's oil dependence, its lack of substantial military forces in the region, its fundamental security dependence upon the US, and the limits on its ability to shape events in the ME, whether in the Israeli-Palestinian conflict, the Iraqi-Iranian war or elsewhere, all constrain the Community's impact and political credit as a major, independent actor. Quite apart from the EEC's own specific attributes, including problems of agreement and lack of a political secretariat to direct its cumbersome political co-operation machinery, the broader limits on the room for manoeuvre by individual European states means that these constraints are likely to prove enduring.

Robert J. Lieber

NOTES

1. For an account of the reduction in the British sanctions, see *The New York Times (NYT)*, 30 May 1980.
2. See, e.g., French Embassy Press and Information Division, "France's Position on the American Hostages in Iran," PP/80/5. New York, June 1980.
3. For a discussion of the inception of the Euro-Arab dialogue, see Robert J. Lieber, *Oil and the Middle East War: Europe in the Energy Crisis* (Cambridge, Mass.: Harvard Center for International Affairs, 1976). The interim period is discussed in Udo Steinbach's paper "Western European and EEC Policies Towards Mediterranean and Middle Eastern Countries," in *Middle East Contemporary Survey*, Vol. 11, 1977–78, (New York and London: Holmes & Meier, 1979), especially pp. 42–45.
4. See Dominique Moïsi, "Europe and the Middle East Conflict", paper presented to the Conference on the Middle East and the Western Alliance, Center for International and Strategic Affairs, UCLA, 21–22 February 1980, p. 21.
5. *Le Monde*, Paris, 14 and 15 November 1980.
6. President Carter's veto warning is quoted in *NYT*, 1 June 1980.
7. *Le Monde*, 28 August 1980.
8. *NYT*, 21 August and 16 September 1980.
9. The texts of the EEC statement and of the official Israeli and PLO reactions are reprinted in *Survival*, London, September/October 1980, pp. 227–230.
10. Quoted in *Le Monde*, 28 June 1980. By contrast, for an analysis which stresses the importance of energy and oil, see Robert J. Lieber, "Energy, Economies and Security in Alliance Perspective," *International Security*, Cambridge, Mass., Spring 1980; and "Energy Policies of the Fifth Republic: Autonomy Versus Constraints," in William G. Andrews and Stanley Hoffmann (eds.) *The Fifth Republic at Twenty* (N.Y.: State University of New York Press, 1981).
11. Abba Eban, "The West Bank: Why Have Europe's Diplomats Played Such an Unimpressive Role?" *The Times*, London, 22 June 1980.

France and the Middle East[1]

Asked how he perceived the international role of a middle-size power like France, the Foreign Minister M. François-Poncet, replied: "The expression middle-size does not satisfy me: it contains an element of resignation that is not part of our national character. There are in the world two Super Powers and, just after, great traditional powers like France. . . ."[2] The Middle East is for France an essential piece of a global political project characterized by the attempt to transcend a purely regional role. In a world divided by blocs, France could see itself as a potential mediator between East and West and, since the concept evolved, between North and South. For France, therefore, the ME could represent an ideally suited region. Strategically, it is East-West, while economically, it can be said to be North-South.

Recent developments—such as the Iraqi-Iranian war, the Soviet military intervention in Afghanistan, the general instability of the Gulf countries, the stalemate of the peace negotiations between Israel and Egypt, and even the extension of Middle Eastern terrorism in Europe—though they have not modified the essence of French policy, have created new challenges and new opportunities for it. They have also exposed the inner limits and contradictions of French aims.

Because of its economic and strategic importance, the ME has become, in the last few years, the main theatre of conflict between East and West. It may again become, as in 1956, 1967 and 1973, a potential source of division among the Western allies. However, one element has definitely changed. What used to be merely French policy in the ME has now become largely a common European policy, partly thanks to French efforts.[3] This is not the place to discuss the relative weight of French influence, the dynamics of European co-operation, the self-isolation process of Israel and the growing energy needs of the West in the making of a common European position vis-à-vis the ME. However, such a common European policy has not replaced the traditional bilateral relationship between European and Middle Eastern countries. Within the European Economic Community (EEC) partnership competitiveness persists. While agreeing on general political statements, the European countries are not above competing with each other for the sake of privileged access to oil or for markets.

CONTINUITY AS POLICY

The ME is a region in which France has traditional interests and influence. The continuity of its policy in the region since 1967 is underlined by the sharpness with which French spokesmen repudiate the accusation that their diplomacy is purely mercantilistic and dominated by their interest in oil.[4] After it was liberated from the Algerian entanglement, France sought to re-establish its traditional influence in the Arab world, a prerequisite to achieve influence in the Third World. Such a move implied curtailing the overly close relationship with Israel based on a common anti-Arab position. Neglecting the feeling and sensitivity of public opinion and the majority of the political class, and even some administrative reluctance (translated in the "Vedettes de Cherbourg" incident), France became, after 1967, the first European country to establish a special relationship with the Arab world—providing it with military assistance, and giving it political and diplomatic support at the United Nations (UN). While defending the principle of

Israel's right to exist, France has gone as far as possible in the direction of the Arab world. It therefore originally dissociated itself from the rest of the Europeans and expressed the wish that they would follow—provided France retained its leading edge, and its role was sufficiently different to distinguish France "from the pack."

In concrete terms France's ME policy in recent years has had two significant elements:

(1) France became the first EEC member country to emphasize the importance of the Palestinian "national" question—no longer seen as a refugee problem. Already in his first presidential campaign, Giscard d'Estaing was stressing the Palestinian factor as the key to solving the conflict. He acted on this analysis by allowing Palestine Liberation Organization (PLO) representation in Paris in 1975, arranging a series of meetings between PLO leaders and French officials, including the visits of Fārūq Qaddūmī to Paris. At the same time the French retain two reservations on the Palestinian question:

(a) They use the expression *patrie* (homeland), not State, when speaking of Palestinian rights.

(b) They have not yet agreed to receive Yāsir 'Arafāt in Paris without conditions, although they would like to be the first EEC country to receive him if his visit were to be seen as a positive step toward peace, i.e. if 'Arafāt was willing to offer something in exchange—e.g. acceptance of something equivalent to Resolution 242. The French were not prepared to agree to give 'Arafāt the stamp of official legitimacy in exchange for a visit of only symbolic value.

(2) France has maintained an aloof position towards the peace process since 1977 and remains opposed to negotiations from which it is excluded, as in the Geneva talks. It pays only minimum lip-service to the American initiatives, their reservations summarized by the formula: "A global solution," not a separate peace. No precise alternative solutions were offered, except that the French would prefer a formula for negotiations preferably in a UN Security Council framework of which they would be a part. France, alone among the Nine, was very reserved about Sādāt's first visit to Jerusalem. The Government's failure to appreciate the full emotional and symbolic value of his gesture was criticized even in some French circles generally favourable to its ME policy.

Prime Minister Begin's interpretation of the Camp David accords with respect to the West Bank, the subsequent stalemate in the autonomy talks, and the refusal of Arab States to follow Egypt's lead in recognizing Israel could only reinforce France's scepticism and provide *a posteriori* justification for its initial scepticism.

The statements made by President Giscard d'Estaing during his visit to the Gulf in the Spring of 1980 simply went further in the direction of established French policy. The President, for the first time, used the term "self-determination" as the right of Palestinians—a term which had previously been used by the West Germans as early as 1974, the Belgians and the Irish in 1979. But, coming from the French with memories of the Algerian experience, "self-determination" equated with independence. In his Amman statement, Giscard d'Estaing went further towards recognizing the PLO's right to be one of the parties in a framework of international negotiations.

100

The Venice Declaration by the Nine in June 1980, though a compromise text moderated by US pressures, illustrated the direction in which the French wished its partners to go. The Declaration put even greater emphasis on the importance of finding a solution to the Palestinian problem, and the PLO was mentioned for the first time as a key to any political solution. (For text of Venice Declaration and further discussion, see essay on the European Community and the ME.)

Apart from its leading role in Europe on the Palestinian question, French policy is also noted for its important element of arms sales which forms part of its political approach to trade.[5] Unlike the Germans, the French believe they can secure markets by political declarations and diplomatic stances. This approach has proved somewhat frustrating in expanding French markets in general—if one excludes the sale of weapons, a field in which France has proved its competitiveness.[6] The delivery of planes to Iraq, in spite of its war with Iran, showed how much importance France attaches to fulfilling its military contracts. France's policy towards Iraq was welcomed in the US as it apparently prevented Baghdad from falling back into the Soviets' arms. Much more serious in the long run is France's sales of nuclear equipment to Iraq, which verges on irresponsibility.

FRANCE AND THE "DIVISION OF LABOUR"

In private the French give a functional interpretation to their ME policy which fits in with "the division of labour" argument. According to this view, it is essential for the West to maintain contacts with both the moderate and radical Arab regimes. Since the US is so close to Israel and Egypt, France feels it is important to maintain links with those countries which refuse to co-operate in the Egypt-Israeli peace process and which also happen to be oil-producing countries. While acknowledging differences of approach between the French and other West Europeans, the Americans would welcome a growing European presence in the Gulf to complement their effort; but they do so without always recognizing the fact that the Europeans are politically welcome in the oil-producing countries because, *inter alia,* of their support of the Palestinian cause. Though limited, the French military role is far from negligible. French troops in Djibouti have so far acted as a deterrent to Ethiopian ambitions. The intervention of a small French police force at the request of Saudi Arabia in Mecca proved to be decisive, but it may be difficult to repeat and could produce the very result they sought to avoid, i.e. reawaken past colonial frustration. Still, a country like France benefits from the very limitation of its military capacity; like Britain, their help and advice is more acceptable precisely because they are not Super Powers—and none of the Gulf countries have any illusion as to their capacity to replace the US. They would, in fact, wish the Americans to be less visible and more credible, while allowing a larger role to suitable West European partners.

FRANCE AND THE MIDDLE-EAST: AN ASSESSMENT

France's position in the ME conflict can no longer be dissociated from that of Europe. The mere fact that one can use the expression—Europe *vis-à-vis* the ME conflict—marks a new phenonemon, and the numerous joint statements of the Nine of the problems of the region since 1973 indicate their closer co-operation along the lines of France's declared position. However, the statements of the Nine have been mainly declaratory, with little concrete, direct impact on the situation in the ME. European Governments, like a Greek chorus, have shown a tendency to comment on events whenever they judge that something important has happened.

France and the other West Europeans are limited in their capacity to act effectively in the Arab-Israeli conflict because of two constraints. Militarily their security still rests largely on the US and economically they will remain dependent for many more years to come on the Arab oil-producing countries. From the military point of view—still the essential dimension of the conflict—France and the rest of the West Europeans do not carry enought weight compared with the Super Powers. On the diplomatic level, it is difficult for the Europeans to exert a mediating independent role, since at least one of the parties to the conflict, Israel, denies them such a role.

However, a European initiative could be indirectly useful by giving a new incentive to the Camp David process if it were presented more as complementary to, rather than as an alternative, to it. The visit paid by President Sādāt to the European Assembly in February 1981 illustrates the limited, but nevertheless significant role that the Europeans could play.

Colonel Qadhdhāfī's intervention in Chad illustrated a potential contradiction in French policy. Its ambition of having a global role embracing the Mediterranean, the ME and Africa, has given birth to a new diplomatic catchword: the trilogue. This suggests a long-term project to link the Euro-Arab dialogue and the Europe-African co-operation, and to consolidate the triangular relations between Europe, Africa and the ME. However, so far from combining harmoniously, France's African and ME policies seemed to clash the moment Qadhdhāfī's ambitions, frustrated in the ME, turned toward the African continent. Is it more important for France to maintain, at any cost, its privileged economic links with Libya or to preserve its image and interests in Africa? The choice of the latter alternative probably helps to explain the beginnings of a new *rapprochement* between Egypt and France: nothing unifies two countries more than a common foe.

One cannot, as some Americans do, describe French policy in the ME as being influenced by mercantilism alone. France does not have to stoop for oil. Its economic needs are part of a wider *realpolitik* framework in which prestige and political influence are equally, if not more, important than its economic interests. French policy is conceived as the fulfilment of a traditional role whose reactivation seems justified by reality (security and economy), and one favoured by the Arab actors themselves. It remains to be said that France's ambition may go beyond France's capacity, if not Europe's capacity—at least as long as Europe does not exist as a united force. One can also question the intellectual basis of the French approach to the ME conflict. Ultimately, the essential question remains the same as in 1948: is there an Israeli/Palestinian conflict—an assumption which, in many ways underlies the intellectual basis of the French policy; or is it an Arab/Israeli conflict, symbolizing the impossibility of reconciling Islam and the West, incarnated by Israel? If the latter is the case, a European presence to protect Western interests in countries where America's presence is not welcome, may prove in vain. It would be the West, not only America, that is rejected.

Whatever its inherent legitimacy, the Palestinian problem will have been used by all as a convenient political and intellectual alibi: by the French to get political influence and oil; by the Arabs to further their interests and to protect their regimes. There is no answer to this fundamental question, but I deeply believe that without a solution to the Palestinian problem, peace cannot be guaranteed.

Dominique Moïsi

NOTES
1. This article draws in part from a paper I presented at a conference organized by the Center for International and Strategic Affairs at UCLA on "The Middle-East and the Western Alliance", 21–23 February 1980. The proceedings of the Conference are to be published by Allen and Unwin.
2. Jean François-Poncet, "Diplomatie française, quel cadre conceptuel?", *Politique Internationale* No. 6, Paris, Hiver 1979–80, p. 9. Translated by the author.
3. cf. Dominique Moïsi, "L'Europe et le conflit israelo-arabe", *Politique Etrangère*, No. 4, Paris, 1980.
4. French Oil supplies come from Saudi Arabia (32.87%), Iraq (23.43%), Nigeria (10.05%), Abū Dhabi (5.71%), Algeria (4.33%), Kuwait (3.98%), Iran (2.53%), Qatar (2.37%), Libya (1.91%); period January-June 1980.
5. cf. Edward Kolodziej, "France and the Arms Trade", *International Affairs,* London, January 1980.
6. French arms sales to the ME represented, in 1979, 60% of France's global military exports. France's recent naval contracts with Saudi Arabia and with Qatar will push French arms sales from 23 bn francs to a much higher level.

Dilemmas and Problems for China in the Middle East

The Russian intervention in Afghanistan in one sense enhanced the credibility of China's insistent warnings about the expansionist tendencies of "Soviet hegemonism"; but in another sense it exacerbated problems and tensions in China's foreign policy as a whole, and in the Middle East in particular.

These problems arose because of the tendency of China's leaders to subordinate specific bilateral foreign relations issues to questions concerning the supposed Soviet global threat. Considerations concerning the perceived Soviet challenge in the ME impelled China to support (with some reservations) the Camp David peace process. This, of course, raised problems for China in maintaining good relations with the Palestine Liberation Organization (PLO) and with some of the governments of the Arab Rejectionist Front. It would hardly have served Chinese interests if these turned even more strongly towards the Soviet Union.

In terms of great power relations, the Russian military intervention in Afghanistan caused the suspension of Sino-Soviet governmental talks and brought China and the US closer together. However, this latest example of what the Chinese regarded as Russian expansionism intensified Chinese calls for an anti-hegemonist international united front since they regarded it as essential that local conflicts in various parts of the world should be subordinated (if not settled) to the over-riding need to unite in resistance to the Soviet danger.

During the course of 1980, China's leaders identified a coherent strategy behind recent Soviet moves. In their view the Soviet Union was engaged in nothing less than a "Southward drive" to gain control over the Gulf and the key sea routes extending from the Horn of Africa in the West to South-East Asia (including the Straits of Malacca) in the East. In this perspective, the Soviet and Vietnamese military occupations of Afghanistan and Kampuchea (Cambodia) were linked not only as examples of unacceptable military intervention in the affairs of neighbouring countries, but also as part of the general strategy of the "Southward drive".

From a Chinese perspective there was both a method and a purpose to Russian "opportunism". Local conflicts were perceived as serving Soviet interests, which led China's leaders to imply that the Soviet Union had instigated them. Thus, just as Soviet commentators accused the US of being behind the war between Iraq and Iran, so Chinese commentators poured scorn on this allegation and, in turn, argued that it was the Russians who sought to exploit the conflict to their own ends. Thus the Russian claim was dismissed as "Moscow's attempt . . . to mislead the public and fish in troubled water". One Chinese commentator went on to argue: "It is known to all that the turmoil in the Gulf region cannot do any harm to the oil-exporting Soviet Union; on the contrary, it will only pave the way for the Soviet Union to step in at this sensitive region, upon which it has long kept a covetous eye".[1] He concluded hopefully: "This cannot but draw the attention of the world's peace-loving countries".

Unfortunately for China's foreign policy-makers, the shifting sands of ME politics do not lend themselves to such a coherent and single-minded approach. So far from China being seen as a disinterested external power, which has consistently supported the "just cause" of the Arabs and which has been their constant ally against interventionist external forces, it has often been perceived in the past by governments in the area as having very definite great power interests of its own

104

and of having been an unpredictable and often wayward friend of the Arab cause, seeking in fact to subordinate Arab interests to its own. Currently, China is frequently seen by the Arab countries as obsessed by the Soviet Union; its support for the Camp David process is considered by some (probably wrongly) to be a result of the domestic shift to the Right in China following the death of Mao.[2]

China's new leaders' support (which, as we shall see, is not unqualified) for the Camp David process is in fact wholly consistent with the Chinese Communist approach to the ME. They have always regarded the region from a geopolitical point of view as of great significance for China's national security concerns, as well as for determining the global balance of power.[3] Consequently, China's leaders have tended to regard the local conflicts in the ME as secondary in importance to external intervention by the two Super Powers. Indeed, China's leaders have at times asserted that it is the tension between the two Super Powers which has caused them to keep alive the enduring local conflicts.

The Chinese leaders have maintained that these conflicts could have been resolved but for the two Super Powers. In the 1950s the Chinese leaders regarded the US as the main threat as an expansionist power and, therefore, as the main enemy to China and indeed to the Arab people; in the 1970s it is the Soviet Union which is seen to be the major threat. At the beginning of the 1980s, the Soviet threat was seen to have intensified. Thus if the 1950s required an anti-American international united front so, in the Chinese view, an anti-Soviet front is called for in the current period. For example, a *People's Daily* commentator argued on 1 August 1980 that while the US has a "clear bias for Israel", the Soviet Union "tries hard to maintain a state of 'no war, no peace' in the ME so as to gain strategic positions and control of the region's oil resources. That would give it leverage against the West, outflank Western Europe, overtake the US and, ultimately, dominate the world."[4] Contrary to certain Arab views, an explanation for the Chinese support of the Camp David accords does not require an exercise in Pekingology. It was seen as the most promising prospect for a peaceful settlement of the Arab-Israeli conflict which, at the same time, excluded the Soviet Union from the peace process itself.

Following the 1973 Arab-Israeli war (which has come to influence quite a few Chinese military strategists on the new character of modern warfare), China's leaders have stopped encouraging Arab leaders to settle the conflict by armed force. In their view such an approach would only benefit the Soviet Union as the one credible alternative arms supplier to the Americans. China could not compete in this league. Thus Peking put such weight as it possesses behind President Sādāt. (He, after all, had been the first Third World leader to expel a mammoth Soviet presence from his country on the ground that his country's independence was being stifled). Against the charges that Sādāt was betraying the larger Arab cause, the Chinese pointed to his proclaimed commitment to the recovery of lost Arab lands, restoration of Palestinian peoples' national rights and an overall settlement. But, above all, the Chinese stressed that Sādāt "held direct negotiations with Israel to get rid of Soviet control over the ME peace talks." They argued, perhaps less convincingly, that "in a certain sense this also weakens the US manipulations of the talks".[5]

BRIDGING THE GAP WITH THE PLO

China's leaders sought to ensure that their endorsement of Sādāt's approach did not lead to a breach with the PLO. After all, China was the first non-Arab state to allow the PLO to establish a diplomatic mission in its capital, and its leaders have taken pride in their consistent support for the Palestinian cause. Moreover, China had an interest in ensuring that the PLO did not turn exclusively to Moscow. The Chinese had initially maintained that it was only some Arab countries and the PLO who opposed the Camp David process, while the others either had reservations about it, or supported it.[6] Libya, however, openly broke with China on the issue.[7] A Palestinian delegation which visited China a year after Sādāt's visit to Jerusalem, expressed its "astonishment" at China's support for Camp David at the "expense of our people and our cause".[8] Beginning in April 1979 the Chinese sought to bridge the gap by arguing that the Egypt-Israel Treaty was but the "first step" towards an overall settlement. Sādāt was depicted as working towards that objective, but was being obstructed by the American bias towards Israel and the "wanton stand" of the Begin Government. China then went on to endorse explicitly, for the first time, the "right of the Palestinian people to set up their own State".

Thereafter, the Chinese endorsed a supposedly "new way to solve the ME problem", as suggested by some in Western Europe and the US; this "aimed at urging the PLO to recognize Israel's right to exist and at urging Israel to deal with the PLO".[9] In October 1979, China's most prominent ME specialist, the Vice-Foreign Minister, He Ying, paid a visit to several supposedly moderate Arab countries in an effort to reconcile them to Egypt's position along Chinese lines. He also met with PLO leaders. When a delegation led by Khālid al-Fāhūm, President of the Palestine National Council, returned his visit in the following month, it was told: "So long as the Palestinian people stick to their aims, adopt practical steps and combine their principled position with a flexible strategy their struggle will have a bright future". As well as being advised to be "practical" and "flexible", the PLO was commended for "the remarkable results" which its "diplomatic activities" had achieved in a "short time."[10] The Palestinians, however, were apparently unconvinced and called for a denunciation of the Egyptian-Israeli peace treaty.[11]

The Russian invasion of Afghanistan impelled the Chinese to try even harder to bridge the gap. Soon after the establishment of diplomatic relations between Egypt and Israel in February 1980, the Chinese quoting Arab and other Third World sources, began to argue that "the Palestinian problem is the crux of the Arab-Israeli conflict and that, so long as it remains unsolved, there can be no peace and security in the ME". Typically, however, this point was explained in terms of Chinese appreciation of the imperatives of global geopolitics. The commentary explained: "The current situation calls for all forces in the world to unite against the thrust of the Soviet hegemonists in the Gulf and in the ME, so it is all the more necessary to contain the Israeli expansionists and strive for a settlement of the Palestinian problem". In addition to endorsing the argument that this problem was the "crux" of instability in the ME, the Chinese commentary also adopted the essence of the Egyptian position that the US was the only force capable of exerting sufficient influence on Israel to acquiesce to Palestinian demands. Moreover, the Chinese sought to square the circle by arguing that, only by pressurizing Israel on the Palestinian issue, could the US hope to succeed in the professed Carter goal of countering the Soviet challenge in the Gulf. It is worth quoting the same Xinhua News Agency commentary at length on this:

"In the US, after President Carter put forth his strategy of countering Soviet challenges in the Gulf area, some people pointed out that if the US did not bring pressure to bear on Israel and if the Palestinian question was not resolved speedily, the strategy would not be effective.

Robert Byrd, leader of the Democratic Party in the US Senate, said that as long as there was the Palestinian question, our ability to co-operate with Arab countries in meeting the common danger of possible Soviet expansionism is hampered.

The Carter Administration has recently officially criticized the Israeli authorities for settling Jewish people in Khālid and reiterated that it would attach importance to the Palestinian question. But, up to now, no major step has been taken.

Diplomatic observers here [i.e., Cairo] are watching with concern how far Washington will go on this vital question."[12]

In other words, a new line had emerged. Its essence was that the Palestine issue was the crux of the ME problem, whose solution had been made urgent by the Russian invasion of Afghanistan, and that America alone had the power to exert sufficient pressure on Israel. This new line was obviously regarded by China's leaders as the way of bridging the gap between the Egyptian approach, largely supported by China, and the Rejectionist Front in general and the PLO in particular.

At this point the divisions in the Palestinian Camp affected relations with China. The more narrowly-based and "radical" Popular Front for the Liberation of Palestine (PFLP) openly broke with China, whereas the more broadly-based and "moderate" al-Fath majority faction still sought to keep open the Chinese door. An al-Fath delegation, led by Abū Jihād, visited China in August and issued a joint communiqué claiming mutual "satisfaction" with the meeting and talks. The communiqué reaffirmed Chinese support for the Palestinian cause and Palestinian "national rights"; while the Palestinian side expressed "praise" for China's "principled stand on the ME question" and "thanked" China for its "genuine aid and support". The communiqué went on to recognize the Palestinian issue as "the core of the ME question", and endorsed the PLO as the "sole legitimate representative of the Palestinian people". It called for an "early" settlement and demanded Israeli recognition of the Palestinian right to statehood and of the PLO's "right to participation in the effort to seek a comprehension and just settlement of the ME question".[13]

Thus, the communiqué skilfully managed to reach an agreement which papered over the differences between the two sides so that the Chinese did not have to disavow the Egyptian effort, nor did the al-Fath have to endorse it. Nevertheless, the differences between the two sides became manifest when the same delegation went on to North Korea the following day, where its leader spoke of their "common struggle against US imperialists and the Zionists".[14] For its part, the PFLP eschewed China altogether. It sent a delegation in September to Vietnam and to Vietnamese-dominated Phnom Penh where its leader, Abū 'Alī Mustafā, said that the "Palestinian people would always remain on the side of the Kampuchean people in the struggle against the US imperialists, *Chinese expansionists* and international reactionaries" (emphasis added).[15]

Later Chinese commentaries noted that the American election process and the significance of the Jewish vote meant that no substantive progress would be expected on the Palestinian issue (still regarded as the core of the ME question) before 1981. In the Chinese view, urgent as its resolution was, this was ultimately dependent upon the ability and willingness of the American Administration to put sufficient pressure on Israel.[16] Meanwhile, Chinese Foreign Ministry spokesmen denied claims that an offer had been made to train and arm 30,000 men of the PLO,[17] or that any Chinese contacts or relations had been established with

Israel.[18] Nevertheless, rumours persisted that contacts had been made. Indeed, an unlikely rumour received wide currency that China was about to complete a $2 bn arms deal with Israel.[19] Perhaps one reason for the persistence of these rumours from unnamed sources (which were repeated and magnified in the Soviet media) was the apparent underlying logic of the Chinese position of opposition to the Soviet Union. The persistance of these rumours or, perhaps more significant, the insistence of Chinese formal denials is itself an indication of Peking's difficulties in bridging the gap with the PLO.

LINKAGE BETWEEN FAR AND MIDDLE EASTERN PROBLEMS

A new complexity in China's relations with the countries of the ME arose in 1980 from the way in which its own conflict with Vietnam became a new factor in the international politics of the ME. In view of China's criticism of the triangular links between South Yemen, Ethiopia and the Soviet Union, it was perhaps hardly surprising that a close diplomatic relationship should be established between South Yemen and Vietnam. A Vietnamese delegation, headed by the legendary General Vo Nguyen Giap, paid an official visit to South Yemen from 10–12 November 1980. A joint communiqué expressed mutual support for the positions of the two sides which, of course, coincided with those of the Soviet Union and criticized the Chinese as "international reactionaries."[20] As if to illustrate the differences, General Giap's visit to South Yemen coincided with a visit to Somalia by China's veteran Vice-Premier, Li Xiannian, who declared on the same day: "China and Somalia agree, by and large, in their view on such major world issues as the Gulf area, Afghanistan and Kampuchea."[21]

In view of Libya's hostility to China's position it was hardly surprising that Peking should publicly note the concern voiced by several African countries at the Libyan "invasion" of Chad.[22] But the position of Syria—as a country bordering on Israel and with claims (legitimate in China's eyes) to the Golan Heights and holding the rein in the Lebanon war—was altogether more complex from a Chinese perspective. The Syrian announcement to withdraw from the Lebanon (so far not implemented) was largely blamed in a Chinese commentary on a prior visit to Damascus by the Soviet Foreign Minister and Politburo member, Andrei Gromyko.[23] The announced merger between Syria and Libya elicited no comment from Chinese sources. However, Chinese commentaries drew great satisfaction from the apparently successful mediation of Saudi Arabia between Jordan and Syria following the massing of troops along their common border.[24]

It was fortunate from a Chinese perspective that Afghanistan was a Muslim as well as a non-aligned country, since it made it that more difficult for fellow-Muslim countries in the ME to side with the Russians. In particular it meant that, however great the hatred by Iranian Mullahs for the US as "the great Satan", they had no difficulty in resisting Russian blandishments.[25] It also meant that China could safely leave the lobbying on the relevant United Nations votes on Kampuchea and its linkage with Afghanistan to the Association of South East Asian Nations (ASEAN) countries. India's recognition of the Heng Semrin regime in Kampuchea remained an idiosyncratic, quixotic gesture without any significant follow-up in the ME. On the surface, the Chinese did not have to engage in any major diplomatic manoeuvering. As against that, the latent differences between China and some of the ASEAN countries may yet emerge into the open, and the linkage to be established with ME countries may turn on the continued resistance capacities of the Afghani tribesmen. The problem for China's leaders is that they lack sufficient leverage on the parties concerned to effectively determine outcomes. In that sense they are, in effect, prisoners of events and must await others to act on issues which they regard as vital to themselves.

Taiwan is another issue in which Chinese regional interests in the Far East have a direct impact on their ME relations. The Saudi Royal House has long eschewed formal relations with the "godless" government in Peking, preferring instead to maintain diplomatic relations with the Taiwan authorities. The latter have also benefited from arms purchases from Israel and, notwithstanding China's diplomatic relations with Oman, they too have excellent commercial relations.[26]

CONCLUSIONS

The Russian invasion of Afghanistan has made the ME even more salient from a Chinese perspective. However, lacking sufficient access to the region or sufficient economic, military and political influence, China has sought to rely on the Islamic and nationalist aspirations of the local countries to resist further Russian incursions. But, in a more immediate sense, China has become even more dependent upon American readiness to act with greater authority and self-confidence in the region. As the Chinese themselves have recognized, this has not been possible in an American Presidential election year. As a result, China's active diplomacy over the past year may be described as having been a holding exercise in which vigorous attempts have been made to give least offence to the Rejectionist Front while still supporting the Sādāt initiative. This has raised the greatest difficulty in relations with the PLO. The two sides have hovered on the brink of a break and, indeed, the PFLP faction has to all intents and purposes itself initiated a breach. But the main centrist faction, the al-Fatḥ, joined with the Chinese in papering over the cracks. While it may be argued that China can, at best, only marginally affect ME outcomes it would still be a dangerous step for the PLO to sever relations with Peking. Moreover, there may be many forces in the ME which quietly agree in their own way with the Chinese position that the Soviet Union constitutes the main danger, and that much depends on whether Israel can be pressurized by the US to change course.

Michael B. Yahuda

NOTES

1. Xinhua News Agency commentary, 24 September 1980, in BBC Summary of World Broadcasts (BBC SWB) FE/6533/A4/1.
2. See "China's Cynical Switch from Support for PLO", *Events*, London, 23 March 1979 p. 23.
3. For an excellent and comprehensive account see Yitzhak Shichor, *The Middle East in China's Foreign Policy 1949–77*, Cambridge University Press, 1979, pp. 1–8 and 162–3.
4. *Beijing Review*, Peking, No. 32, 11 August 1980, p. 10.
5. Xinhua commentary, 4 March 1978.
6. Peking Home Service, 28 February 1979 in BBC SWB, FE/6060/A4/1.
7. On 6 January the Libyan General People's Congress cut off trade and other co-operative relations with China, see BBC SWB, Part 4, ME/6312/A/11.
8. Cited in Yitzhak Shichor, "Just Stand and Just Struggle: China and the Peace Process in the Middle East", p. 11 to be published in *Australian Journal of Chinese Affairs*, Australian National University Press, Canberra.
9. Xinhua commentary, 22 August 1979.

10. "Middle East: Hua Guofeng Reaffirms Three Principles" in *Beijing Review* No. 48, 30 November 1979, pp. 8–9 and *People's Daily* commentary, Peking, 1 December 1979.
11. Yitzhak Shichor, "Just Struggle . . .", *op. cit.* p. 15.
12. "Settlement of Palestinian Issue Becomes Urgent" Xinhua commentator from Cairo. *Beijing Review* No. 10, 10 March 1980 p. 29.
13. Xinhua, 26 August 1980 in BBC SWB, FE/6508/A4/2.
14. *Ibid.*, FE/6508/A4/2.
15. Vietnam News Agency, Hanoi, 21 September 1980 in BBC SWB, FE/6542/A4/3.
16. Xinhua commentary, 23 August 1980 from Washington correspondent.
17. BBC SWB, FE/6534/A4/2.
18. *Beijing Review*, No. 30, 28 July 1980, p. 8; and *ibid.* No. 35, 1 September 1980, p. 13.
19. *Newsweek*, New York, 24 November 1980; repeated in the same week in *Encounter*, London.
20. BBC SWB, FE/6575/A4/1 and 2, 14 November 1980.
21. *Ibid.*, FE/6575/A5/1.
22. Beijing Home Service, 14 November 1980, in BBC SWB FE/6581/A4/2.
23. Quoting foreign news services a Chinese commentary blamed the decision to withdraw Syrian forces and thus again create turmoil in the Lebanon on Foreign Minister Gromyko's recent visit to Damascus. His alleged interest was to divert attention from Moscow's intervention in Afghanistan to the Israel-Egypt peace agreement. *Beijing Review*, No. 9, 3 March 1980, p. 12.
24. Commentary, "Syria-Jordan Border", *Beijing Review*, No. 51, 22 December 1980, p. 10.
25. "Iran Refuses Soviet Military Aid" *Beijing Review*, No. 4, 28 January 1980, p. 11 and "The Iranians Did Right", *ibid.*, No. 36, 8 September 1980, p. 14.
26. Paul Wilson, "A Diplomatic Dike is Breached", *Far Eastern Economic Review Week*, Hong Kong, 26 December 1980 to 1 January 1981, pp. 8–9.

African States and the Middle East

Africa is politically closely linked to the Middle East through four international groupings with overlapping memberships: the Organization of African Unity (OAU), the League of Arab States (LAS), the Organization of the Islamic Conference (OIC), and the Non-aligned movement. These do not constitute, except in the very loosest sense, an alliance; but they do provide important world platforms for African and Arab leaders; at the same time these links make it inevitable that each of the member-states is drawn into every contentious issue facing any of their number in every corner of the Third World.

Since Israel finds itself automatically excluded from belonging to any of these international groupings, it is placed at a strong disadvantage *vis-à-vis* this influential international sub-system, whose members also constitute a powerful lobby within the United Nations (UN). Despite the schismatic nature of each of the four groupings, all of them can be counted upon to adopt, more or less, hostile attitudes towards almost any criticizable aspect of Israeli policy, with one exception: its claim to exist as a sovereign state (at least within the 1967 borders) is strongly upheld by the great majority of OAU members and a smaller, but still, large majority of the Non-aligned nations. Moreover, on this single issue even the LAS finds itself divided since Egypt's peace agreement with Israel; but even before then most of the LAS members had given, at least, nominal support to this principle by their acceptance of Resolution 242.

If Israel is to regain the position it held in the Third World before 1973, it is to the African grouping in this Third World network of relationships that it must look for a breakthrough. However, hopes of such a shift flowing out of the establishment of diplomatic links between Cairo and Jerusalem remain unfulfilled. On the other hand, efforts to drive Israel into an even tighter corner in 1980 were also unsuccessful—despite the failure of the Palestinian autonomy talks, the Jerusalem Law and the policy of thickening Jewish settlements on the West Bank. The majority of African leaders—even those well-disposed to Israel—saw all these issues as being extremely provocative.

Perhaps fortunately for Israel, African leaders were less preoccupied in 1980 with its policies, or even with the Palestinian question, than with four other issues affecting their relations with the Arab and Islamic worlds, as well as with the West and the Communists: Afghanistan, the Iraqi-Iranian war, Colonel Qadhdhāfī's Islamic crusade and, above all, with the terrifying impact on their economies of higher oil prices and the huge rise in the cost of imports from industrial countries.

AFGHANISTAN AND THE GULF AREA

The African countries were very largely united in taking a strongly critical view of the Soviet Union's military intervention in Afghanistan. Only three of them (Angola, Mozambique and Ethiopia) cast their votes against the condemnatory resolution passed by the UN General Assembly. The great majority saw the attack as an invasion of a small Third World country by a Super Power. The fact that Afghanistan was a Muslim nation was an added reason for the Islamic African countries to condemn the Russians. But the dominant theme in African reactions was the perennial fear that Third World crises—Afghanistan, the Iraqi-Iranian war and the Gulf area after the Shah's overthrow—would be exploited by the Super

Powers. This theme was strongly expressed by Tanzania's President Julius Nyerere:

"Following the invasion of Afghanistan by Soviet troops, the US has been stepping up its naval presence in the Indian Ocean. They have sought, and been granted, military bases on the East-African coast; this is of concern to all of us in the Indian Ocean region, especially to us in East Africa. Moreover, whatever is done by us, the weak nations, to oppose oppression, is judged by the Super Powers in relation to their own tug-of-war, without regard to the aspirations of those involved. All of this means that we live in an extremely dangerous world. It is evident that such disputes, the way that they are viewed by the Super Powers and the manner in which they are tackling them, threaten the Non-aligned countries and the independence of small nations. This concerns us. The strength of a small nation like ours lies in its membership of a group of similar small nations who refuse to be pulled this way or that by the Super Powers."[1]

Only Senegal in black Africa took sides in the Iraq-Iran conflict, which Africans saw as an unmitigated disaster. Wars between Third World countries—especially prominent, radical states—are always upsetting to the Non-aligned: their image of themselves is that they are not as greedy, selfish or power-hungry as the major powers; that they set a greater store by human values and better understand the importance of not allowing war to destroy their precious resources. In the case of the Iraqi-Iranian war they also feared the consequences for themselves if a prolonged conflict led to another substantial rise in the price of oil—and, as already mentioned, they were anxious about the risk of Super Power involvement in the conflict. For all these reasons they threw their full weight behind the various efforts at mediation.

Most African countries were also remarkably silent about developments in Khomeyni's Iran and the unsettling effects on the surrounding Gulf area. There was no significant comment about the taking of the American hostages, but some criticism of the US effort to release them by the use of force. Such criticism as was offered, was directed at the Super Powers—urging, and warning, them not to become involved in the Iranian revolution, and not to build up their military forces in the Gulf area. America's renewed interest in acquiring military bases in the Gulf, Red Sea and Indian Ocean regions was widely criticized by anti-Soviet African leaders as well as by those more predictably likely to adopt a critical attitude. Their objections were two-fold: the acquisition of bases by either of the Super Powers provides a pretext for the other to seek similar facilities to maintain the military balance; and that bases, whether American or Russian, are potential threats to governments in the regions which happen to be opposed to the policies of the occupying power.

RADICAL ISLAM AS A DIVISIVE FACTOR

The political element of Islam was never a serious factor in disturbing Afro-Arab relations until Colonel Qadhdhāfī launched his militant Islamic mission into Saharan Africa in late 1980, and created a specific Islamic Legion to fulfil his objectives—variously described as aiming at a Libyan-dominated Islamic Empire in the Sahara or a campaign to enhance the political role of Muslim communities in black Africa. The Libyan leader's intervention in countries like Uganda, under Amin's rule, were generally treated as typical of his maverick policies; but his

112

military intervention in Chad and his proposals to unify it with Libya stirred African leaders to reassess his role—more especially as his Chadian adventure coincided with the exposure of attempts at subversion in countries like the Gambia, Mali, Senegal, the Central African Republic, Niger and, it was strongly suspected, even in the Muslim northern areas of Nigeria. In a matter of days, francophone and anglophone African leaders joined in an unusual display of unity to denounce Qadhdhāfī's Islamic fanaticism and his attempts to subvert his neighbours. These criticisms were voiced by Muslims no less than by Christians; the fact that a number of Arab States—like Sudan, Tunisia, Morocco and Egypt—also joined in denouncing Qadhdhāfī helped prevent the Libyan leader's role from becoming a divisive issue between Africans and Arabs. Nevertheless, Qadhdhāfī's peculiar brand of radical Islam suddenly became as disturbing to Muslims as to non-Muslims in the African region.

AFRO-ARAB RELATIONS
Strenuous but largely unsuccessful efforts were made during 1980 to revive the close political ties between the OAU and the LAS, which had been disrupted in 1979 by the expulsion of Egypt from the Arab League. (See *Middle East Contemporary Survey* [*MECS*] 1979–80, pp. 75–79.) In his report to the OAU Council of Ministers' meeting in Addis Ababa in February 1980, the Secretary-General, Edem Kodjo, spoke of the "abortive meetings" held to restore Afro-Arab co-operation. The Council reaffirmed "the principle according to which OAU member-states have the right to be invited to, and participate in all meetings of Afro-Arab co-operation." This decision was a rebuff to the LAS because of its continued refusal to allow Egypt to be present at their meetings with the OAU. The Council of Ministers also called for further consultations to end this impasse and to arrange for the holding of the Fifth Session of the Standing Commission of the OAU and LAS, the First Session of the Joint Afro-Arab Ministerial Conference, and the Second Session of the Afro-Arab Summit Conference. (No summit had been held, despite repeated efforts, since the first one in 1976.)

Edem Kodjo held the first round of his new consultations with the LAS in Tunis from 19–24 March 1980. He described the consultations[2] as an effort to find "ways and means of ironing out the differences which, earlier on, had led to the repeated postponement of joint Afro-Arab meetings, at the request of the Arab League, especially the Joint Conference of Arab and African Ministers of Information, the Fifth Session of the Standing Commission and the First Session of the Joint Afro-Arab Ministerial Conference. Kodjo outlined the OAU stand on Egypt's right to attend all Afro-Arab co-operation meetings, while Chedli Klibi, Secretary-General of the LAS, reiterated his organization's stand as defined in the resolutions of the Council of the Arab League in Baghdad. He pointed out that the Baghdad resolution was "aimed especially at excluding Egypt from joint Afro-Arab activities and meetings." (Later, when reporting on his consultations to the Council of Ministers, Kodjo pointed out: "It should especially be emphasized that it was this problem which was at the origin of the postponement *sine die* of the First Ordinary Session of the Joint Afro-Arab Ministerial meeting scheduled to be held in Tripoli in January 1980.) Since there could be no possible meeting point on this central issue, the first round of consultations ended with the two Secretaries-General saying that "considering the present political situation, it was still premature to attempt to convene joint Afro-Arab meetings, either at Ministerial or Summit level." At the same time they reaffirmed the need to do everything possible to maintain and sustain "the torch of Afro-Arab co-operation", and

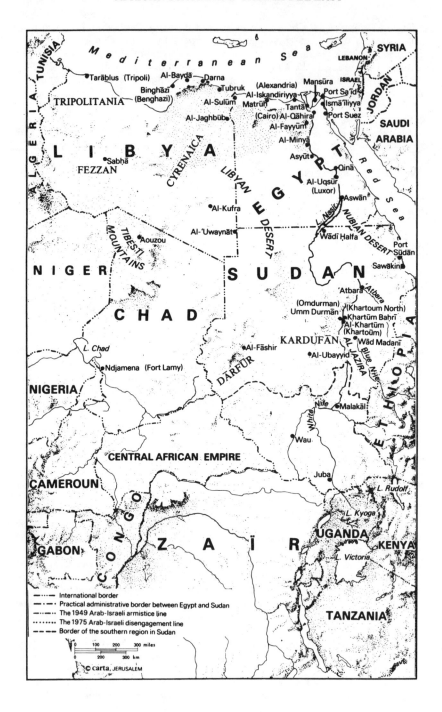

proposed a way out of the impasse: meetings to be held outside the framework of the LAS. These would take the form of joint consultations between African and Arab economic and financial bodies such as the Arab National Development Funds, the African Development Bank (ADB), the Arab Bank for Economic Development in Africa (BADEA) and the Economic Commission for Africa (ECA). The purpose of these meetings would be to identify suitable areas for co-operation, to co-ordinate project studies and arrange for their financing. The substance of this proposal was, in fact, first made by the Council of Ministers in Monrovia in 1979.

Edem Kodjo's second round of consultations took place in Tripoli from 22–24 March. The choice of this venue was because the Libyan Government was to have hosted the First Afro-Arab Ministerial Conference, cancelled at the request of the LAS because of the Egyptian issue. The Libyans predictably reiterated the LAS stand on boycotting Egypt, ruling out any joint meetings where they would be present.

At both the Tunis and Tripoli meetings, Kodjo and Klibi also discussed the difference between the Libyans and Tunisians over the Gafsa episode in January 1980. (See essay on inter-Arab relations.) They agreed to support efforts to help settle the dispute. (The OAU also set up a special committee to investigate the Tunisian complaints against Libya; its inconclusive findings formed part of the Secretary-General's report to the Council of Ministers' meeting in Freetown in July 1980.)

Kodjo and Klibi met for a third round of consultations in Tunis from 30 May to 1 June 1980. Their discussions ranged over the situation in Southern Africa and the political problems of the ME. While no progress was made in ending the impasse over Egypt's role in Afro-Arab co-operation, they agreed on "the urgent need to review the structural machinery of Afro-Arab co-operation," and proposed that periodic meetings should be held between African and Arab specialized technical institutions including bodies with similar, or complementary, objectives. They also agreed on "priority actions" to reactivate Afro-Arab co-operation in three areas:

(1) *Political Co-operation*

To co-ordinate efforts to "harmonize the positions" of the two organizations (OAU and LAS) for a just and equitable solution to be found to the ME problem on the one hand, and the liberation of Namibia and elimination of apartheid in South Africa on the other.

To co-operate with Arab financial institutions to provide effective and rapid assistance to the new Republic of Zimbabwe.

To recommend that the Co-ordinating Committee should meet at least twice a year "to define the political orientation of this co-operation and to co-ordinate the different activities of Afro-Arab co-operation." The first meeting would be held at the end of July 1980.

To establish a Standing Advisory Technical Committee, composed of specialized African and Arab institutions or bodies concerned with implementing the co-operation programme.

To organize periodic consultation meetings between the OAU and LAS. Kodjo invited the Arab League to send a delegation to the next joint meeting to be held in Addis Ababa.

(This formula for overcoming the impasse between the two bodies skirted around the question of Egypt's role: if it could not be present at the proposed consultation meetings on the LAS ticket, what was to prevent it from attending as an OAU member? No clarification was offered on this point.)

115

To define a legal framework to govern the "excellent relations of co-operation" between the OAU and LAS. A joint commission was to prepare a draft agreement in time for the next joint meeting.

(2) *Trade Co-operation*

The Arab Chamber of Commerce's representative emphasized the "slow flow of trade" between Arab and African countries; it was therefore decided to invite bodies like ADB, BADEA and the ECA to undertake, as early as possible, a detailed study into the possibilities of improving this situation.

The President and Director-General of BADEA, Dr Chedli Ayari, said that no new International Economic Order could be established outside, and without, Afro-Arab co-operation. It was agreed to convene an economic conference in Kenya in January 1981 with representatives from the African and Arab private sectors.

It was further agreed to harmonize the decisions of the OAU Economic Summit held in Lagos and the Economic Summit of the Arab League due to be held in Amman "to establish an additional framework between the African and Arab economic strategies."

A final recommendation was to prepare a study for the establishment of a Guarantee and Investments Funds "to promote Arab private investment in Africa, as well as to promote Afro-Arab private trade."

(3) *Cultural Co-operation*

It was agreed to study ways of establishing a Cultural Fund and an Afro-Arab Cultural Research Centre.

Klibi proposed that the OAU Secretary-General should extend his visits and consultations to those Arab countries which are not members of the OAU in order to extend "the framework of exchange of information and experience between the two regions."

Edem Kodjo presented a report on the results of his consultations to the OAU Council of Ministers' Meeting held in Freetown from 18–28 June 1980. At the end of the meeting a resolution was adopted authorizing the Secretary-General to continue his negotiations with the LAS Secretary-General for the purpose, *inter alia*, of facilitating the resumption of the activities of the Co-ordinating Commission for Afro-Arab Co-operation. The resolution also endorsed the proposals that African and Arab economic and financial institutions should collaborate in making detailed studies on the flow of trade between the two regions; to establish an Investments Guarantee Fund; and to establish a Cultural Fund and Afro-Arab Cultural Research Centre. One entirely new recommendation was for an Afro-Arab Co-operation Department to be established within the OAU Secretariat, subject to suitable financial and administrative arrangements being made. Libya's renewed invitation to host the (postponed) first joint Afro-Arab Ministerial Conference was accepted. (Again, no reference was made to the problem of getting over Egypt's participation.)

Chedli Klibi described the progress made in his consultations with Edem Kodjo as having given a fresh impetus to Afro-Arab co-operation. "We need each other more than ever" he told Karl Lavrencic in an interview.[3] "We Arabs welcome African support in regard to Palestine, and they require our assistance in respect to their problems, especially in Southern Africa." Klibi also stressed the importance of Afro-Arab co-operation in securing a bigger say for the Third World in the International Monetary Fund (IMF) and World Bank.

A different aspect of the importance of Afro-Arab co-operation was stressed by Ablatif al-Hamad, the managing director of the Kuwait Fund. Speaking of Africa's great potential for development, he said: "One day this potential will be useful to

116

the Arabs. By assisting Africa now we may be helping our children and grandchildren."[4]

AFRICAN-ISRAELI RELATIONS

The question of re-establishing diplomatic relations between African countries and Israel received more prominence in 1980 than at any time since all but three of the OAU member-states (Malawi, Swaziland and Lesotho) broke their ties at the end of 1973. However, apart from Egypt, no practical steps were taken to resume the broken ties. But *sub rosa* diplomatic and commercial ties further improved; countries like Ivory Coast, Zaire, Ghana and Kenya have made little effort to conceal these relations.

In Kenya's case, though, the warmth of the old relations that had existed in President Jomo Kenyatta's lifetime cooled off considerably under his successor, President Daniel arap Moi. Following up his earlier success in attracting a loan worth c.£450m from Saudi Arabia in 1979 and a reported gift of c.£5m, Moi's visit to Iraq brought a loan of just under £200m and, more important, an agreement to supply Kenya with half its annual oil imports. In addition to obtaining this valuable guaranteed source of supplies, the agreement eliminated middlemen: Iraq's state oil corporation is to sell directly to Kenya's new state oil corporation. (The Iraqi-Iranian war cast a cloud over the advantages of this arrangement.) The cooling off in the formerly close relations with Israel began after President Moi's 1979 visit to Saudi Arabia but more significantly after his Iraqi deal. Nevertheless, Israel still maintains a diplomatic presence within the Swiss embassy in Nairobi and *El Al* continues to make scheduled flights through Nairobi *en route* to South Africa.

But if Israel's relations deteriorated with Kenya, they visibly improved with Nigeria since the return to civilian rule. Even under the military regime, economic ties had grown steadily stronger, with an estimated 3,000 Israeli technicians working in the country on a variety of projects. President Shagari—who is known to be personally well-disposed to Israel, even though he is himself a Muslim—disclaimed widespread reports in January 1980 that Nigeria was about to re-establish formal ties.[5] He recalled that his country had ended diplomatic relations with Israel on principle because it was occupying African lands, a situation which had not substantially changed. The President added that even if Nigeria were to overlook the ME situation, the fact that Israel still maintains good relations with "our enemy, apartheid South Africa" would make any form of reconciliation impossible. In any event, he concluded, the matter is a problem for the OAU. Despite Shagari's refutation, his Minister of External Affairs, Professor Ishaya Audu, found it necessary a month later to repeat the President's denial; but at the same time he made the significant statement that Nigeria's only condition for a resumption of relations would be a change in Israel's relations with South Africa. He added that OAU members might be able to decide their own policy towards Israel after the next summit of African Heads of State due to be held in Freetown in July. Notwithstanding these statements of official policy, public demands for ending the rift with Israel continued. The national president of Nigeria's Union of Journalists, Michael Asaju, claimed in an interview with Radio Israel on 22 July 1980 that Israelis would be contributing to building the country's new capital at Abuja, and said he felt "optimistic that diplomatic ties would soon be resumed." Asaju added: "Currently, there is a very strong agitation and demand among Nigerians that Nigeria should restore diplomatic ties with Israel."[6]

A campaign favouring ties with Jerusalem was launched by a new Ghana-Israel Association, which was formed in July 1980. Welcoming this development, the

117

Believer editorialized that the country's divorce with Israel "has done this country and her people no good."[7]

A more surprising indication of the changing tide in African opinion towards renewing relations with Israel came from Liberia's radical Foreign Minister, G. Bacchus Matthews.[8] Addressing the UN General Assembly on 26 September, he declared:

> "My Government believes that the time has come for all States that have severed diplomatic links with Israel to begin a re-examination of their policy with a view towards the establishment of some links, however limited, that will facilitate communication."

On his last visit to Africa as US Ambassador to the UN, Andrew Young canvassed support for ending the diplomatic boycott of Israel.[9] Among those whose support he sought was Tanzania's President Julius Nyerere. After their meeting Nyerere told a Press conference:

> "We do recognize the existence of the State of Israel", but added that Israel's existence was no longer the central issue because "I don't see how anyone can threaten the existence of Israel as a State. The real problem is whether the Palestinians are going to have a home of their own."

Nyerere also rejected Young's argument that black African States should play a moderating role in the ME, saying that present peace efforts precluded the active involvement of Tanzania.

A more trenchant statement of his views about Israel's policies was delivered by Nyerere on a later occasion:

> "The Middle East dispute has not yet been resolved and it is still of very grave concern to all the people in the region. Israel is still occupying large tracts of Arab land and the Palestinians have no homeland. We well understand what our own independence, and the independence of our brothers in the South, mean. But the bitterness resulting from the occupation of part of our country, the Kagera, cannot be compared to the Arab's bitterness at Israel's occupation of their lands. And the bitterness that provoked the struggle in Mozambique and Angola, or in Zimbabwe and Namibia, cannot be compared to the Palestinian bitterness. Our brothers in the South are fighting because they are being denied self-rule in their own countries. But the Palestinians are bitter because they are being chased away from their homeland, thus becoming stateless nomads. The situation in the ME and the disputes between the Super Powers constitute a grave threat to world peace."[10]

The issue of restoring relations with Israel was expected to be brought up at the OAU summit in Freetown in July 1980 but nobody, in fact, raised the question in any of the discussions. The OAU resolutions repeated the pattern of those adopted at the previous summit held in Monrovia in 1979. (See *MECS* 1978–79, pp. 76–77.) On this occasion no attempt was made, as at the previous summit, to seek Egypt's suspension from the OAU because of its agreements with Israel; nor was there any direct repudiation of the Camp David accords. The African leaders continued to give their wholehearted support to the PLO and to the Palestinians' right to a state of their own. Several resolutions fiercely criticized Israel for its links with South Africa, especially over the sale of arms.

The new chairman of the OAU, Sierra Leone's President, Siaka Stevens (known in the past for his friendly attitude to Israel), was particularly sharp in his criticism of the Begin Government's policies towards the Palestinians. After the passage of the Jerusalem Law, he sent a strong protest to the UN Secretary-General in his capacity as OAU Chairman, in which he warned:

"This act by the Israeli authorities cannot but obstruct efforts being made to arrive at a just and lasting peace in the ME."[11]

There were reports that Arab delegations would seek to challenge Israel's credentials at the opening of the UN General Assembly in September 1980. But this putative move failed to win support from the Africa Group at the UN. One reputedly influential African diplomat, who refused to be named, said that the Africans had warned the Arabs that they would balk at any attempt to oust the Israelis.[12]

AFRICAN-ARAB ECONOMIC RELATIONS

The 18th session of BADEA's board of directors, held in Khartoum from 28–29 October 1980, announced that the current year's aid operations would amount to $72m, bringing its total commitments since the Bank was founded in 1975, to $383.63m. Combined with the Bank's emergency aid operations, its overall commitments stood at $605.374m.

The actual amount of Arab aid to Africa is difficult to calculate with any degree of accuracy because apart from the various Arab aid funds, unknown sums are allocated through bilateral agreements.[13] The Kuwait Fund for Arab Economic Development (KFAED) approved $89.9m for non-Arab Africa in 1979 cf. $32 m in 1978; of the ten beneficiaries, six were non-Muslim. The Saudi Development Fund donated c. $50m in soft loans and grants to non-Arab Africa in 1980, a drop of almost half from the preceding year. The mainly Arab Organization of Petroleum Exporting Countries (OPEC) Fund approved over $209m in loans to black Africa between 1976/79, and over $900m to the Third World as a whole; another $683m was given to other development agencies. Among the 13 OPEC loans announced in October 1980, totalling $22m, five were for non-Arab Africa. Arab funds are also channelled through the European Economic Community (EEC) in joint-financing projects. According to EEC sources, these funds amounted to c.$1.1 bn out of a total of $3.87 bn. The Arab element came to 36% against the EEC's 31% and the World Bank's 12%, the rest being made up by the recipient countries themselves.[14]

While pro-Arab sources lay stress on the magnitude of the aid figures, critics analyse them in terms of the oil-producing states' ability to provide aid. A third viewpoint is that of the recipient states themselves, which is well summed up in the following comment:

"Aid from Islamic and Arab States to the African continent in terms of percentage of the Gross National Product of the donors is impressive when compared with that from the industrialized countries. But the same impression is not necessarily made on the poorer members of the OAU, who look at the massive capital investments made with oil money in the West, and wonder whether they could not hope for more to come their way."[15]

119

Sharper and more open criticism of the oil producers has, not unexpectedly, grown among African leaders, as their own economies have continued to slump badly under the double impact of higher oil costs, and the rising cost of importing essential goods from industrialized nations. Typical of this criticism is the comment made by Mozambique's Finance Minister, Rui Baltazar Alves, when addressing the Front for the Liberation of Mozambique (FRELIMO) Central Committee:

"Each time the petroleum exporters meet, we are shaken by a brutal price increase. Our exports do not keep up with this sinister dance of numbers."[16]

However, the Arabs too, are beginning to voice more open criticism of what happens to the aid they give. In a splash article headed "Swindles disturb Arab donors," the editor of *Voice of the Arab World (Voice)*, Claud Morris, wrote:

"All the sincere efforts in aid for Africa do not alter the fact that in cases now coming to light for every $1m of aid, less than $100,000 find effective application in countries like Zambia and Zaire. . . . An observer of the scene told *Voice:* 'the true facts about those areas to which generous Arab aid is given would shock figures like King Khālid of Saudi Arabia, Shaykh Zāyid of Abū Dhabi and Shaykh Khalīfa of Qatar.' "[17]

A characteristic African riposte would be that Shaykhs who live in glass palaces should not be the first to cast stones.

Colin Legum

NOTES
1. R Dar-es-Salaam, 23 July 1980.
2. Report of the OAU Secretary-General on Afro-Arab Co-operation, CM/1056 (XXXY).
3. *Voice of the Arab World (Voice)*, London, 1 November 1980.
4. *Ibid.*
5. *West Africa*, London, 21 January 1980.
6. *Ibid*, 11 February 1980.
7. Quoted on R Accra, 16 July 1980.
8. R Monrovia, 17 September 1980.
9. *International Herald Tribune (IHT)*, Paris, 20 September 1980.
10. R Dar-es-Salaam, 23 July 1980.
11. *West Africa*, 18 August 1980.
12. Quoted in *IHT*, 22 September 1980.
13. *Voice*, 1 November 1980.
14. *The Middle East*, London, September 1980.
15. *West Africa*, 26 January 1981.
16. *The Guardian*, London, 22 December 1980.
17. *Voice*, 1 July 1980.

Developments in the Maghrib and their Middle East Dimensions

Domestic developments within the Maghrib during 1980 all involved internal consolidation of regimes in power, after a previous year characterized by regime change in many countries. Morocco's tenacious monarchy once more turned an occasion of political challenge into a manifestation of solidarity through two constitutional referenda and a series of amnesties. Algeria's new regime also turned a review session by the single party into a consolidation of President Chedli Benjedid's own power. In Tunisia, a new Prime Minister rapidly improved his own position as a liberal leader and the heir-presumptive to the ailing President, Ḥabīb Bourguiba. Mauritania's military regime tried to weed out its internal opponents and move ahead out of a time of domestic, social and economic troubles.

In their relations among themselves, the states of the Maghrib were, above all, preoccupied by war—Morocco's defence of its new Saharan provinces against the political and military attacks of Algerian- and Libyan-backed Polisario attacks, and Tunisia's political consolidation against the attack on Gafsa by Libya. The Maghribi States also had an eye on strengthening their own positions in the conflicts in the Arab and Islamic arena: Algeria used the Steadfastness Front to support the Polisario; Morocco led the al-Quds (Jerusalem) Committee as a way of gaining Arab support for its Saharan position; all took sides in the Arab Summit in Amman in line with their previous alliances and positions. In addition, Algeria developed a new aspect of its global role by serving as intermediary in the US-Iranian hostage negotiations.

INTERNAL AFFAIRS IN 1980

MOROCCO'S CONSTITUTIONAL PLEBISCITE

Elections have always troubled King Ḥasan II since they legitimize political forces that he has to work with and which implicitly challenge his position as sole focus of national will and unity. In a time of war, they can be particularly uncertain and even unsettling. Yet the King is proud of his constitutional monarchy and parliamentary government. He therefore proposed a constitutional amendment prolonging the life of the National Assembly, elected in 1977, from four to six years.[1] The new elections in 1983 will be held at the same time as the regularly scheduled communal elections. The National Assembly has two-thirds of its members directly elected, and one-third elected indirectly by professional and local assemblies. The amendment was submitted to referendum on 30 May. The National Independents Group favoured the amendment; the Istiqlal party favoured it conditionally; the National Union of Socialist Forces (USFP) called for a boycott; and the Progress and Socialism (Communist) Party was opposed. The amendment passed with 96.7% voting in favour. The USFP plans to boycott the Assembly after its initial term expires in June 1981.

The King also proposed a change in the status of the Crown Prince—his son, Prince Muḥammad, age 16[2]—by lowering the age of majority from 18 to 16, and by proposing that the presidency of the Regency Council should be held by the first president of the Supreme Court and no longer by the closest male relative of the

King (his brother, Prince Moulay 'Abdallah). Party positions on this issue were the same as on prolonging the life of parliament except that the USFP took no stand. The amendment passed on 23 May with 99.7% voting in favour. The vote was construed officially as another expression of self-determination by the formerly-Spanish Saharan provinces, which took part in the referendum, and particularly by the new province of Wed al-Dahab (formerly Spanish southern Rio de Oro and later Mauritanian Tiris al-Gharbiyya).

The year began with student and labour unrest.[3] At the end of January, the National Union of Moroccan Students called strikes over a number of political issues, protesting political arrests and the Camp David agreements. Arrests of strikers were followed by new strikes, until the Government decided to suspend scholarships of students on strike. In February, the Moroccan Labour Union and the Democratic Labour Confederation called strikes to protest the cost of living. The Government began discussions with labour leaders and created an Economic and Social Council to institutionalize these contacts. Once these disturbances were brought under control, the King used a number of national and religious holidays between March (Feast of the Throne) and August (Anniversary of Muḥammad V's exile) to amnesty several hundred prisoners, including political prisoners, mostly more radical supporters of the USFP.[4] About 150 political prisoners remain, most of them Marxist-Leninist "Frontists" whose opposition includes support of the Polisario in the Sahara. Once again, the King was able to manipulate the political system to produce renewed solidarity for his throne and his Saharan policy, and to isolate opposition.

ALGERIA'S CONSOLIDATION IN 1980

When Col. Chedli Benjedid (Shādhilī Ibn Jadīd) was elected President in early 1979, he was supported by a shadow group of army officer-colleagues who were prepared to find other candidates and other ways of putting them in power if the new President did not provide effective leadership. The procedural issues of selection having been taken care of, the State and Party apparatus turned to the substantive issues of consumer benefits and sound management which the country demanded. An extraordinary congress of the National Liberation Front (FLN) was planned for June to handle these issues which had plagued the preceding regime of Houari Boumedienne, and to put the decision-making capabilities of the new President to the hard test of solving a decade of problems. Benjedid rose to the challenge by asserting his control of the political system.

On 13 January, the Council of Ministers was reshuffled, some older figures removed and younger technicians brought in; the Interior Ministry was separated from the Prime Ministry (Muḥammad Benahmad Abdelghani) and given to a rising ally (Boualem Benhamouda); the senior Minister-Counsellors to the President were eliminated. Then, Benjedid's major competition during the presidential elections, Col. Muḥammad Salih Yahyawi, was removed as Party leader and replaced by a Party functionary, Muḥammad Sharīf Messaadia. In early May, the 160-member Central Committee of the FLN passed a resolution giving full powers to the President to carry out all structural reforms in the party which he judged necessary. By the time 3,998 Congress delegates met from 15–19 June, Benjedid was in full charge.[5] New statutes gave him greater control over the Party. Policy debates focussed on criticisms of the "ruling class;" pressures in favour of greater democracy and more effective links between party and people; and demands for greater consumer-oriented policies and social programmes, all against a background of confrontation between those who favoured maintaining and improving the "revolutionary accomplishments" and those who saw the moment appropriate to expand the private sector. The Congress adopted resolutions supporting a consumer-oriented Five Year Plan (1980–84), and confirming the breakup of the State heavy industry for petroleum (Sonatrach) into smaller components. It was followed by three further institutional consolidations.[6] The cumbersome 17-member Political Bureau was reduced to seven members, representating major factions but without the higher policy pretensions and attributions of the larger body. The members in addition to the President are Rabat Bitah, 55, historic chief and National Assembly President; Col. 'Abdallah Belhouchet, 56, army Inspector-General and Vice-Minister of Defence; Col. Yahyawī, 48, former party leader and representative of the populist Left; 'Abd al-'Azīz Bouteflika, 43, former Foreign Minister and representative of the liberals; Muḥammad Sa'īd Mazouzi, 56, head of the FLN economic and social commission, a Kabyle (Berber); and Benhamouda, 47, Interior Minister and representative of the Arabists. The Government was again reshuffled to bring in younger technicians to replace older politicians and military, in mid-July. At the same time, Benjedid reinforced the military's control over the army. While retaining the Defence Ministry for himself, he named two Vice-Ministers—Col. Belhouchet, a former military security chief, and Col. Kasdi Merbah, a former Political Bureau member. He also appointed Col. Mustafā Belloucif as Secretary-General of the Ministry. At the same time he announced the creation of a General Staff, which had been abolished by Boumedienne in 1969. Benjedid's policy is one of restricting the various power groups to their own sectors of activity, and allowing them policy input into areas of their competence, but under his consolidated control. One indication of Benjedid's new style and assurance was his liberation on 30 October of the former President, Aḥmad ben Bella, after 15 years of prison and house arrest.[7]

The regime faced a more fundamental problem than that of consolidating the President's position—the re-emergence of ethnic politics.[8] The Berber unrest of April was in part a reaction against earlier promises by the regime to push ahead with Arabization and, in part, merely collective umbrage at an inept administrative decision; but it was also an indication of potential rebellion if Kabyles are ever discriminated against. The immediate incident giving rise to the April troubles was the refusal to allow a lecture by the noted Kabyle poet, Mouloud Mammeri, on "Early Kabyle Poems" at the University of Tizi Ouzou in Kabylia on 10 March. A student strike turned into a general strike in Tizi Ouzou by 16 April; the strikers came into confrontation with the police a week later, and 24 of those arrested were arraigned before a State Security Court. The general strike was renewed in Tizi Ouzou on 18 May, and a strike occurred at the University of Algiers on the following day. The confrontation gradually dissipated, in part because the school year ran out and, in part, because of the moderate approach of Dr Abdelkaq Brerhi, the Minister of Higher Education, who made a number of visits to the dissident region in April and May to talk with the strikers. The FLN Central Committee, in its May meeting, reaffirmed its decision to proceed with Arabization.[9] The problem did not reappear during the year, but it reminded the Government that "democratization" meant listening to the pressure of the Berber minority as well as to the Islamic fundamentalists.

TUNISIAN SUCCESSION POLITICS
The political manoeuvring for Presidential succession in Tunisia, which has been going on since Bourguiba's illness in 1969, took a new turn in the beginning of 1980 when the heir-presumptive to the 77-year old President was eliminated for medical reasons and the need for a new political heir provided the opportunity to bring in a

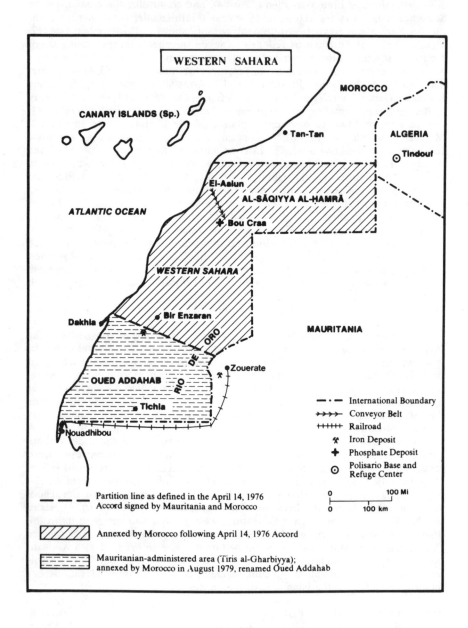

WESTERN SAHARA

MOROCCO

CANARY ISLANDS (Sp.)

Tan-Tan

ALGERIA

Tindouf

El-Aaiun

AL-SÂQIYYA AL-HAMRÂ

ATLANTIC OCEAN

Bou Craa

WESTERN SAHARA

Bir Enzaran

Dakhla

RIO DE ORO

MAURITANIA

Zouerate

OUED ADDAHAB

Tichla

Nouadhibou

— · — International Boundary
>>>>> Conveyor Belt
+++++ Railroad
⚒ Iron Deposit
✚ Phosphate Deposit
⊙ Polisario Base and Refuge Center

— — — Partition line as defined in the April 14, 1976 Accord signed by Mauritania and Morocco

0   100 Mi
0   100 km

////// Annexed by Morocco following April 14, 1976 Accord

Mauritanian-administered area (Tiris al-Gharbiyya); annexed by Morocco in August 1979, renamed Oued Addahab

124

new generation and to reopen doors to excluded political tendencies. At the end of February, the Prime Minister, Hedi Nouira (Hādī Nuwayra), 69, next in line for the Presidency, was admitted to hospital for a circulatory ailment. The Education Minister, Muḥammad Mazālī, 54, was appointed caretaker of government affairs. On 23 April, when it appeared that Nouira was permanently incapacitated, Mazālī was appointed Prime Minister, completely changing the interplay of alliances and factions—liberals against conservatives, Nouira's technicians against Socialist Destour Party (PSD) aparatechniks, French-speakers vs Arabists, and various personal factions.

The Government that came in with Mazālī in April contained some subtle changes, including the demotion of the former PSD director, Muḥammad Sayah, to Housing and Equipment Minister; and the inclusion of one formerly excluded liberal, Sadok ben Jama', in another minor Ministry, that of Transport. The latter represented an important second step in the reintegration of the liberals who had been excluded from the ruling party and the Tunisian political system in the early 1970s. The first step was taken on 8 March when the PSD Political Bureau, in response to the liberal Democratic Socialist Movement's expressions of support for the regime during the Libyan attack on Gafsa, lifted the exclusion imposed on eight former leading party members because of their appeals for party democracy.[10] The third step came on 3 December when a new Cabinet reshuffle was announced which included a much higher-level liberal, Beji Qaid es-Sebsi, a former Defence Minister and Ambassador to Paris, who became Minister-delegate of the President to the Prime Minister.[11] At the same time, Mazālī's former Cabinet director, Mezri Chekir, was named to the Civil Service Ministry. Mansour Moalla, a former Minister-delegate for Planning, who had resigned when the liberals were excluded in 1974, was named Minister of Planning and Finance. On the other hand, two important figures in the Nouira-Sayah era—the former Economics and Agriculture Minister, Ḥasan Belkhoudja, and the former Interior Minister, Taher Belkhoudja—were restored to Government positions as Foreign and Information Ministers respectively, while one of Bourguiba's personal companions, Bechir Zarg Layoun (Zarq al-'Ayun), was named chairman of a new PSD Consultative Council of former militants with ex officio participation on the party's Central Committee. Mazālī's Tunisia also sought to restore representation to important sectors of society. In August, he announced that elections to the General Union of Tunisian Students (UGET) would be free and open; and in August and December he freed and pardoned all political prisoners and most labour union members arrested for the riots of January 1978—except the former UGET Secretary-General, Ḥabīb Achour, who remains the only Tunisian under house arrest.[12]

The result of the personnnel changes during the year was typical Tunisian balancing politics. While Mazālī carefully consolidated his position, Bourguiba ensured that counter-balancing stalwarts should also be kept in the picture; the opening to the liberals was—for the moment—limited to co-opting leading members but not yet giving recognition to a competing party, the Democratic Socialist Movement—as its leader, the former Interior Minister, Aḥmad Mestiri, would wish.

MAURITANIAN SEARCH FOR WELL-BEING

On 4 January 1980, the Mauritanian Government underwent another "internal coup d'état" to work out the political conflicts within the Military Committee for National Security (CMNS) which had come to power in July 1978. Muḥammad Khouna Ould Haydalla, Prime Minister and Defence Minister, took over the presidency and the leadership of the CMNS. In April he further consolidated his power by changing the Interior Minister and the heads of all the military services (army chief of staff, *gendarmerie,* national security, and national guard). His policy has been to steer between pro-Moroccan and pro-Algerian factions, avoiding pro-business and pro-socialist extremes, and enacting policies that satisfy both the French-speaking Blacks in the South and the Arabic-speaking Moors in the North—a difficult balancing act.

EXTERNAL AFFAIRS

ARAB WAR AND DIPLOMACY IN THE SAHARA

The war between Morocco and the Popular Front for the Liberation of Sāqiyya al-Ḥamrā and Rio de Oro (Polisario Front), supported by Algeria and Libya, took a decided turn in favour of Morocco during 1980; but events on the diplomatic front moved—somewhat contradictorily—toward a Polisario success. The military swing began in early November 1979 when the King reorganized the military command structure and launched a new campaign by a 6,000-man mobile force called *Ohoud,* under the independent command of Gen. Aḥmad Dlimi to supplement the previous structure of garrison forces under the control of Rabat. In early 1980, a second column, *Zellaqa,* joined *Ohoud,* but in mid-March the forces were caught off-guard by a major Polisario offensive in the Warqziz mountain chain in eastern Tarfaya province within the pre-1975 boundaries of Morocco. However, by early May the two columns had regained the initiative in the same area. At the end of June they were joined by a third force, *al-Araq.*

The military operations, which had reached the classic guerrilla peak by escalating into a conventional military confrontation around the turn of the year, thus again returned to the guerrilla level. The Polisario continues to raid towns and outposts in both southern Morocco and in the Moroccan Sahara, but they have not attained any notable successes in these attacks and they have lost both bases and freedom of movement in the Saharan area. One indication of the restricted options available to the Polisario military compaign was the increase in Polisario attacks on Spanish fishing vessels after June; such attacks have high diplomatic visibility and are an attempt to undermine Spanish-Moroccan fishing agreements as well as to assert sovereignty by the Saharan Arab Democratic Republic (SADR) over Saharan territorial waters; but they have not attained their diplomatic aims with the Spanish.[13] The military weakness of the Polisario contrasts with its military supplies, which continue to flow from initially Soviet sources through Algeria and Libya. During 1980, the Libyan supply role increased markedly, leaving Algeria in a position of sanctuary and diplomatic mentor.

Diplomatically, Polisario fortunes reached a high point in mid-1980 and continued uncertainly thereafter.[14] On 3 July the SADR received its 26th African recognition during the summit meeting of the Organization of African Unity (OAU) in Freetown; this provided it with the simple majority it needed for admission into the 51-member Organization. However, Morocco immediately raised a procedural question, demanding that the question of whether the SADR qualified as a ''state'' within the OAU definition should be decided by a two-thirds vote. The question of membership was put off to allow an OAU Committee of Wisemen to make one final attempt to move toward a diplomatic settlement through ''open discussions with all interested parties''—meaning that Morocco would meet with the Polisario, but also that elected and tribal representatives and members of the pro-Moroccan Association of Natives of Sāqiyya al-Ḥamrā and Rio de Oro (Aosario) would be heard as well. The OAU's resolution also called for

126

the holding of a self-determination referendum; but in their meeting in early September in Freetown the OAU Committee indicated that the referendum need not be preceded by Moroccan military or administrative withdrawal. Although the United Nations passed another resolution in its Autumn session affirming the sole representative character of the Polisario and calling for a self-determination referendum, it is possible that the highwater mark of diplomatic support for SADR has been reached—unless the necessary eight additional OAU votes are obtained to define SADR as a "state". At the same time, it is noteworthy that Algeria agreed, and reportedly pressed the Polisario to agree, to the referendum without Moroccan withdrawal. Morocco still opposes a referendum; but the gap preventing a political solution has been slightly narrowed.

The Arab League has long been paralysed on the Saharan issue. It has supported Morocco since 1960 but habitually seeks to avoid conflicts among its members. However, the radical Arab faction—meeting as the Steadfastness Front in Tripoli from 15–21 April—traded positions of importance among its members (Algeria, Libya, Syria, South Yemen and the Palestine Liberation Organization [PLO]); among its decisions was the agreement to recognize SADR. Morocco thereupon broke diplomatic relations with Libya which, though main supplier of the Polisario, had heretofore withheld recognition, and pressed the local PLO representative into a denial that PLO recognition was official; this, in turn, brought a denial of the denial by the PLO representative in Algiers. The status of Moroccan-Syrian and Moroccan-PLO relations remains troubled and ambiguous, but the Steadfastness Front's position has not made a major impact on the Saharan situation.

LIBYAN ATTACK ON TUNISIA

Libya's messianic policy toward the Arab world took a concrete expression on 27 January when a 50-man commando, originating in Libya, made an attack on the southern Tunisian town of Gafsa, in which 48 were killed including three of the raiders; another 111 were wounded.[15] About 20 of the attackers were Tunisians living in Tunisia, while the rest were Tunisians, Libyans and others coming from Libya via Rome and Algiers. They had been trained in Libya. On 14 March, the trial of 60 people implicated in the raid, including seven still at large, opened before the State Security Court. Evidence during the trial indicated that the goal of the attack was to trigger off a popular uprising that would overthrow the regime, and also confirmed the complicity of Libya and of some Algerian authorities. On 27 March, the Court delivered 15 death sentences (including two on individuals still at large), and ten life sentences. Their appeal was rejected, and the 13 were executed on 17 April.

Instead of triggering popular rebellion, the attack was turned into a domestic victory for the Tunisian regime which received strong statements of support from the important but illegal opposition parties, the Democratic Socialist Movement (MDS) of Aḥmad Mestiri and the Popular Union Movement of Aḥmad ben Salāḥ. Two days after the attack, France sent two *Transall* cargo planes and two *Puma* helicopters with military supplies; and two days later the US agreed to send additional helicopters and troop transports for the Tunisian army. The French military assistance team finally left on 12 March.

Tunisia sent missions to present its case to Arab States in early February. The Minister of Information went to Algiers where a satisfactory understanding was reached; the Education Minister visited Iraq, Syria, Lebanon and Jordan; the Foreign Minister toured the Gulf States, and the National Assembly President went to Morocco and Mauritania. Libya denied it had any role in the attack, vigorously assailed the French military assistance, expelled Tunisian workers from Libya, and called for a meeting of the Arab League to discuss Franco-Tunisian aggression. Tunisia, too, called for a meeting of the Arab League. A week later it complained of additional Libyan provocation over the installation of a Libyan-licensed oil rig at the edge of Tunisian territorial waters. The League met in extraordinary session in Tunis on 27 February; after a two-day session it adopted a declaration of principles (non-interference, inter-Arab solutions) which had no positive effect on the problem of Libyan-Tunisian relations. (For details, see essay on inter-Arab relations.)

THE MAGHRIB AMONG THE ARABS

All the North African countries remained with the Arab League majority, except for Algeria, which developed a broader basis of good relations with other Arab States. Towards the end of March President Benjedid undertook a rapid trip through Syria, Jordan, Iraq, Saudi Arabia, South and North Yemen, the Emirates, Qatar and Bahrain, Kuwait, and Libya.[16] The visit was the first made by the new President to the Arab world, although he had previously visited a number of African countries south of the Sahara. It was seen as part of his campaign to consolidate his personal position at home, and also as a move to reassure the Arab League members of Algeria's primary Arab concerns and of its interest in Arab unity on the Israeli issue.

The next major confrontation within the Arab camp following the Tripoli Steadfastness meeting also divided the North African countries. Algeria joined the other Steadfastness members in support of the Syrian boycott of the Amman summit of the Arab League at the end of November; while Morocco, Mauritania and Tunisia attended the summit. They supported Iraq's position, opposed the Camp David process, criticized Resolution 242, and agreed to a modest economic development plan for Arab League members.

Algeria's careful membership in the radical Arab group had unexpected benefits toward the end of 1980 when Algeria became the intermediary in the US-Iranian hostage negotiations. Although Algeria had previously acted as mediator (between Iran and Iraq in 1975, and between Morocco and Mauritania in 1969–72), it had never intervened in a conflict in which a great power was involved. Although the role of mediator can carry problems with it, it was a welcome opportunity for the Benjedid regime to show itself as a "responsible radical", thus gaining an audience for its positions in the ME and the Sahara, and developing close personal relations in the West to compete with those of Morocco, Egypt and Israel. However, all its personal contacts left the American Government after the change in administration, and the Reagan Government had little sympathy for Algerian policies.

Morocco also insured its position among the majority of Arab States by presiding over the al-Quds (Jerusalem) Committee of the Islamic Conference Organization. The Committee met on 18 August in Casablanca to recommend the use of measures, including boycott, against countries supporting the Israeli stand on the future of Jerusalem. In February, King Ḥasan went to Mecca for the Omra and used the opportunity to discuss the question of Jerusalem with the Saudi Arabian leaders. He followed this by a visit to President Saddām Ḥusayn in Baghdad. In early May, a representative of the King again visited Saudi Arabia and Iraq, as well as the Gulf States, to consult on the activities of the al-Quds Committee. Just before the trip, on 28 April, the King announced some new twists on his ME attitudes by supporting sectorial solutions to the Palestine problem, notably urging the PLO to seek a solution on the West Bank, Gaza and Jerusalem without awaiting a solution on the Golan Heights.[17] Another important link between the Maghrib and the rest of the Arab world was the financial support that oil states were giving to non-oil states, principally to Morocco and Mauritania, to enable them to pursue their policies.[18] Saudi Arabia is the primary supporter of Morocco. The amount of its annual grants is unconfirmed, but the figure of $1bn has been advanced. This probably includes paying the $232.5m bill for the US authorization at the end of 1980 for reconnaissance planes, F-5E fighters and helicopters. Saudi aid to Morocco had been interrupted during 1978 as a mark of displeasure with Ḥasan's support for Sādāt; it was restored only when Ḥasan criticized the Camp David process. Saudi Arabia has also promised $100m to Mauritania, of which half was paid in early 1980. Iraq promised a grant of $5m and a loan of $15m in September 1979, and a mixed loan and grant of $100m was negotiated by President Ould Haydalla in Baghdad in May 1980.

THE IMMEDIATE OUTLOOK

The New Year began with stable governments in all the countries of the Maghrib and with pertinent efforts by them all to maintain that stability. The Libyan threat had turned from Tunisia to Chad, while still remaining active behind the Polisario. Because of the unlikelihood of a military solution, the conflict in the Sahara might be seen to be edging toward a political solution, although its terms remain unclear. The absence of movement in the ME peace process and the unlikelihood of any renewed activity until late in 1981, after a new Israeli Government is elected, should give North African states time to improve their relations among themselves before new causes of disruption can arise.

I. William Zartman

NOTES
1. *Le Monde*, Paris, 15, 23 May 1980.
2. *Ibid*, 9, 25 May 1980.
3. *Ibid*, 7, 9, 21 February 1980.
4. *Ibid*, 23 August 1980.
5. *Ibid*, 17, 20 May, 1 July 1980; *Afrique-Asie*, Paris, 4 August 1980.
6. *Le Monde*, 17 July 1980; *Jeune Afrique*, No. 1021, Paris, 30 July 1980, p. 31; *Marches Tropicaux et Méditerranéens*, Paris, 25 July 1980; *Africa Confidential*, Vol. XXI, No. 18, London, 3 September 1980, p. 1.
7. *New York Times*, 1, 2 November 1980; *Le Monde*, 6 November 1980.
8. *Le Monde*, 22, 23, 29, 30 April, 6, 15 May, 5 June 1980.
9. *Ibid*, 5 January, 15 February, 11 May 1980; Gilbert GrandGuillaume, "Relance de l'Arabisation en Algerie?" *Maghreb-Machrek Monde Arabe*, No. 88, Paris, pp. 51–62.
10. *Le Monde*, 11 March 1980.
11. *Jeune Afrique*, 1041: 23, 17 December 1980.
12. *Le Monde*, 5, 6, 7, 9 August, 12 November 1980.
13. *Ibid*, 1, 10, 13, 28 June, 1, 28 October 1980.
14. Details on the Saharan war and diplomacy come from I. William Zartman *Ripe for Resolution*, Yale University Press, New Haven, forthcoming 1981.
15. *Le Monde* presented daily accounts during the extended crisis.
16. *Le Monde*, 21 March, 4 April 1980; *Afrique-Asie*, 14 April 1980.
17. *Le Monde*, 30 April 1980.
18. James Markham, "Ḥasan's Quagmire" *New York Times Magazine*, 27 April 1980; *Washington Post*, 29 October 1979, *Le Monde*, 31 March 1980.

PART III
Middle East Economic Issues

Middle East Oil: An Economic Analysis*

During the past decade the view that has come to prevail is that the Organization of Petroleum Exporting Countries (OPEC) was largely instrumental in causing the major oil price increases of 1973–74 and again in 1979–80; and that the dominant group within the Organization—the major Arab oil exporters, and Saudi Arabia, in particular—do not "need" all the oil revenues, and are therefore able to reduce production and, thereby, raise prices almost at will. A corollary of this view is that these countries (again with the emphasis on Saudi Arabia) must be induced by political means and concessions to maintain or raise production to levels desired by the West, and to moderate price rises. These views have been buttressed—both in the West and in the OPEC countries—by numerous forecasts projecting long-term oil shortages which would necessarily entail higher real prices (i.e. corrected for inflation); increased dependence on OPEC and, in particular, on Middle East oil; and huge and growing financial surpluses accumulated primarily by the ME oil exporters. The political and economic implications of these forecasts are well known.

It is the thesis of this writer that the underlying trends in the oil and energy markets are largely determined by economic forces. Furthermore, that the Saudis, and other ME oil exporters, determine their oil policies largely on the basis of *their* perceptions of their own economic interests. This does not rule out political factors. The economic policies of *any* government are influenced by a host of social and political factors. However, since oil is literally the lifeblood of the ME oil-exporting countries, their production and pricing policies are determined by their economic interests, as *they* view them. By and large, many analysts have seriously underestimated the strength of the economic forces unleashed by the major oil price increases. These have tended effectively to reduce the demand for OPEC and ME oil. Furthermore, the massive revenues flowing to the oil exporters have stimulated internal demand for expenditures on a wide range of imported goods and services. This, in turn, has greatly increased the dependence of the ME countries on a continued massive flow of oil revenues. It is to the nature and strength of these economic forces that we wish to address ourselves.

AN EVALUATION OF THE RISE IN OIL PRICES BETWEEN 1970 AND THE OCTOBER WAR 1973

OPEC was established in 1960—but oil prices were stable throughout the decade. They were, in fact, somewhat lower than during the 1950s. In real terms, i.e. measured in constant prices, there was a steady decline. In the energy markets the consequences were both a tendency towards energy-intensive goods and services, and a substitution of petroleum for other sources of energy—especially coal. Between 1970 and 1 October 1973 oil prices rose by c. 120%.[1] A number of market factors were instrumental in raising oil prices, primarily the US oil production which peaked in 1970. A steady decline followed until Alaskan oil began to flow in 1977. Venezuelan production also peaked in 1970, primarily for technical reasons. There was a subsequent steady decline until 1979. Libyan production also began to decline after 1970—primarily for technical reasons. The downtrend was reversed in 1976. The nationalization of the Iraq Petroleum Company in 1972 led to a

*The author wishes to express his sincere gratitude to the Littauer Foundation, and to its President, Mr Harry Starr, for the research grant, in support of this study.

133

sharp reduction in production. Since 1975 (until the outbreak of the Iraqi-Iranian war in September 1980) production had risen very sharply. All of these unrelated events drastically altered the world oil market, and prices began to rise sharply in the two or three years before the 1973 war.

THE OCTOBER 1973 WAR AND THE ARAB OIL EMBARGO

About a week after the outbreak of the war, the Gulf oil producers announced a major price increase and at about the same time the Arab members of OPEC announced an embargo on oil shipments to the US and the Netherlands. It is clear in retrospect, however, that what more than anything else sent oil prices soaring in the spot market to levels about three times the official OPEC prices was the Arab decision to reduce oil production by 25% and to cut production subsequently by 5% per month in order to bring increasing pressure on the US in particular to favour their side in the conflict with Israel. At the OPEC meeting towards the end of December 1973 the decision was made to raise official prices from c. $5 per barrel to $11.65 as of 1 January 1974. In mid-March 1974, the Arab oil embargo was officially ended.

What did actually take place during this period? Arab oil production as a whole during the last quarter of 1973 was c. 9% lower than during the first nine months of the year. Iraqi production was 6% higher. As compared with the last quarter of 1972, Arab oil production was actually higher. Saudi oil production in the last quarter of 1973 was 11% lower than during the first nine months of the year, but was 4% higher than in the corresponding quarter in the previous year. While the embargo had called for continued cutbacks in production (and exports), Arab oil production during the first quarter of 1974 was, as a whole, 4% higher than in the previous quarter; it included a Saudi increase of 11%. Abū Dhabi, Kuwait and Algeria also increased production in the first quarter of 1974.[2]

Without entirely discounting political factors, it is clear in retrospect, that at least the Saudis had ample economic motivations for the cutback in production in the last quarter of 1973, and the subsequent increase in the first quarter of 1974. A US Senate Foreign Relations Committee Report published in 1979 notes that:

> "In the early 1970s, Aramco production skyrocketed, increasing from 3.2m barrels per day [mbd] in January 1970 to 8.3 mbd in September 1973 . . . This large increase in Aramco productions from 5.4 mbd in May 1972 to 8.3 mbd in September 1973 occurred primarily in two major Saudi Arabian fields, Berri and Ghawar. But in both fields Aramco's plans for water injection fell behind schedule . . . Many experts believe that production below the critical gas saturation point causes some damage to ultimate recovery."

In other words, the Saudi authorities were concerned that unless the rate of oil extraction was reduced, and pressure was restored in these oil fields, they would suffer permanent damage. The report noted that pressure in these fields was restored and that Saudi production resumed its upward climb as of January 1974.[3]

On an annual basis it is also clear in retrospect, that there was no underlying oil shortage in 1973. World oil production increased by 9.3%, while consumption grew by 8.0%. Excluding the communist countries (the Soviet bloc and China) the gap between the increment in production and in consumption was even wider—9.4% and 7.6% respectively. The Saudi increase in production in 1973 was unusually large—an unprecedented 1.6 mbd, which has not been matched since that time. Production also rose sharply in 1973 in Iraq and the United Arab Emirates (UAE); there were smaller increases in Qatar and Algeria. Entire Arab oil production rose by 14.6% in 1973 cf. an increase of 7.0% in non-Arab production.[4] It is clear that whatever oil shortages existed were caused in no small measure by large-scale stockpiling. This was stimulated by the fear of shortages, and the expectation of still higher prices. The announcement of the Arab oil embargo and the expectation of large and continued cutbacks tended to push prices to far higher levels.

NEW TRENDS IN THE OIL AND ENERGY MARKETS SINCE 1973

The escalation in oil prices in 1973–74 resulted in a plethora of prognoses of gloom for the oil-importing countries. A number of forecasts were made in 1974 about the future accumulation of OPEC financial surpluses (petrodollars) and, especially, by the small-population major ME producers, with Saudi Arabia out in front. The range of forecasts of OPEC cumulative surpluses was between $650 bn and $750 bn by 1980, with a continuation of current account surpluses (i.e. a further accumulation of financial assets) well into the 1980s. Even as late as 1977 a US Senate committee, basing itself on testimony offered by the Treasury, stated:

> "The smaller Persian Gulf States, Saudi Arabia, Kuwait, and the UAE . . . have tiny populations and non-industrial economies which can absorb only a tiny fraction of their annual petrodollar revenues . . . there is no reason to believe that this pattern of accumulating surpluses and chronic deficits for the oil importers will be reversed in the near future. The grim conclusion of the US Treasury is that the OPEC countries will continue to pile up excess revenues of over $40 bn per year, perhaps for the next two decades."[5]

It is important to note that this, and other, forecasts were based on their perception of economic trends, not on any foreknowledge of political convulsions—such as the Iranian revolution which drastically raised world oil prices in 1979–80, or the Iraqi-Iranian war which erupted in September 1980.

OPEC current account surpluses had in fact been declining quite rapidly after 1974. In 1978 the OPEC countries, as a whole, had no current surplus. Saudi Arabia had a deficit of $750m in its balance of payments (the current account), and its fiscal accounts showed far greater deficits. There was every indication—prior to the Iranian revolution—that this trend would continue; not only the larger-population OPEC countries, but Saudi Arabia and some other small-population oil exporters would be incurring deficits in their balance of payments.

What is important is not the forecasting errors of the past, but their sources. Conceptually the errors were of two kinds. First, the failure to perceive the magnitude of the changes which would take place and the rapidity of these changes in the oil and energy markets, as a consequence of the major oil price increases in 1973–74. Second, the economists who made these forecasts apparently had little knowledge of the economic policies and problems of the major small population ME oil exporters. They assumed that these countries did not "need" and were unable to spend (or to absorb) the massive oil revenues accruing to them in the aftermath of the 1973–74 oil price increases. We shall first examine the changes in the oil and energy markets since 1973, and then analyse economic developments in the ME oil-exporting countries, focusing primarily on Saudi Arabia.

It will be recalled that the forecasts were for an increasing world dependence on OPEC oil. OPEC production in 1980 (27.5 mbd) was significantly lower than in 1973 (31.3 mbd). OPEC exports had declined even more sharply, by c. 5 mbd. Internal consumption in the OPEC countries has been rising very sharply. On the other hand, non-OPEC production has risen from 27.2 mbd in 1973 to 35.6 mbd in 1980. Excluding the communist countries, the rise in non-OPEC production was from 17.1 mbd in 1973 to 20.9 mbd in 1980. The increase in non-OPEC production, outside of the communist countries, began in 1977. The small increase in world consumption has been more than satisfied by non-OPEC sources since 1973. This trend was accelerated by the second "oil shock" in 1979–80; but the trend was apparent in 1978—prior to the Iranian revolution.[6]

What were the factors underlying these changes? Historically, the consumption of primary energy (petroleum, natural gas, coal, hydro and nuclear power— the other sources of energy are currently insignificant) had been rising more-or-less proportionately with the rise in real GNP. This relationship held for the US economy. Though there were wide variations from country to country, this relationship held for the world as a whole. The US alone consumed c. 30% of the world's primary energy and about the same percentage of world oil. It was difficult in 1974 (and even currently) to forecast the nature of this relationship as a consequence of the sharp increases in oil prices in 1973–74. In fact, all the forecasts turned out to be highly pessimistic—from the point of view of the oil consumers. A report of the US House of Representatives, published in 1979, noted:

"The relationship of fuel (energy) consumption to national product is the single largest uncertainty in long-term forecasting . . . Every two years the most extreme (optimistic) expectations of reduced energy use have gained increasingly wide acceptance."[7]

In addition to the largely unforeseen rate of improvement in energy efficiency, there was a marked reversal of the previous trend in the composition of the "basket" of energy sources. Since oil prices had been declining steadily in real terms during the decades prior to 1973, the trend was towards the substitution of oil (the cheaper energy source) for other sources of energy, primarily coal. Thus, for the world, gross product had been rising in real terms by an average annual rate of 4–5%, and energy consumption rose by c. the same rate during the decades prior to 1973. As a result of the substitution effect, oil consumption was rising by 7–8% p.a. Since 1973 the substitution effect has been working in the opposite direction, namely, the substitution of other energy sources for oil. However, while this was true for the world since 1973, in the US itself the policy of oil price controls tended to increase the ratio of oil consumption within total energy consumption, until 1977. The subsequent gradual decontrol of oil prices reversed the US trend; there was a sharp decrease in the share of oil in total US energy consumption between 1977 and 1980. Since the US is such a large consumer of oil, the world trend towards substituting conventional sources of energy for oil has been strongly reinforced.

The combined effects of improvement in energy efficiency and the substitution of other sources of energy for oil are readily apparent from an examination of American trends as well as in other major oil-consuming countries and the rest of the world. While it is true that the decline, or small increase, in oil consumption has been in part due to the lower rate of economic growth in the US and in other countries since 1973, the main factors were the improvement in energy efficiency and the substitution effect.

In the US the rate of GNP growth between 1973 and 1980 was 2.5% p.a. cf. 3.5% p.a. over the previous seven years. The total growth of the economy was over 19% between 1973 and 1980; energy consumption increased by less than 2%; oil consumption was almost 3% lower in 1980. Put differently, given the lower growth rate of the US economy since 1973—had the previous trends prevailed—US oil consumption would have been c. 6 mbd higher than it actually was in 1980; imports might have been close to 13 mbd in 1980, rather than 6.9 mbd.[8]

In Japan, the world's second largest oil-importing country after the US, the trends were even stronger. It enjoyed a higher rate of growth of GNP, as compared with America. Its 1979 GNP was 27% higher than in 1973; its energy consumption had increased by 7.3%; and its oil consumption was unchanged. In 1980 its GNP rose by 5.7% and its oil consumption declined by more than 7%. In Germany, the world's third largest oil-importing country, GNP increased by 15.7% between 1973 and 1979; energy consumption by 7.6%; and oil consumption was 2% lower in 1979. In 1980 its GNP increased by 2.7% while oil consumption dropped by 10.5%.[9]

For Western Europe as a whole, oil consumption in 1979 was 2% below its 1973 level; gross product had grown by 16.5% during this period.[10] In 1980 the drop in oil consumption was more than 10% despite continued economic growth.[11]

For the world as a whole, oil consumption increased by an average annual rate of 2% between 1973 and 1979 cf. 7–8% p.a. before 1973. Given the sharp decline in oil consumption in the Western industrialized countries in 1980, there is every reason to assume that world oil consumption declined significantly in 1980—possibly in the order of 5%, back to the level prevailing in 1977.

In addition to its impact on energy efficiency and oil substitution, the sharp oil price increases of 1973–74, and again in 1979–80, stimulated far more intensive exploration for, and development of oil and natural gas in the non-OPEC countries. There is, of course, a time lag between exploration and actual oil production. The effects of the 1973–74 oil price increases became increasingly apparent after 1976. These included the Alaskan oil pipeline, the rapid development of North Sea oil (the UK and Norway), the huge discoveries in Mexico as well as many smaller discoveries. Non-OPEC production (excluding the communist countries) rose from 16.4 mbd in 1976 to 20.9 mbd in 1980. At the same time OPEC production declined from 31.1 mbd to 27.3 mbd. ME oil production reached a peak in 1977—25.3 mbd, declining to 21.2 mbd in 1980.[12] Non-OPEC oil was, in effect, displacing OPEC oil within the context of a stagnant market.

The combined effect of all these economic forces was a strongly downward pressure on real oil prices. Even nominal oil prices were beginning to decline before the Iranian revolution reduced that country's oil production in the last quarter of 1978. Between early 1974 and the end of 1978, real oil prices declined by c. 25%. The oil glut that emerged towards the end of 1977, and which became increasingly prevalent during the first nine months of 1978, was the occasion for widespread discounting by various OPEC countries. In some cases, the discounts were official; in other cases, it took the form of inexpensive credit and barter arrangements. Libya, Iraq, Algeria, Nigeria, and even Kuwait were cutting prices.[13] If the OPEC countries did not decide to raise prices between mid-1977 and the end of 1978, it was simply a recognition of market forces: they were unable to do so in the face of the growing oil glut, and the "cheating" by many of its members. Though the Saudis were not discounting, their oil was being sold in the spot market below official prices.[14]

The sharp oil price increases during 1979 were not due to any underlying shortages. There was massive stockpiling occasioned by fears of shortages. It appears that stocks had been run down somewhat during the latter part of 1978. The oil surpluses and price discounting had made stockpiling unprofitable for the oil companies. The Iranian revolution, which sharply reduced production as of October 1978 and stopped oil exports in December 1978, was the occasion for massive stockpiling. The new Government which took over in Iran in early 1979 was widely viewed as unstable, and even the lower level of Iranian production which had been anticipated was, at best, uncertain. The resumption of Iranian production in March 1979 did little to allay the oil buyers' concerns. Furthermore, there were fears that the "Islamic Revolution" would spread to other ME oil exporting countries. The siege in Mecca in November 1979 heightened fears that the world's major oil exporter was in the throes of revolution and instability. The Soviet invasion of Afghanistan towards the end of 1979 further exacerbated the apprehensions of the oil-consuming countries. The result was a mad scramble for oil and massive stockpiling. An examination of the increment in world production and consumption confirms this view. Despite the far lower level of Iranian oil production in 1979, world oil production rose by 4.2% while world oil consumption increased by 1.2%. Excluding the communist countries (the Soviet bloc and China) the gap between the increment in production and in consumption was even wider—4.6% and 0.2% respectively. By the end of 1979 stockpiles had reached unprecedented levels. During the course of 1980, until the outbreak of the Iraqi-Iranian war in September 1980, there were increasing signs of an oil glut; discounting by some OPEC members was becoming prevalent.

It will be recalled that the "conventional wisdom" had been—and is—that the small-population Arab oil exporters would willingly and readily reduce production in times of oil surpluses. This did not take place in 1975 when there was an oil glut and price discounting, nor during the year preceding the Iranian revolution when price discounting was even more prevalent. In order to better understand the oil policies of these countries, it is necessary to examine their internal economic policies and development, especially since 1973. Saudi Arabia alone accounted for 25% of OPEC production in 1973 and 37% in 1980. Its share of ME oil (the Arab members of OPEC and Iran) rose from 32% in 1973 to 48% in 1980. Hence, we shall focus mainly on economic policies, development and problems in Saudi Arabia, with a few brief remarks about other larger ME oil producers.

SAUDI ARABIA—A CASE STUDY OF EXPENDITURES CHASING REVENUES

Between 1960 and 1970 Saudi oil revenues quadrupled. Measured in constant dollars, 1970 oil revenues were 3.3 times their 1960 level. The rapid growth in oil revenues was due mainly to the rise in oil exports and, to some extent, to revisions of the agreement with Aramco (the American consortium of oil companies operating in Saudi Arabia) allocating an increasing share of profits to the Government. Oil prices were stable during the 1960s. Saudi budgetary expenditures and imports initially lagged behind the rapid growth in revenues. (Since non-oil production in the country is very small, increasing expenditures call forth an almost corresponding growth in imports, with a relatively short time lag.) By the end of the decade, expenditures and imports had risen to such high levels that they were incurring deficits in their fiscal accounts and in their balance of payments (the current account, i.e. the export of goods and services, minus the import of goods and services, and transfers). An American scholar who studied the Saudi economy of the 1960s concluded that:

> "The experience of Saudi Arabia during the 1960s suggests that both the desire and the capability of increasing spending rapidly were present . . . and that the gap between (rising) revenues and expenditures closed whenever the Saudis had time to adjust to the new levels of income and wealth."[15]

My own study of the Saudi economy confirms these conclusions with respect to the 1970s—at far higher levels of revenues and expenditures.[16]

Deficits are anathema to the Saudi authorities and it is, therefore, easy to explain the doubling of oil production by the Saudis between 1970 and 1973. As noted earlier, the decline in oil production in the US, Venezuela, Libya and, subsequently, in other oil-producing countries, provided the Saudis with a ready market for their oil. The rise in oil prices between 1970 and 1973 made the Saudis all the more anxious to raise production rapidly. Oil revenues rose from $1.2 bn in 1970 to $4.3 bn in 1973. Fiscal and balance of payments surpluses were again the norm, and once again the Saudis raised their expenditure levels. The very sharp oil price increases towards the end of 1973 and as of 1 January 1974, brought about a "flood" of revenues—which had not been anticipated, rising from $4.3 bn in 1973 to $22.6 bn in 1974.[17] The quantum leap in revenues in 1974 was largely due to the escalation in oil prices. What is noteworthy is that the Saudis raised their production by almost 1 mbd in 1974, following the unprecedented 1.6 mbd increase in 1973—despite the fact world oil consumption had declined and an oil glut was emerging. The UAE was one of the few other OPEC members which raised production in that year. Most OPEC producers were constrained to lower production.

The Saudi leadership, determined not to permit financial surpluses to accumulate, called in US consultants to suggest a new Development Plan since the previous Plan was coming to a close. The Second Development Plan (mid-1975 to mid-1980) called for total expenditures of $142 bn during the five-year period, or an average annual outlay of over $28 bn. This was the level of governmental revenues in fiscal 1974–75, the year preceding the new Plan. Oil revenues paid by Aramco and some smaller oil companies operating in the country accounted for 94% of fiscal revenues, with the bulk of the balance accruing from interest and dividends derived from foreign assets held abroad. What is apparent is that the dimensions of the new Plan were commensurate with the far higher level of revenues. The goals of the Plan included:

> "A high rate of economic growth (of the non-oil sectors); maximizing earnings from oil *over the long-term* (emphasis added); reducing economic dependence on export of crude oil . . . developing human resources (education and training) . . . The Development strategy consists of three key elements: (1) Diversification of the economic base through emphasis on increasing agricultural and industrial production. (2) Rapid development of the Kingdom's [indigenous] manpower resources. (3) Development of the economic regions of the country by a wide distribution of productive investment and social programmes."[18]

Conceptually one might view the planned expenditures as consisting of four broad components. (1) Investment in infrastructure—transportation and communications, electricity, water (mainly desalination), educational and health facilities, housing and urban development. (2) A major build-up and modernization of the military forces. (3) Current expenditure on the bureaucracy, health, education, social welfare, etc. (4) The development of industry and, to some extent, agriculture; in other words, the diversification of the economy with a view to reducing its overwhelming dependence on oil.[19]

What ensued was an influx of foreign contractors and of a foreign labour force to build and implement the various projects envisaged by the Plan. There was massive construction of roads, ports, airports, electric power plants, water desalination, telephones, schools, hospitals, etc. The bureaucracy mushroomed far beyond levels envisaged by the planners. There were massive imports of modern military equipment, and "military cities" were constructed in various parts of the country. Social welfare programmes were rapidly expanded. There was an astronomic rise in governmental expenditures and of imports (goods and services). Revenues were continuing to rise, albeit relatively slowly—from $28.5 bn in fiscal 1974–75 to $39.3 bn in 1978–79. However, expenditures rose far more rapidly. The fiscal surplus declined from a peak of $18.8 bn in 1974–75 to $8.9 bn in 1976–77. In the third year of the Plan (1977–78) a deficit of $4.1 bn emerged. The Ministry of Finance and the Governor of the Central Bank (the Saudi Arabian Monetary Agency) were particularly concerned; orders were issued to the various Ministries to curtail expenditures to no more than 70% of the original allocations. These attempts were apparently not very successful. In the fourth year of the Plan (1978–79) the fiscal deficit was even larger, $4.6 bn.[20]

As might be expected, the balance of payments showed similar trends. The current account surplus rose from $2.2 bn in 1973 to $22.2 bn in 1974. However, imports rose very rapidly and the surplus was dwindling. In 1978 there was a deficit of $751m.[21] The financial problem is also apparent from an examination of the foreign assets of the Central Bank, which include the international reserves. Initially they were rising rapidly; but between the end of the first quarter of 1978 and mid-1979, there was a rapid decline of over $6 bn, from a peak of $61.6 bn to $55.5 bn.[22]

What had happened was not only the almost inexorable rise in expenditures and imports, but a decline in oil revenues in 1978. As noted earlier, the oil glut in 1978 and the widespread discounting by other OPEC members had compelled the Saudis to curtail their oil exports. When the Iranian revolution reduced production, beginning with October 1978, and brought about a complete cessation of its oil exports in December 1978, it required no urging on anyone's part to induce the Saudis to raise production and exports. They did so with alacrity. Nor did they oppose oil price increases at that time. Their short-term financial needs were, in their view, pressing. What is noteworthy is that despite the sharp increase in Saudi exports beginning with the last quarter of 1978, and higher prices in 1979, their deficit in fiscal 1978–79 (ending May 1979) was even larger than in the previous year. Expenditures were continuing to rise—despite the admonitions of the Ministry of Finance. Official foreign assets continued to decline until mid-1979. Subsequently, as a result of a continuing high level of production and a further sharp escalation in oil prices during the course of 1979, fiscal and balance of payments surpluses emerged again.

Preliminary estimates for fiscal 1979–80 indicate that budgetary revenues rose very sharply from $39.3 bn in the previous year to $68.7 bn. The increase was almost solely from higher oil revenues; the balance, a $1 bn increase in interest and dividends received from foreign assets. Expenditures climbed by $16 bn cf. an increase of $2.3 bn in the previous year. The Saudi authorities were following their "traditional" policy of raising expenditures rapidly. However, since revenues had increased by almost $30 bn in fiscal 1979–80 cf. an increase of $1.8 bn in the previous fiscal year—a fiscal surplus of $9 bn emerged.

In the Saudi balance of payments developments were quite similar. The sharply higher oil prices in 1979 and the higher rate of production raised oil exports from $37 bn in 1978 to $57.8 bn in 1979. Receipts from dividends and interest on foreign assets held abroad also increased by over $1 bn. Imports rose rapidly—by almost $11 bn in 1979; but the sharp rise in export revenues altered the balance on current account from a deficit of $751m in 1978 to a surplus of $10,856m in 1979.

The magnitude and growth of Saudi imports can be illustrated by a comparison with Iran under the Shah. Various studies made during the post-1973 period had included Iran, with its much larger population among the "large absorbers" of revenues, i.e., that their current account surpluses would be small or insignificant. It had included Saudi Arabia among the "small absorbers", i.e., that it would not be able to spend a large share of its oil revenues and would accumulate massive current account surpluses. Iran, with a population of c. 35m, imported $22.9 bn worth of goods and services in 1977. Saudi Arabia, with a population of c. 6m (including foreigners) imported $29.6 bn. Thus, Saudi imports per capita were about seven times those of Iran. Under the Shah, Iran was also a major buyer of sophisticated and costly military equipment. Two years later Saudi imports had increased by $21.6 bn to $51.2 bn in 1979. Viewed differently, Saudi export revenues in 1979 were twice their 1974 level; but the current account surplus in 1979 was only half of that in 1974. The Saudis were again following their "traditional" policy of raising expenditures and imports rapidly to meet rising revenues.

This policy is again indicated both in the current projected budget for fiscal 1980–81 and in their new Five-Year Plan (1980–85). The Budget, announced in May 1980, anticipated an increase in revenues of $17.0 bn, and the planned increase in expenditures was $16.1 bn.[23] The continued rise in prices since May 1980, and still higher production levels after the outbreak of the Iraqi-Iranian war in September 1980, most probably means that revenues will be much higher than projected for the fiscal year ending in May 1981; and though expenditures might rise further, one can anticipate a much larger fiscal surplus. By March 1981, the Saudis had not yet published the balance of payments for 1980. But there is every reason to believe that there was a major rise in the current account surplus in that year. Will this persist?

The Third Five-Year Plan (1980–85) was announced in May 1980. Total planned expenditures (including military) are $391 bn, or two and three-quarters times planned expenditures under the previous Plan. Actual expenditures during the 1975–80 period had been c. $200 bn, but many of the projects in the Plan were not initiated; others were curtailed in scope; many were still in the process of implementation and others were dropped. In the latest Plan $236 bn are allocated to the civilian sectors, including both capital and current spending, and $156 bn for military expenditures, including a relatively small allocation for foreign aid. Aside from the huge allocations for military expenditures, spending will be increased for education and health and for what is termed human resource development, desalination and other water projects as well as other infrastructural investments. The latest Plan puts a greater emphasis on industrial and some agricultural development.[24] Even in real terms (i.e., corrected for inflation) the level of planned expenditures is far higher than in the 1975–80 Plan. It will come as no surprise if actual expenditures again exceed planned expenditures. More im-

141

portant, the far higher level of spending does not by any means assure the fulfilment of the goals set by the planners. What is particularly problematic are the plans for the diversification of the economy, i.e., the development of a non-oil economy which would contribute significantly towards import-substitution and non-oil exports, and bring about a marked reduction in the country's almost total dependence on oil.

WHY DO SAUDI EXPENDITURES AND IMPORTS RISE SO RAPIDLY?

Notwithstanding the huge financial resources of Saudi Arabia, the country is in many respects similar to other under-developed countries. This applies in particular to the level of skills, managerial competence, etc. Though there are individual Saudis who have attained high levels of administrative competence, they are far too few in number, especially given the responsibility of allocating and supervising the expenditure of the massive oil revenues. No data on corruption are issued by any country; Saudi Arabia is no exception. But the opportunities for corruption on a large scale lead observers to believe that it is very prevalent. No disclosure is made of the allocations by the Saudis to the large and proliferating Royal Family and their consorts. What is probably of greater magnitude are the "commissions" paid by foreign companies to Saudi intermediaries (many from the Royal Family) whose "good offices" are usually a pre-requisite for obtaining a contract for implementing projects. What is more, the system of intermediaries and commissions, in which leading Saudis are involved, creates built-in pressures for undertaking projects which might be of little or no benefit to the country, and a preference for high-cost projects which would enhance the commission paid to the intermediaries.[25]

More objective considerations which impel the Saudis to increase expenditures include the following:

(1) Fears of revolution from within and attacks from without—hence the escalation in military expenditures, including internal security; this is also an important motivation for much of its foreign aid.

(2) Internal pressures to raise living standards.

(3) Awareness and concern regarding the longer-term future of the oil market; hence the drive to diversify the economy.

(4) The very large size of the country, and the geographic dispersal of the population.

(5) The overwhelming dependence on a foreign labour force which entails high costs.

Fears underlying escalating military expenditures were expressed by Aḥmad Zakī Yamānī in 1978 when he stated that never before "has a country had such a valuable resource [oil] and been so ill-equipped to defend it."[26] Official statistics do not include an itemization of actual Budgetary spending, but there is no reason to assume that planned military expenditures were not fully utilized—or even exceeded. The military budget had risen very rapidly from $0.5 bn in fiscal 1971–72 to $9 bn in 1977–78. The Second Development Plan (1975–80) had allocated $22.2 bn for military spending. In fact, the annual Budgets for this period called for a total of $53.1 bn for the military during this period. Part of the escalation in outlays was due to higher prices for sophisticated military equipment purchased abroad, and to the rising costs of construction of the "military cities." But, for the most part, it appears to represent a real increase.[27] The Iranian

142

revolution, the siege in Mecca, the Soviet invasion of Afghanistan and the Iraqi-Iranian war all served to increase Saudi fears of revolution, subversion and foreign attacks—stimulating further increases in military spending. For the current fiscal year (1980–81) the Budget calls for an allocation of $20.9 bn for the military.

The magnitude of Saudi foreign aid is not very clear. The balance of payments indicated that this ranged between $3 bn and $4 bn p.a. between 1975 and 1979.[28] These figures include both grants and loans. However, foreign estimates of Saudi concessional aid (grants plus long-term low interest loans) are far lower, indicating a total of $5.8 bn in 1977–79 as compared with the Saudi figures of $11.3 bn for this three-year period.[29] The large discrepancy between the two estimates may be due, at least in part, to the Saudi inclusion of military aid as well as economic assistance.

Much of Saudi foreign aid is determined by its perceptions of its own security problems such as, for example, aid to North Yemen. In other cases, where the Saudis feel less urgency over their own security, actual aid disbursements are far less than those promised publicly.[30]

Another facet of the country's rapid growth in expenditures is the rising expectations of the Saudi population. It is certainly aware of the massive oil revenues flowing into the country and of the opulence of its rulers and of others who have amassed fortunes. After the Iranian revolution foreign observers suggested that the Saudis would learn the lesson that large-scale spending tends to augment the destabilizing forces in their society, and curtail spending. The evidence indicates that quite the contrary has happened. The authorities have continued to raise expenditures on a host of projects designed to raise living standards, as well as to provide various subsidies. In the words of the Saudi Minister of Planning:

> "The problems in Iran weren't caused by economic development, but by the lack of it . . . Iran had a huge navy but no houses . . . [Saudi Arabia has tried] to create a middle class . . . the basis for political stability . . . and I don't think our development has been too fast . . . If I had to do it over again I would do it the same way."[31]

While we know that average per capita income is very high, there are no authoritative data on the distribution of income and wealth. Unofficial reports state that "the inequalities in income are perhaps unprecedented in history."[32] Since there is no prospect of income redistribution under the existing regime, the only solution is to increase disbursements from the Treasury.[33] The 1980–85 Plan clearly reflects these views, with major increases in spending on social welfare.[34] This includes housing, electricity, water, telephones, health and education, and a host of direct and indirect subsidies. In the Saudi context these are very costly undertakings.

The country's size (about one-third of the continental US) and the wide dispersal of its small population, add significant costs in terms of transportation and communications, electrification, etc. The known oil reserves are located only in the eastern party of the country in the Gulf area. Though this part of the country has grown rapidly, most of the population resides in other parts of the country. Extending the gas-gathering project to the West and laying a cross-country pipeline had added to total outlays. Furthermore, they have added significantly to military expenditures.

THE SAUDI DIVERSIFICATION PLANS AND THE LABOUR FORCE

While outsiders might view Saudi oil revenues with envy, its leaders are well aware of the dangers inherent in their almost complete dependence on oil. Various industries have been, or are in the process of being, established. A special government commission was set up with a mandate to develop two major industrial complexes—in Jubayl, on the eastern coast, and in Yanbu', on the western coast. Both are based on petrochemicals and on the utilization of the energy and feedstock provided by the major gas-gathering project. The authorities are anxious to persuade multi-nationals to come in as partners in these ventures; however, before 1979, the foreign companies felt that these industries would not be profitable despite cheap energy, feedstock and a range of subsidies. Their particular concern was with labour problems, especially since Saudis with the requisite skills are few, and are enticed by far more lucrative opportunities in other occupations, and foreign labour is both problematic and very costly. The 1979 oil crisis persuaded the Saudi authorities to offer hard-to-resist incentives to induce foreign companies to enter into partnerships in these ventures, including long-term guarantees of oil supplies at official prices.[35] The fact that since 1979 the Saudis have been selling their oil at prices significantly lower than those of other exporters, has been persuasive; some foreign companies have concluded agreements while others are still negotiating.[36]

Since the potential labour force is small, the authorities have emphasized the development of capital-intensive industries. But these usually require high levels of technical and managerial skills, which are in very short supply among Saudis. Foreign specialists therefore remain very sceptical. The following evaluation is quite typical:

> "Many of the industrial projects, both small and large . . . are not competitive . . . most of the heavy industries now operating have been disastrous, and there is little reason to suppose that new ones will be different . . . the implications for the country's future are obviously momentous."[37]

Official Saudi figures for the population and the labour force are generally considered unreliable—grossly overestimating the population and greatly underestimating the number of foreign workers. Unofficial population estimates indicate c. 4m Saudis.[38] Since women are almost completely excluded from the labour force (they are permitted to work only with other females), the potential labour force, excluding children, is c. 1m. This includes the armed forces and internal security, and the bloated bureaucracy. Even more relevant is the quality of manpower. There are, of course, individual Saudis who have acquired education and skills, as well as administrative and managerial competence; but they are far too few for a rapidly expanding modern economy. While in other developing countries there are strong economic incentives to acquire modern skills, the Saudi economic and political system provides powerful disincentives. The problems are not only those of building a modern economy, but of operating and maintaining the infrastructure and of production in the modern industrial and agricultural sectors. The authorities are very much aware of the problem. They have built technical schools and have attempted to attract young people to these schools as well as to industry providing for on-the-job training by foreign technicians. In this effort the Saudi leadership has been singularly unsuccessful. Some foreign observers attribute this reluctance to social mores; others note that there are far more lucrative alternatives for the more capable Saudis, e.g. government service and utilizing "connections" for private gain, entering into business ventures with foreigners, or

144

acting as intermediaries for foreigners in obtaining contracts. Since Saudi laws require that business ventures have majority Saudi ownership, foreigners must seek local partners for their ventures.[39]

The foreign labour force includes unskilled and semi-skilled workers, technical, professional and managerial personnel. The unskilled and semi-skilled are generally from the poor Arab countries, as well as from Asian and African countries. The most highly-skilled technical and managerial personnel are more frequently from Western Europe and North America. All foreigners are permitted to enter only with temporary work permits. Only in very rare cases are foreigners permitted to acquire Saudi citizenship. Unofficial estimates of the size of the foreign labour force range from 1.5m to 2.5m. According to the Director-General of the Ministry of Labour, three-quarters of the labour force was foreign towards the end of 1979.[40] This is a far cry from the planners' expectations in 1975 when they had projected that by 1980 the foreign labour force would number c. 800,000 and constitute only 35% of the country's manpower resources.

The Saudis view foreigners with apprehension for both social and political reasons. From time to time, there are drives to apprehend and expel the tens of thousands of Muslims from the poor countries, who enter the country as pilgrims and then stay on in search of jobs as casual labourers in construction, services and other menial jobs. "Draconian laws govern work permits. It is not uncommon to see Egyptians fleeing through the streets from Saudi policemen only to end . . . at the airport" (for expulsion from the country).[41] The result of these measures is an upsurge in wage rates for labourers.[42] On the other hand, the high-level technical and managerial personnel, mainly Westerners, are reluctant to come to Saudi Arabia, or to remain for any length of time because of social and other restrictions. To overcome this reluctance, foreign contractors must pay three to four times what it would cost to employ them in the US. Thus, the non-economic constraints add significantly to the costs of projects as well as to production.[43] A Congressional report (1979) estimated that the costs of construction in Saudi Arabia were two-and-a-half to three times those of the US.[44]

The Saudis' reluctance to acquire modern technical and managerial skills, and the country's overwhelming dependence on foreigners, concurrent with their resentment of foreigners, puts into serious question the viability of the diversification programme. The leadership is aware of the problem. In the words of the Deputy Minister of Industry: "The problem now in Saudi Arabia is manpower."[45] The 1980–85 Development Plan puts greater emphasis on developing an indigenous labour force, and calls for a standstill in the size of the foreign labour force.[46] However, under the best of circumstances it takes decades or generations to educate and train a modern labour force—and Saudi Arabia is hardly moving in that direction. A British analyst noted in 1980 that:

> "Despite a growing xenophobia, there is no sign that the Saudi manpower crisis is doing anything but going from bad to worse . . . the showpiece vocational training centres have been almost utterly neglected . . . An inflated and inefficient bureaucracy is a drain on the private sector, attracting graduates, with short hours, slothful work, the chance of a dizzying rise, and a blind eye turned towards private business interests. [Civil servants engaged in private business or in obtaining 'commissions'] . . . Where there are Saudis in the private sector, they are frequently promoted above their heads. Every firm likes to show off having one [Saudi]. Inefficiency results . . . The State cannot stop giving things away, but it is a clear impediment to developing a productive society."[47]

OTHER MAJOR MIDDLE EAST OIL EXPORTING COUNTRIES

In Iran there was a far lower rate of oil production and exports even after the new revolutionary government was established in early 1979. During the course of 1980—prior to the war—production was falling almost steadily. In the second half of 1979 it was 3.6 mbd cf. 5.8 mbd in the same period in 1977. During the first half of 1980 there was a further drop to 2.1 mbd. In July–August 1980 production averaged 1.4 mbd. The result was increasing internal economic problems.[48] The war reduced oil production and has further exacerbated the country's economic problems. There is little doubt that internal pressures will induce the Iranians to make every effort to raise oil exports as rapidly as possible.

Iran and Algeria have usually been considered by analysts as among the OPEC members which are "large absorbers" of revenues. Iraq had reached a level of 3.5 mbd in 1979, and was expanding productive capacity before the outbreak of the war in September 1980. Libya, the UAE and Kuwait have, in recent years, been producing c. 2 mbd. They were usually viewed as being among the "small absorbers" of revenues. Hence, in the conventional view, they like Saudi Arabia, could and would readily curtail production during periods of oil surpluses. A brief look at the economies of these countries and their oil policies is instructive.

IRAQ

Potential oil reserves are believed to be vast, probably exceeded in the ME only by those of Saudi Arabia.[49] In the early 1960s the Government annulled the concession for oil exploration granted to the consortium of Western oil companies, the Iraq Petroleum Company. Only a small area (c. 1% of the land area) where there were producing wells, was left to the foreign company. The result was a decade in which hardly any exploration was undertaken. In 1972 the Iraq Petroleum Company was completely nationalized and oil production declined. There was a subsequent strong drive to explore and develop oil resources, and production began to rise. In 1979 production was 3.5 mbd, double the production rate of 1971—the peak year before nationalization. The 1979 increase in production was particularly large, 850,000 b/d. While a number of ME producers were curtailing production during the first eight months of 1980 (i.e., before the Iraqi-Iranian war), and an oil glut was becoming increasingly prevalent, Iraq (and Saudi Arabia) continued to raise production. In view of the doubling of oil prices during 1979, this may appear to be surprising. However, ambitions for economic development and the serious problems faced, especially in the agricultural sector, together with its military ambitions, required huge expenditures and imports. This was the prime determinant of its oil policy. There were reports that a major expansion of its productive capacity was under way, planned to reach 8 mbd by the end of 1983.[50] This would put Iraq into a not-too-distant second place to Saudi Arabia, whose sustainable capacity was c. 10.5 mbd in 1980, with development under way for expansion by c. 2 mbd.[51]

Reports from meetings of OPEC have usually depicted Iraq as a "price hawk." If one examines Iraqi actions, a different conclusion emerges. In times of oil surpluses, such as in 1975 and in 1978, the Iraqis succeeded in raising production and exports by offering official and unofficial discounts; this pattern was again repeated during the first eight months of 1980 when oil surpluses were becoming increasingly prevalent. At more recent meetings of OPEC the Iraqis appear to have adopted a more moderate stance.[52] Apparently, like the Saudis, they have become more aware of the longer-term adverse effects of oil price increases on future oil consumption generally, and demand for ME oil in particular. Iraq's huge oil potential makes them even more concerned with the longer-term effects of oil price increases.

No one can predict the end of the Iraqi-Iranian war, but there are clear indications that Iraq (and, even more so, Iran) is feeling the economic impact of the conflict. Iraq's potential exports via the pipelines through Syria and Turkey are over 2 mbd; it appears that Iraq is endeavouring to maximize its exports through these pipelines, even in the midst of the conflict. Its other major pipeline, via the Gulf, was closed as a result of the hostilities. When hostilities cease, or abate, they will surely make every effort to maximize production and exports as rapidly as possible. With a population of c. 12m (1980) and ambitious economic and military goals, they have every motive to pursue this policy. It may come as a surprise to some observers that Syria had agreed to Iraqi pumping through the Syrian pipeline in view of its hostility towards Iraq and its pro-Iranian position. But for those familiar with the history of Iraqi-Syrian relations during the last few decades, such developments come as no surprise. Economic factors are rather potent in the decision-making of both countries.

LIBYA
The overthrow of the Monarchy in 1969 and the advent of Qadhdhāfī were viewed with apprehension by the West. After 1970 there was a steady decline in oil production; by 1975 it was less than 1.5 mbd, down sharply from its peak rate of 3.3 mbd in 1970. The factors underlying this sharp drop have often been ascribed to "conservation" measures, Libya's anti-Western stance and disputes with the Western oil companies operating in the country. Without negating these factors, there is no doubt that there were more objective technical reasons for the decline. Many of the oil wells discovered in the 1960s had passed their prime; many more wells were needed than in the past to produce even at the lower level of production prevailing in the mid-1970s.[53]

Despite the sharp oil price increases in 1973–4, expenditures and imports had risen so sharply by 1975 that Libya's international reserves and net foreign assets began to decline quite sharply.[54] Subsequently, there was a significant increase in oil production. In times of oil surpluses, the Libyans were among the price discounters—despite their "hawkish" stand in OPEC.

The Libyans have ambitious economic development plans, and their political-military ambitions in the international arena are very costly. Despite the sharp rise in oil prices in 1979, the Libyans raised production, and have been exerting pressure on the Western oil companies operating in the country to expand their exploration and development activities. Their announced goals are to raise oil production, as their perceived revenue needs tend to grow.[55] What is particularly noteworthy is a statement by the Libyan Oil Minister in 1979 that leaving oil in the ground is a poor alternative for Libya since the costs of development (construction, imported equipment etc.) tend to rise far more rapidly than oil prices.[56] However outsiders may view Libya's political goals, their oil policy is quite pragmatic. Notwithstanding its anti-American stance, it has been selling about one-third of its oil to the US (1977–79 average).

THE UNITED ARAB EMIRATES
Oil production is dominated by Abū Dhabi, with Dubai a distant second. The only other Emirate with some oil production is Sharjah; but it is insignificant. There was a steady rise in oil production until 1978. What is noteworthy is that UAE production continued to rise even in 1974–75 when an oil glut was prevalent.

147

There was a small cutback in production—from a peak of 2 mbd in 1977 to 1.8 mbd in 1978 and 1979. In many respects the pattern of development and in expenditures is similar to Saudi Arabia's. The foreign population is even more predominant, constituting c. 85% of an estimated 1.3m people in the federation. Expenditures were rising rapidly. In 1975 the budgetary surplus was $1,947m. By 1977 the surplus had declined to $886m, and in 1978 a deficit of $193m emerged.[57] The 1978 cutback in production was not because of surplus revenues, but because of the advice of technical consultants, in order to prevent damage to the long-term productivity of some of the oil fields.[58] The sharp oil price increases of 1979–80 again created large financial surpluses. However, the 1980 Budget calls for major increases in spending, including military, developmental and current expenditures.[59] Though there are differences in details, the pattern is similar to that found in other small-population Arab oil-exporting countries.

KUWAIT

Of the major Arab oil-producing countries—those producing c. 2 mbd or more—Kuwait has been relatively prudent in its spending. As in the other small-population Arab oil-producing countries, the labour force (excluding the highly-inflated bureaucracy) is overwhelmingly foreign. Official population estimates are 1.3m in 1980, of which c. 60% is foreign. Unofficial estimates are that the foreign population may be about half a million higher.[60] The Kuwaiti policies regarding foreigners are similar to those prevailing in the other Arab oil-exporting countries.

Though governmental expenditures have risen rapidly, the Kuwaiti authorities have, as a matter of policy, set aside a reserve fund "For Future Generations." Their relatively small current and developmental expenditures may be due, in part, to its territory. Nonetheless, expenditures have risen quite rapidly from c. $3 bn in fiscal 1974–75 to c. $6 bn in fiscal 1978–79. They were scheduled to rise to $8.6 bn in fiscal 1979–80. However, revenues rose far more rapidly as a result of the major oil price increases in 1973–74 and in 1979–80, despite lower production levels. Production peaked in 1972 at 3.3 mbd. Between 1975 and 1978 production ranged between 2.1 mbd and 2.2 mbd. Following an increase to 2.6 mbd in 1979, they curtailed production to c. 1.7 mbd in 1980.

The major oil price increases, combined with relatively moderate spending increases, succeeded in raising Kuwaiti official foreign assets very rapidly—from $2 bn in 1974 to c. $45 bn by the end of 1979, and probably over $50 bn by the end of 1980.[61] In absolute terms, Kuwaiti official foreign assets at the end of 1980 were about one half those of Saudi Arabia. However, in relation to the levels of governmental expenditures, they were far larger. Possibly alone among the larger Arab oil-producing countries, Kuwait can withstand a lengthy curtailment of oil exports in response to an oil glut. The large oil price increases of 1979–80 and the cushion of very large official foreign assets permitted the Kuwaiti authorities to respond to the 1980 oil glut by reducing production and exports quite sharply. However, Kuwait has little room for further cutbacks in oil production. There is a "technical" floor for its production, necessitated by the utilization of the associated gas required to provide the energy needed for electric power, water desalination, etc. This "technical" floor was estimated to be c. 1.5 mbd. During the oil glut in 1978 Kuwait was among the price discounters.[62]

SAUDI OIL POLICY AND OPEC

OPEC is widely viewed as a potent cartel which can manipulate production and oil prices, almost at will. But is this really so? There are very diverse interests in

148

OPEC. Some members, with relatively small oil reserves, are far more concerned with short-term considerations. The fact that sharply rising oil prices might be (and are) counter-productive to oil demand in the longer run—and for OPEC oil in particular—is of little concern to these countries. This is especially the case for those countries with the economic potential for diversification and a reduction in dependence on oil revenues in the relatively near future. Others—particularly Saudi Arabia, with vast known oil reserves, and with little prospect of successful diversification in the foreseeable future—are more concerned with the longer-run impact of escalating oil prices. Every country has both short-term and longer-term economic interests; the two often conflict. However, the weights given to short-run and long-run considerations vary greatly from one country to another, and may also vary within the same country over time. At no time in its history has OPEC succeeded in setting an effective common policy for allocating production and export quotas. This weakness becomes apparent in times of oil surpluses. What has ensued has usually been a scramble for sales through price discounts. The oil glut, which was becoming increasingly prevalent during the year preceding the Iranian revolution was abruptly ended by the cessation of Iranian exports towards the end of 1978. In 1978—before the last quarter of the year—Iran had been the second largest exporter, with sales of c. 5 mbd cf. Saudi exports of c. 7.5 mbd at that time. The oil glut in 1980 was again ended, at least temporarily, by the Iraqi-Iranian war in September 1980.

Analysts consider Saudi Arabia as the key to oil developments generally. In view of the changes in the oil and energy markets and Saudi internal policies and problems, what can be said of Saudi oil policy, both with respect to production and pricing?

In determining its oil policy, Saudi decision-makers face certain realities. These include the vast oil reserves; the changes in the world oil and energy markets brought about by the "oil-shocks" of 1973–74 and 1979–80; the failure of its diversification plans; the current and perceived future revenue needs; and the actions of other OPEC members.

While it is a truism that petroleum is the life-blood of the Saudi economy, it is less obvious that this is true not only at this time, but for the foreseeable future. This derives from the country's inability to diversify its economy in order to provide alternative sources of significant income for the reasons already noted. The corollary of this proposition is that Saudi Arabia's almost total dependence on oil will continue into the indefinite future. It is this fact of life which lies at the root of Saudi Arabia's relative price moderation. They have seen the impact of the "oil shock" of 1973–74 and even more so of 1979–80, and are concerned. The world trend away from oil, and especially from ME oil, must arouse their concern.

Shaykh Yamānī has spoken of the fundamental divergence of interests between his country and other OPEC members. Using Algeria as his example, he noted that the latter's oil reserves are small and that its production will decline rapidly during the 1980s. Hence, Algeria, unconcerned with the longer run, pushes for the highest possible price today. Saudi Arabia, he emphasized, is in an entirely different position and must be concerned with the longer-run impact of oil price increases on future demand for oil. He stated that computer projections indicated that "a point has been reached beyond which it would go against Saudi Arabia" to increase oil prices.[63] He is apparently far less confident of the forecasts made during the 1970s that demand for oil generally, and ME oil in particular, will continue to rise. The decline in demand for ME oil since 1977, and the rise in non-OPEC oil supplies, must arouse Saudi concern.

It may very well be that there have been occasions when short-run economic

149

considerations were more weighty for Saudi decision-makers. The fiscal and balance of payments problems of the country in 1978, and the rapid decline in official foreign assets, may have impelled the leadership to look with favour upon the oil price increases announced by OPEC towards the end of 1978. The Iranian revolution literally saved the Saudis from serious economic problems. It was subsequently reported that the Central Bank had estimated in 1978 that, by mid-1980, its foreign assets would have declined to one half the 1977 figure. At the end of 1977, Saudi foreign assets were $59.4 bn.[64] The rise in production since the last quarter of 1978, and the higher prices as of January 1979, succeeded in reversing the downtrend in foreign assets only after mid-1979. The fiscal deficit for 1978–79 (ending in May 1979) was even higher than in the previous year.

However, since 1979, the Saudis have made a sharp departure from previous pricing policy by keeping their official prices a few dollars below those of other oil-exporters. By and large, until that time (with the exception of the first half of 1977), there had been price uniformity in OPEC for similar grades of oil, with Saudi light oil (the marker crude) setting the pattern for other oil prices. What lies behind this policy? Two factors suggest themselves. The first is the heightened Saudi concern regarding the longer-run impact of the very sharp oil price increases during 1979. Since Saudi exports constitute an important share of world oil exports, their lower prices must necessarily have some moderating influence on price increases. The second factor is more short-run. The Saudis were anticipating that the large-scale stockpiling taking place during 1979, and the impact of the price increases, would bring about an oil glut in the near future. Their previous experience had been that when oil surpluses become prevalent, other OPEC members discount prices. Their experience in 1978 was particularly disturbing. During the first nine months of the year (before the Iranian revolution) Saudi production was 16% below that of the comparable period a year earlier, while in the rest of OPEC the decline was a mere 2%. The Saudis were most unhappy with this situation. Shaykh Yamānī publicly accused a number of other OPEC members of price discounting below the official prices.[65] The financial problems encountered by the Saudis during this period have already been noted. The oil glut which the Saudis correctly anticipated would emerge in 1980 (before the Iraqi-Iranian war) left them unconcerned. A number of OPEC members were lowering prices, such as by the cancellation of so-called surcharges.[66] This time, Saudi exports were not affected; their prices were, in any case, lower. At the time of writing (March 1981) the Saudis continue to maintain lower prices. This is not surprising in view of the expectation of the Saudi Oil Minister of an oil glut in 1981 and 1982.[67]

Given the growing desire, or need, for increasing revenues and their awareness of the adverse longer-run effects of significant oil price increases in real terms, the Saudi option is to enhance oil production and exports. This, indeed, has been their policy at least since the early 1970s. They have availed themselves of market opportunities to increase sales, and have cut back only where conditions compelled them to do so. The net effect of the Saudi policy has been to increase their exports sharply during the 1970s, in the face of a shrinking OPEC and ME oil market.[68] The Saudi announcement noted earlier that they were expanding productive capacity by 2 mbd is in consonance with this policy.

The Saudi leadership is aware of the dangers inherent in their failure to diversify the economy. In his above-mentioned lecture in Saudi Arabia in early 1981, Yamānī stated:

"If we don't do that [diversify the economy] we will reach a time when there will be a violent explosion in the country . . . [and with respect to oil pricing] don't shorten the life of oil as a source of energy before our industrialization is complete and other sources of revenue established."[69]

However, the Saudi leadership is surely aware of the enormous difficulties and poor prospects of their diversification plans. Given their perceived revenue needs, a good insurance policy is to make every attempt to moderate further price increases, and to capture as big a share as possible of the oil market.

CONCLUSIONS

An analysis of ME oil must necessarily focus on the oil and energy markets generally as well as on internal developments and their policy implications in the major ME oil-exporting countries. The "oil shocks" of 1973–74 and 1979–80 brought about fundamental changes in the world oil and energy markets at a far more rapid pace than had been envisaged. The rate of improvement in energy efficiency and in the substitution of other conventional sources of energy for oil have combined to bring about a sharp slowdown in the growth rate of oil consumption. In the Western industrialized countries, oil consumption was lower in 1980 than in 1973. There are indications that economic forces will bring about similar changes in the communist countries and in the under-developed countries which import oil. On the other hand, the far higher oil prices have stimulated a very intensive search for oil and gas, especially in areas outside the ME. The growth in non-ME oil supplies between 1973 and 1980 has more than satisfied the small increment in world oil consumption.

No attempt will be made here to assess future supply and demand for oil. Regrettably, the guesstimates made by so many serious researchers have proved to be very wide of the mark—almost invariably on the pessimistic side, from the point of view of the oil-importing countries. All projections of future supply and demand for oil depend crucially on estimates of future changes in energy efficiency, on the substitution effect, and on guesses of future discoveries of oil and gas. Supply and demand elasticities have been seriously under-estimated in the past. With respect to the future all we can say is that elasticities tend to increase over time. The effect of the latest oil price increases will most probably be felt during the coming years. However, though precise estimates may not be very feasible, we can detect the underlying trends; these clearly indicate a continued slowdown in the rate of growth of demand for oil, if not an absolute decline; and continued growth in non-OPEC and non-ME oil and gas supplies. These should bring about downward pressure on real oil prices, at the very least. This is what economic forces would seem to indicate.

In the ME oil countries generally, the sharp rise in oil revenues has raised the threshold of expenditures and imports to levels which were, at one time, believed to be most improbable. Economists have long theorized regarding the relationship between personal income and consumption. Generally-speaking, personal consumption tends to rise at about the same rate as income, with a relatively short time lag. It would appear that the same relationship exists with respect to income and expenditure in the public sector. Whether foreign observers view these expenditures as "wise" or "efficient" is immaterial from the point of view of our analysis. What is relevant is that it is extremely difficult, and politically hazardous, for a government to reduce its expenditures from whatever levels they have reached. In the case of Saudi Arabia, in particular, we have noted that expenditures tend to develop a momentum of their own. In the words of one analyst of the Saudi economy: "The great investment and spending machine set up in 1975–80 [the Development Plan] has a momentum that is almost unstoppable."[70] With the possible exception of Kuwait, this appears to be the case in the other major ME oil-exporting countries as well. In terms of oil policy, what is relevant are the revenues of the Treasury and the Central Bank. The fact that members of the Royal Family, and others, have amassed private fortunes does not solve the financial problems faced by the Ministry of Finance. Under the existing regimes there is no prospect of these private fortunes being utilized to finance public expenditures. There are no personal income taxes in these countries, let alone other forms of redistribution of wealth and income.

As by far the leading oil exporter, the Saudis are particularly concerned with the longer term effects of major oil price increases. The Saudis' possession of huge oil reserves and their failure to diversify the economy, makes them all the more concerned with the future of the oil market. Hence their relative price moderation and their policy of capturing as large as possible a share of the shrinking OPEC and ME oil market. Their lower prices since 1979, and their expansion of productive capacity are consistent with their economic interests.

Clearly, any future political-military "explosion" in any major oil-exporting country would again tend to raise prices. However, they would also tend to accelerate the trends away from oil generally and from ME oil, in particular. The possibilities of such an "explosion" occurring can certainly not be dismissed. The effects of the last two events—the Iranian revolution, and the Iraqi-Iranian war—are still being felt. On the other hand, the increasing economic difficulties faced by Iran, even before the recent war, and even more so since the war, can only strengthen the regime's determination to increase oil production and exports as soon as possible. Iraq has followed a policy of expanding productive capacity and exports since the mid-1970s. The civilian and military losses incurred by the Iraqis can only add to the impetus for higher oil production and exports.

In December 1980 Shaykh Yamānī stated that "Iran and Iraq will have to export as much as possible . . . [no less than 7 mbd] . . . there will be a [world oil] surplus—definitely—unless political events interrupt the flow of oil again." He cited increased non-OPEC production, conservation (energy efficiency) and the use of alternative energy sources.[71] Yamānī appears to be concerned with these developments, and the possibility that Saudi Arabia would have no choice but to reduce its production drastically.[72] If extended over a longer period, the results could be serious for Saudi Arabia. Its official foreign assets, which may have reached $100 bn by the end of 1980, were equivalent to somewhat over one year's spending. From the point of view of the oil consumers the implications—barring political convulsions—are for downward pressure on real and, possibly even nominal, oil prices. If the major oil price increases have not killed the goose that lays the golden eggs, they have at least inflicted some serious wounds. It will not be surprising if the importance of ME oil continues to diminish, at least in relative terms, during the coming years.

Eliyahu Kanovsky

NOTES

1. The sources used in this study are official national and international publications, unless otherwise stated. This study is based, in part, on my more detailed study, completed at the end of 1978 "Deficits in Saudi Arabia: Their Meaning and Possible Implications" in *Middle East Contemporary Survey (MECS)* 1977–78. For that part of this study which summarizes and repeats some of the principal findings of the earlier study, the sources will not be repeated.
2. *Petroleum Economist (PE)*, London, various issues.
3. A Staff Report to the Subcommittee on International Economic Policy of the Committee on Foreign Relations, US Senate *The Future of Saudi Arabian Oil Production*, April 1979, Washington, D.C., pp. 25–29.
4. Data on oil and energy production and consumption are from the annual *BP Statistical Review of the World Oil Industry*, London; *PE;* the US Department of Energy *Monthly Energy Review*, Washington, D.C.
5. Subcommittee on Foreign Economic Policy of the Committee on Foreign Relations; US Senate, *International Debt, the Banks and US Foreign Policy*, August 1977, Washington, D.C., pp. 33–4.
6. See "Oil Statistics," Table 1 in this volume.
7. The House of Representatives, the US Congress, *Intelligence on the World Energy Future* December 1979, Washington, D.C., p. 5.
8. The calculations were based on GNP estimates of the US Department of Commerce, and oil and energy data in the *Monthly Energy Review* of the US Department of Energy.
9. The GNP figures for Japan and West Germany are from the International Monetary Fund (IMF) *International Financial Statistics (IFS)*, February 1981. For 1980 the estimates are based on the first three quarters of the year. The figures for energy and oil consumption between 1973 and 1979 are from *BP Statistical Review of the World Oil Industry*, 1979. The 1980 figures are based on data for the first seven or eight months of the year—as compared with the same period in the previous year, in the US Department of Energy *Monthly Energy Review*, January 1981, p. 92.
10. The data for economic growth refer to GDP rather than GNP. In reality these two measures change at nearly the same rate in these countries. See OECD, *Main Economic Indicators*, various issues.
11. *New York Times (NYT)*, International Economic Survey, 8 February 1981, p. 14.
12. See "Oil Statistics," Table 1.
13. *Business Week*, New York, 30 January 1978, p. 32; 20 February 1978, pp. 41–2; *Events*, London, 21 April 1978, p. 38; *The Middle East (ME)*, London, August 1978, pp. 73–4; Economist Intelligence Unit *Quarterly Economic Review (QER): Oil in the Middle East*, No. 1, London, 1978, p. 2.
14. *Middle East Economic Digest (MEED)*, London, 16 September 1977, p. 20.
15. D. A. Wells *Saudi Arabian Development Strategy* American Enterprise Institute for Public Policy Research, Washington, D.C., 1976, p. 20.
16. See Eliyahu Kanovsky "Deficits in Saudi Arabia: Their Meaning and Possible Implications" in *MECS* 1977–78, pp. 318–59. The sources used in the above study are primarily official Saudi publications and official international publications, such as those of the IMF. In this study I have also used these sources for revised and updated data.
17. See "Oil Statistics," Table 4.
18. *Summary of Saudi Arabian Five Year Development Plan (1975–80)* US-Saudi Arabian Commission on Joint Economic Co-operation, Washington, D.C., 1975, pp. 1–19.
19. For greater detail the reader is referred to the above mentioned study "Deficits in Saudi Arabia: Their Meaning and Possible Implications."
20. See "Oil Statistics," Table 2.
21. See "Oil Statistics," Table 3. The fiscal accounts are given in accordance with the Muslim calendar; the balance of payments figures are in accordance with the more common calendar year.
22. IMF, *IFS*, January 1981, pp. 334–5.
23. See "Oil Statistics," Tables 2 and 3.

24. The Economist Intelligence Unit *QER: Saudi Arabia*, No 3, 1980; *MEED*, Special Report—Saudi Arabia, July 1980, pp. 7, 25–9.
25. T. H. Moran *Oil Prices and the Future of OPEC*, Resources for the Future, Washington, D.C., 1978, pp. 20–8.
26. *Fortune*, New York, 31 July 1978, p. 113.
27. See "Oil Statistics," Table 2.
28. See "Oil Statistics," Table 3, and note 4 above.
29. *The Financial Times (FT):* Survey—Saudi Arabia, London, July 1980, p. IV.
30. *Middle East Currency Report*, London, February–March 1978, p. 51.
31. *The Wall Street Journal (WSJ)*, New York, 30 January 1981, p. 25.
32. *FT:* Survey—Saudi Arabia, 28 April 1980, p. X.
33. *Ibid.*
34. *MEED*, 7 November 1980, p. 5.
35. *FT*, 23 April 1979.
36. *NYT*, 17 October 1979, p. 35; *Business Week*, 10 July 1978, p. 38.
37. Economist Intelligence Unit, *QER: Saudi Arabia*, No 3, 1978, pp. 11–12.
38. *Middle East Annual Review* 1979, London, p. 335; *NYT*, 11 October 1979, p. D5; *FT*, 26 June 1979, p. VI.
39. *Euromoney*, April 1980, pp. 130–34; Ramon Knauerhase "Saudi Arabia: Our Conservative Muslim Ally" in *Current History*, Washington, January 1980, p. 36; *FT:* Survey—Saudi Arabia, 23 April 1979.
40. Economist Intelligence Unit *QER: Saudi Arabia*, No 1, 1980, p. 14.
41. *FT:* Survey—Saudi Arabia, 28 April 1980, p. XXV.
42. *MEED*, 22 September 1978, p. 33.
43. *WSJ*, 25 October 1980, p. 31.
44. *Activities of the US Army Corps of Engineers in Saudi Arabia;* Hearing Before the Subcommittee on Europe and the Middle East of the Committee on Foreign Affairs; House of Representatives, 25 June 1979, p. 26.
45. *NYT*, 29 December 1980, pp. D1, 5.
46. *MEED*, 7 November 1980, p. 7.
47. *FT:* Survey—Saudi Arabia, 28 April 1980, p. XVI.
48. *ME*, May 1980, p. 69.
49. *ME*, February 1979, p. 106.
50. *ME*, August 1980, p. 53.
51. *The Economist*, London, 19 April 1980, pp. 63–4; *NYT*, 11 December 1980, pp. D1, 6.
52. *NYT*, 23 November 1980, p. 8F.
53. *NYT*, 15 October 1979, p. D1.
54. IMF, *IFS*, February 1981, p. 244.
55. *NYT*, 15 October 1979, pp. D1, 5; *ME*, December 1979, pp. 86, 88.
56. *ME*, July 1979, pp. 82–3.
57. *IMF Survey*, 18 August 1980, p. 250.
58. UAE Currency Board, *Bulletin*, Abū Dhabi, December 1979, p. 56.
59. *The Economist*, Supplement, 13 December 1980, p. 64; *FT*, Supplement-UAE, 23 June 1980, pp. II, VII; *MEED*, 1 August 1980, p. 35.
60. *FT:* Supplement—Kuwait, 25 February 1980, p. VIII.
61. *Ibid*, pp. VIII, IX.
62. *ME*, August 1978, pp. 73–4; *Events*, 29 July 1977, p. 39.
63. *Christian Science Monitor (CSM)*, Boston, 5 February 1981; *WSJ*, 2 February 1981, p. 20.
64. *FT:* Survey—Saudi Arabia, 28 April 1980, p. X; see "Oil Statistics," Table 3. The figures for foreign assets in this table include those of the commerical banks as well as of the Central Bank. The overwhelming share of these assets is in the Central Bank.
65. *The Arab Economist*, Beirut, August 1978, p. 35.
66. *WSJ*, 9 September 1980, pp. 1, 20; *NYT*, 1 October 1980, pp. F1, 11.
67. *NYT*, 11 December 1980, pp. D1, 6.
68. See "Oil Statistics," Table 1.
69. *WSJ*, 2 February 1981, p. 20.

70. *MEED,* 21 December 1979, pp. 59–60.
71. *NYT,* 11 December 1980, pp. D1, 6.
72. *CSM,* 5 February 1981.

Oil Statistics

TABLE 1:   WORLD PETROLEUM PRODUCTION (millions of barrels per day)

	1969	1970	1971	1972	1973	1974	1975	1976	1977	1978	1979	1980 (prel)
Saudi Arabia	3.2	3.9	4.8	6.1	7.7	8.6	7.2	8.8	9.4	8.5	9.8	10.2
Kuwait	2.8	3.0	3.2	3.3	3.1	2.6	2.1	2.2	2.0	2.2	2.6	1.7
UAE	0.6	0.8	1.1	1.2	1.5	1.7	1.7	1.9	2.0	1.8	1.8	1.7
Iraq	1.5	1.6	1.7	1.5	2.0	2.0	2.3	2.4	2.5	2.6	3.5	2.8
Libya	3.1	3.3	2.8	2.2	2.2	1.5	1.5	1.9	2.1	2.0	2.1	1.8
Qatar	0.4	0.4	0.4	0.5	0.6	0.5	0.4	0.5	0.4	0.5	0.5	0.5
Algeria	1.0	1.0	0.8	1.1	1.1	1.0	1.0	1.1	1.2	1.2	1.2	1.0
Iran	3.4	3.8	4.6	5.1	5.9	6.1	5.4	5.9	5.7	5.2	3.1	1.5
Total ME	16.0	17.8	19.4	20.9	24.1	24.0	21.6	24.7	25.3	24.1	24.6	21.2
Total OPEC	21.0	23.6	25.5	27.3	31.3	31.1	27.5	31.1	31.8	30.3	31.3	27.5
USA	10.8	11.3	11.2	11.2	11.0	10.5	10.0	9.7	9.9	10.3	10.2	10.3
Total non-Communist World—excl. OPEC	15.4	16.4	16.5	16.9	17.1	16.6	16.3	16.4	17.5	18.7	20.0	20.9
Communist Countries Total	7.4	8.1	8.7	9.3	10.2	11.0	11.8	12.6	13.3	14.1	14.4	14.8
Non-OPEC	22.8	24.5	25.3	26.2	27.2	27.6	28.2	29.0	30.9	32.8	34.4	35.6
Total World	**43.8**	**48.1**	**50.8**	**53.5**	**58.5**	**58.6**	**55.7**	**60.1**	**62.7**	**63.1**	**65.7**	**63.1**
(percentages)												
Saudi Share of World Oil	7.4	8.0	9.5	11.3	13.2	14.7	13.0	14.6	15.0	13.5	14.9	16.2
OPEC Share of World Oil	48.0	49.1	50.3	51.0	53.5	53.0	49.4	51.7	50.7	48.0	47.6	43.6
ME Share of World Oil	36.5	37.0	38.1	39.1	41.1	40.9	38.8	41.2	40.4	38.2	37.4	33.6
Saudi Share of OPEC Oil	15.5	16.3	18.9	22.2	24.6	27.8	26.2	28.2	29.6	28.2	31.3	37.1

NOTES: 1. The figures include crude oil production as well as natural gas liquids, and very small quantities from shale oil and oil sands.
2. The ME is here defined as the Arab members of OPEC, listed above, plus Iran.
3. OPEC production includes that of the current membership, namely, the ME producers plus Venezuela, Nigeria, Indonesia, Gabon and Ecuador.
4. The Saudi and Kuwaiti figures include their half shares of the Neutral Zone.
5. The Communist countries include the Soviet Union, China, and Eastern Europe.
6. The figures may not add up due to rounding.

SOURCES: *BP Statistical Review of the World Oil Industry 1979* London, 1980. The 1980 figures are based on preliminary estimates in *Oil and Gas Journal*, Tulsa, Oklahoma, 29 December 1980, and *Petroleum Economist*, London, January 1981.

TABLE 2: SAUDI BUDGETS IN FISCAL YEARS (millions of dollars)

Actual Revenues and Expenditures—Unless Otherwise Stated

Fiscal Years	Total Revenues	—of which Oil	Total Expenditures	of which Military	Balance (Cash Basis)
				(Projected)	
1971–72 (22 Aug. 1971 to 9 Aug. 1972)	2628	2316	2250	555	378
1972–73 (10 Aug. 1972 to 29 July 1973)	3900	3424	2952	903	948
1973–74 (30 July 1973 to 19 July 1974)	11748	11061	5831	1523	5917
1974–75 (20 July 1974 to 9 July 1975)	28483	26759	9631	2504	18816
1975–76 (10 July 1975 to 27 June 1976)	29289	26482	18215	6721	11072
1976–77 (28 June 1976 to 16 June 1977)	38515	34332	29632	9039	8884
1977–78 (17 June 1977 to 5 June 1978)	37438	32677	41576	9055	−4138
1978–79 (6 June 1978 to 25 May 1979)	39255	34352	43881	10627	−4625
		Preliminary Estimates			
1979–80 (26 May 1979 to 14 May 1980)	68716	62687	59700	17674	9016
		Budgetary Projections			
1980–81 (15 May 1980 to 4 May 1981)	85750	78750 (est.)	74240	20900	11500

NOTES: 1. The oil revenues are the payments from the foreign oil companies to the Government. The bulk of the other revenues are from dividends and interest received from abroad by the Government.
2. Total expenditures are on a cash basis, and apply to the whole public sector. The balances in the fiscal accounts, surpluses or deficits, are reflected in the changes in government deposits held by the Central Bank.
3. No data are published after the completion of the fiscal year with respect to itemized actual expenditures. The military budgets in this table are those which were planned.
4. Actual revenues in 1980–81 will be higher due to subsequent oil price increases, following the announcement of the Budget in May 1980 and the higher level of production.
SOURCES: Saudi Arabian Monetary Agency *Annual Reports*.

**TABLE 3: SAUDI ARABIA—BALANCE OF PAYMENTS—SELECTED DATA
(millions of dollars)**

	1969	1970	1971	1972	1973	1974	1975	1976	1977	1978	1979
Exports											
Merchandise	1785	2089	3505	4328	7531	30091	27150	35467	40029	36962	57847
Services	235	283	341	464	764	2556	3296	4647	6136	6462	7736
Imports											
Merchandise	825	829	866	1275	2103	3713	5998	10396	14355	20363	24973
Services	1189	1391	2003	1886	3490	5702	7389	12591	15219	19912	26251
Official											
Transfers	93	81	68	157	498	1015	3128	3328	3887	3900	3503
Balance on											
Current Account	−86	71	909	1474	2204	22217	13931	13799	12904	−751	10856
Foreign Assets											
(net)											
End-of-Year	824	957	1760	3154	5082	20130	39323	52255	61401	61668	64838

NOTES: 1. Non-oil merchandise exports are insignificant. In 1978 crude oil accounted for 94.2% of total merchandise exports; the rest was refined oil products. In 1979 the volume of refined oil exports was unchanged; the sharp increase in revenues was due mainly to far higher prices, and also to a greater volume of crude oil exports.
2. Of the service exports in 1978 (invisibles) about $1 bn was on account of tourist expenditures, mainly the pilgrimage; almost all of the balance was on account of dividends and interest receipts from abroad.
3. Service imports include: payments to the foreign oil companies; payments to foreign contractors or consulting firms; payments on account of freight, insurance, etc. to foreign firms; and the remittances of foreign workers, which are, in essence, payments for the importation of labour services. The official Saudi data include the latter under private transfers, but they are, in essence, service imports. The labour-exporting countries, such as Egypt and Jordan, include the receipt of remittances under service exports.
4. Official transfers should, under the usual definition, include only grants made by the Saudi Government to other countries. However, the Saudis include, under the term official transfers, loans as well as grants.
5. The data on foreign assets include those of the banking system, as a whole. As of the end of 1979 the Central Bank held 95% of these assets. The foreign assets include what are defined as the international reserves; however, since the Saudis have changed the definition of the latter term, the figures on foreign assets are a better indicator.

SOURCE: International Monetary Fund *International Financial Statistics*, October 1980, and earlier issues.

158

TABLE 4: SAUDI ARABIAN OIL

	1969	1970	1971	1972	1973	1974	1975	1976	1977	1978	1979
Production (mbd)	3.22	3.80	4.77	6.02	7.60	8.48	7.08	8.58	9.20	8.30	9.53
Crude oil Exports (mbd)	2.79	3.22	4.19	5.43	7.01	7.91	6.59	8.02	8.59	7.69	8.80
Exports of refined products (mbd)	0.43	0.57	0.53	0.57	0.58	0.58	0.48	0.56	0.52	0.49	0.49
Domestic oil consumed (mbd)	14.2	15.5	17.2	20.0	24.9	32.0	42.8	57.8	77.3	104.0	125.0
Proved plus probable oil reserves (billions of barrels)	120.0	123.9	127.5	156.4	164.5	172.5	175.8	177.5	177.6	177.8	177.9
Oil Reserves in years of current Production	110	96	78	75	62	58	71	58	54	60	53
Government oil revenues millions of dollars	949	1214	1885	2745	4340	22574	25676	30748	36540	32234	48400
Oil Revenue per barrel in dollars	0.93	1.03	1.23	1.38	1.70	7.82	10.67	10.48	11.65	11.48	15.06

NOTES: 1. The data include the Saudi half share in the Neutral Zone.
2. Aramco accounts for the bulk of oil production—97.0% in 1979.
3. The data on oil reserves refer to the Aramco concession. These are end-of-year figures.
4. The data on government oil revenues refer to direct payments by the oil companies to the Saudi Treasury.
5. The 1969 figure for proved and probable oil reserves are the author's estimate.
6. The 1979 figure for domestic oil consumption is the author's estimate.
7. The figures for oil reserves (proved plus probable) in years of oil production refer to reserves and production in the Aramco concession area. It should be noted that the figures for oil reserves do not include the potential for further discoveries. In fact, in every year during the past 40 years that Aramco has been operating in the country, the additions to reserves, as a result of new discoveries, have exceeded current production, and hence, oil reserves have risen, though only very slightly in recent years. Oil production in 1976–79 has been unprecedented.

SOURCE: Saudi Arabian Monetary Agency *Annual Report*, various issues.

Eliyahu Kanovsky